CURRICULUM, SCHOOL AND SOCIETY: AN INTRODUCTION TO CURRICULUM STUDIES

Curriculum, School and Society.:

An introduction to Curriculum Studies

Edited by
Philip H. Taylor
University of Birmingham, England

Kenneth A. Tye
Research Division, |I|D|E|A|

with an introduction by
John I. Goodlad
Dean, Graduate School of Education
University of California, Los Angeles

NFER Publishing Company

Published by the NFER Publishing Company Ltd.,
Book Division, 2 Jennings Buildings, Thames Avenue,
Windsor, Berks. SL4 1QS
Registered Office: The Mere, Upton Park, Slough, Berks, SL1 2DQ

First published 1975
© *P. H. Taylor and K. A. Tye*
ISBN 85633 065 5

Printed in Great Britain by
John Gardner (Printers) Ltd., Hawthorne Road, Bootle, Merseyside L20 6JX

Distributed in the USA by Humanities Press Inc.
Hillary House-Fernhill House, Atlantic Highlands,
New Jersey 07716 USA

Contents

ACKNOWLEDGEMENTS

The success of a joint venture depends on more than those whose names appear as its creators. It depends on those who encourage, lend aid and their competencies. There are, thus, many to acknowledge. In particular Brian Holley and Bill Reid who contributed Chapters 3 and 8, and Pam Cotton who worked and re-worked the manuscript. The Publishers too. Without their patience, diligence and readiness to reconsider, this book would not have appeared.

P. H. Taylor
K. A. Tye

INTRODUCTION

John I. Goodlad

The editors have selected a group of readings designed to provide perspective on both the substance of intended learnings and the array of human transactions involved in making these intentions actualities for the students for whom they are intended. Their orientation is to curriculum as a field of study, defined as involving both intentions and transactions. This is a definition with which I identify very readily.

The transactions are many, complex and varied. They include those between some sanctioning body (e.g. citizens of a borough) and some council or school board (involving more often tacit rather than overt agreements or commitments); between this controlling agency and its employed agent (in the United States, the school superintendent); between this agent and sub-levels of authority, the kind and variety varying with the degrees of centralization and decentralization extant in the educational system; and between teachers and their students. Curriculum inquiry encompasses all these in addition to the ends and means of what is transacted. This puts into the curriculum basket much more than many curricularists would like to see there.

Narrower definitions can be and are made, of course. But even if one chooses a more limited definition, there is no denying that curriculum development includes sensitive matters of policy making and of negotiations among many groups of people, in addition to those more technical educational matters of specifying the ends and means of instruction and learning. Planning curricula is philosophical, political, and sociological/anthropological as well as psychological. It includes politics as well as subject matter, human relations as well as pedagogical principles.

Taylor and Tye clearly assume, then, that curriculum planning consists of two inseparable sets of human operations. The first is specifying intentions; the second is getting specified intentions into the ongoing experiences of those for whom they are intended. Since curriculum inquiry embraces both, one net effect is to join what often are separated as curriculum on one hand and instruction on the other. This is a useful fusion.

The common, implied separation of curriculum and instruction has had unfortunate consequences. There are those planners and researchers, primarily psychologists, who see curriculum planning almost solely as a process of arranging sets of stimuli so as to promote maximum efficiency in the learner's interaction with them. Mastery learning is the intended, ideal result. Precise delineation of objectives, selection of stimuli for their attainment, followed by reconstruction of this relationship on the basis of evaluative feedback are the central criteria of curriculum development.

Traditional goals for education generally are assumed. Whether or not these goals are the most significant or relevant tends not to be the central concern. That is for someone else to decide. The curriculum maker is an engineer, largely free from such value questions.

The other half of planning and research is shared by philosophers, some sociologists and anthropologists, many 'subject-matter' specialists and most curriculum generalists. Extremists among them see psychologists as simplistic corrupters of the educational process. Many in this second group are concerned, as a first question, with what should be taught: what knowledge is of most worth and, therefore, worthy of being humanized for general consumption. They nod in the direction of psychology by recognizing as relevant the question of appropriate ends and means for successive stages of human development and by noting that efficiency is of some importance.

This separation of the two groups of curricularists comes out rather clearly in the literature. The psychologists of curriculum cite psychologists in their footnotes, beginning with Thorndike and moving through Brownell, Skinner, Bruner, Gagné and Glazer, for the United States at least. Their literature is relatively cumulative.

The second group (no neat classification is possible) is much more eclectic and divisive. The literature is more fractionated and non-cumulative. It cites, variously, Aristotle, Mead, Whitehead, Dewey, Bobitt and their contemporary (often unwitting) disciples. With the first group, the literature shares from time to time personages such as Piaget and Tyler. And more recently, it includes the writings of many whose fields of allegiance are difficult to define: Schwab, Eisner, Macdonald, Broudy, Husén, Taba. Most of these are unabashed curricularists and their writing usually embraces the whole of curriculum in that it deals with both intentions and transactions.

As stated earlier, embracing intentions and transactions as different components of a complex set of related phenomena is the important contribution of the editors. Taylor and Tye point out, rightly, that intentions are ethereal until fulfilled and that what ultimately is fulfilled often is a far cry from intentions. Both well-conceived intentions and careful attention to the logistics and human elements of transactions from initial conception to ultimate implementation are required in curriculum practice.

The readings they have brought together here support my hypothesis that there is a schism in curriculum thought and practice reflected in the literature. There is a paucity of concern in them for instructional transactions. This is where papers by Gagné, Glazer and L. Tyler (on psychoanalysis and curriculum) could have filled in the gap very nicely.

It seems to me unlikely that Gagné and Glazer (with L. Tyler excepted) would be represented in the journals from which the several pieces were selected, supporting the contention that the gap is a direct product of two separate traditions in curriculum inquiry and literature. There exist, apparently, 'two worlds of curriculum.' 'Tis a pity.

II

By virtue of the Taylor-Tye definition, we see curriculum 'writ large'. We are not introduced only to the quality of the learning opportunity and the logistics of packaging it, important as these are. Moving into the curriculum domain are all those social/political/sociological processes through which values are articulated, goals are formulated and intentions find their way into educational institutions and are modified by the humans who live there. Curriculum study and practice offer good work for philosophers, linguists, mathematicians, natural scientists, behavioural scientists, administrators, teachers, and politicians. But there is no neat discipline, no precisely demarcated sphere of study and practice. This is upsetting to some scholars and conducive to anti-intellectualism among practitioners. But there is no alternative, if we accept the Taylor-Tye postulates regarding the domain of curriculum. The field of curriculum is as diverse and rich as life itself.

Having confronted these postulates, whether or not happily, we are confronted with formidable problems and issues of study and practice. Let us examine five of them.

The first pertains to the source of intentions. Presumably, in a democratic society, intentions spring from the people. But this statement is, to considerable degree, naive. No country has provided equally for all its citizens with respect to being heard. The overwhelming majority are never heard; they do not express an articulate voice in regard to aspirations. Others (leaders) may try to figure out their intentions but usually end up deciding what is best for others (and instrumental to their roles as leaders).

It would appear, then, that there is a little-explored realm of curriculum work involving the study of *what* intentions find their way through the political/social structure, *how* these proceed, and with *what* effects. This kind of study could add to our normative speculation on what *should* be some considerable empirical insight into the consequences of alternative value orientations—for example, the ways in which competing values in our society affect the curriculum.

The second problem pertains to slippage regarding intentions. Studies have revealed the lack of relationship between goals for education such as citizenship, honesty, good work habits, compassion and the like, and the behaviour of outstanding graduates of schools. Success in school is one thing; the practice of ideal behaviours is another. Other studies have revealed the lack of relationship between what many educators espouse and what they do. Clearly, the gap between what the tongue says and what the hand does is monumental.

Here, we have two potentially rewarding realms of curriculum inquiry. First, there is the matter of what happens when practitioners (administrators, supervisors, teachers) attempt to deduce the meaning of intentions. Does the precision of a statement of intentions help to dictate a set of interactions? Does the clarity of the statement help to exclude divergent intentions of the implementers? These are significant, appealing questions which have eluded serious study and the development of a technology for dealing with them. But at least the proper questions are being raised, as we see in subsequent papers.

A third set of issues grows out of the first two. *It pertains to the who of formulating and implementing intentions.* There are questions pertaining to the line between decisions for the constituency sanctioning educational institutions and those for the professional or employee. There are questions pertaining to the degrees of freedom available to those elected 'to protect the public interest.' There are questions pertaining to the lines of demarcating administrative prerogatives and teachers' authority and responsibility in schools.

Who is now making what decisions and what happens to these decisions are relatively unstudied questions. Data regarding them would at least enlighten the question of who should make them by revealing possible discrepancies between the 'is' and the 'ought'.

A fourth set of issues pertains to all those classical questions of selecting, organizing and evaluating the effects of curriculum content—the substance of intentions. For most curricularists, this *is* the field of curriculum. A couple of decades ago, this is what books on curriculum were all about: scope, sequence, integration, continuity, patterns or designs, units of work and the like. Strangely, there has been very little fresh thinking on these matters of late, with the possible exception of evaluation. Because so many of today's established curriculum specialists cut their eye teeth on these questions, they may be bored with them or think them all settled. A renascence of inquiry regarding them would be very much in order.

Finally, we have the matter of identifying the locus of transactions. They occur at a host of decision-making points: between national commissions and local lay authorities, local authorities and various layers of professionals, one layer of professionals *with* another, teachers with their students. At each of these, new sets of values intrude. Curriculum development is not a rational, linear process, with intentions stated from on high moving neatly and systematically through logical processes of deduction to influence the experience of students. As a matter of fact, curriculum planning is more a transactional, socio-political process than it is a rational, substantive one of determining and then logically relating ends and means.

One will not find in what follows much of what constituted curriculum studies two decades ago. There is very little treatment of the conventional commonplaces and very little certainty. But curriculum planning is seen in its complexity and richness. The editors have taken a useful cut across my five sets of issues and several more, fortifying their selection of readings with helpful commentary and suggestions for further reading. A useful, transatlantic dialogue, I would say.

PREFACE: THE AIMS OF THE BOOK

The major aim of this book is to introduce the student of education to the field of curriculum studies through a selection of readings collected and introduced in two parts under eight chapter headings. Each Part has an introduction which lays out the framework within which its four chapters are set. Similarly each Chapter has an introduction which outlines its particular contribution to curriculum studies together with a summary appraisal which aims to note briefly the salient features of the readings selected. This is followed by suggested reading which in each case provides an annotated guide to further relevant work.

For purposes of the book we define curriculum studies to be the study of 'all those activities and enterprises in which curricula are planned, created, adopted, presented, experienced, criticized, attacked, defended and evaluated' (Walker, 1973) and 'curriculum' as the *content* of education both as proposed and intended *and* as proposals and intentions operated upon in practice, in programmes of study and learning experiences transacted in schools and classrooms.

The dual nature of the term 'curriculum' as the answer to the questions: What should be taught? and What is taught? is reflected in the two parts of this book: the first dealing with the *curriculum as intentions* and the second with the *curriculum in transaction*. Within each Part the nature of the two central questions is illustrated by reference to the activities and enterprises in which people engage who are attempting either to answer them, to evaluate the answers or to find what is common to the different ways in which the questions have been and are being answered. In this way theorizing, conceptualization, analysis and research each find a place as methods used within curriculum studies.

It has not been possible to cover every aspect of curriculum studies in this book of guided readings but the major points of focus are presented—value issues and the curriculum, evaluation and theory, curriculum planning and innovation, the curriculum in transaction and curriculum research.

An effort has also been made in the selection of readings to illustrate different but equally valid approaches to the study of the curriculum. There is, for instance, Goodlad's large conspectus of curriculum change in *Curriculum: A Janus Look*, which by taking a large time scale reveals a patterning of behaviour which serves to explain an aspect of the psychopathology of curriculum movements, their inclination to excess. This may be contrasted with Walker's *A Naturalistic Model for Curriculum Development*, where the author attempts to construct a model of an ongoing curricular activity, that of developing a curriculum, which accounts for all the complexities and immediate concerns of those involved. Such contrasts may be found throughout the book and the reader is recommended to seek them out for analysis. It is after all by understanding the different methods of those who have contributed to curriculum studies that the reader will be better fitted not only to make his own contribution but also to appreciate the need in an emerging field of study to keep an open mind about the methods of inquiry and research to be employed.

As we have already implied, any field of study is characterized by two things: its concerns and its methods. In the readings, introductions, appraisals and annotated bibliographies this book attempts to reveal the concerns of the student of the curriculum and the range of methods he employs but it will succeed in doing this fully only if the reader takes time to reflect, to engage in further reading and becomes himself concerned and caught up not only by the questions: What *should* be taught and learned in educational institutions? and What *is* taught and learned in them? but also by their interaction and by the ways in which they are answered by the many people for whom they are a matter of professional concern.

P. H. Taylor
Kenneth A. Tye

Reference

WALKER, D. F. (1973). 'What Curriculum Research?' *J. Curr. St.*, 5, 1.

PART ONE

The Curriculum as Intention

Introduction

Curriculum studies is the study of those practices which concern what is taught and learned in schools and colleges. It attempts to understand how courses of study and the practices associated with them come into being and take the form they do. To do this curriculum studies begins by asking how questions such as *What should be taught and learned?* are answered. Who answers them, in what way, by reference to what values and beliefs, and with what purposes and intentions in mind? Curriculum studies then goes on to ask *What is in fact, taught and learned?* together with questions which aim to search out the relationship between intentions and their level of realization.

Here in Part One, the focus of attention will be on the first of these two questions, especially on how intentions are formulated, on their relationship to values and on their translation into curriculum objectives. The readings in Part One have been selected not only to illustrate how value issues and the curriculum are dealt with but also to show that the study of such issues belongs to the generalized matrix of pedagogy (Walker, 1973) which concerns itself with illuminating things done within the practice of education, with why and how they are done, and with the theories which inform and explain them. This is especially true of Chapter 4.

Finally, Part One is as much concerned to convey the idea that curriculum as the embodiment of valued intentions is an area of study which, though broad, can be subject to rational inquiry.

Reference
WALKER, D. F. (1973). 'What curriculum research?' *J. Curr. St.*, 5, 1, 58–72.

Chapter 1

Values and the Curriculum

Introduction

Until recent years, it was generally accepted that what a group of people
values is best understood by viewing what is taught in its schools. But
as Broudy (1971) suggests, those of us who are concerned with curriculum today may be guilty of having our thinking shaped by notions
of a democracy tuned to another age or perhaps by notions that are
not democratic at all. Social reality and societal values should determine
the ends of schooling and directly or indirectly determine the means of
schooling. Unfortunately, however, the interplay between societal values
on the one hand and the ends and means of schooling on the other of
late has had scant attention paid to it by either curriculum theorists
or practitioners.

The questions which curriculum workers face concerning the role of
values in curriculum development are not new ones. Questions about
the purposes and resultant nature of education have been part and
parcel of Western civilization since its beginnings in Greece. However,
in an age of rapid change marked by dramatic conflict between the
collective good and individual rights, such questions are even more
pressing and even more complex. Thus, at present, it is not enough to
ask the value question, 'What should be taught in our schools?' One
must go further and ask related value questions such as, 'Who should
decide what is taught in our schools?' and 'How should they decide?'
It is appropriate to note, as Goodlad and Richter (1967) do, that the
starting point for curriculum planning must be a set of values derived
from specialists (funded knowledge) and from the interests, beliefs, and
understandings of those who sanction the educational system or
consume education (conventional wisdom). It is also important to

understand how values are authoritatively allocated in and to the institutions of the Western world. This allocation of values is a political process, surrounded by conflict and ever-changing balances of power. The degree to which our schools and school bureaucracies are responsive to this process and at the same time utilize funded knowledge and rational problem solving may in the long run answer the complex question, 'What should be taught in our schools and by whom and how should such decisions be made?' Further, it is only through concern for the relationship between societal values and what happens in schools that curriculum workers can help to bridge the gap between the schools and the societies they serve. It is this relationship with which each of the three papers in this chapter deals.

Each paper approaches the problem of values and the curriculum somewhat differently. Eisner, noting that ours is a time of conflicting ideologies, calls for a revised curriculum in which the sciences, the arts, and values are reconstructed within a mankind perspective so that students are caused to examine their own values and beliefs. He suggests that it is important for students to understand the characteristics of scientific inquiry and its relationship to value questions. He rejects the position of the logical positivists and builds a strong case for the arts as a source of knowledge for students. Further, he argues that the data about mankind should serve as a conceptual thread around which the social studies curriculum is built. Finally, he states that students need to engage directly in axiological inquiry through the consideration of real life situations.

Musgrove starts from much the same position as Eisner. That is, he assumes that society is ever more pluralistic, decentralized, diverse, and heterogeneous. However, he builds from this assumption to a quite different set of conclusions. These conclusions suggest that within the schools there should be a corresponding and unabated subject pluralism and loose confederation of subject departments. There should not be 'integrated' curricula. However, to avoid 'anomie', subject specialists should decide together their common objectives and how each will make his distinctive contributions.

Eisner responds to the question, 'What should be taught in schools?' He suggests that funded knowledge and the needs of mankind, *per se,* dictate the teaching of scientific inquiry, the arts, and values. Musgrove, deals with the question, 'Who should decide what is taught?' It is his strong conviction that subject specialists should make such decisions. Both Eisner and Musgrove address the question, 'How should subject matter be determined?' Substantively, Eisner calls for the use of funded knowledge. Organizationally, Musgrove suggests a loose confederation of diverse academic centers, each specializing in its own field, each free from bureaucratic constraints, and each with its own decision-making power.

References

BROUDY, H. S. (1971). *Democratic Values and Educational Goals*. In: MCCLURE, R. M. (Ed.) *The Curriculum in Retrospect and Prospect*. 20th Year Book. Chicago: NSSE.

GOODLAD, J. I. and RICHTER, M. N. (1967) *The Development of a Conceptual System for Dealing with Problems of Curriculum*. Washington, DC: US Office of Ed. Co-op. Res. Rep. SAE 8024.

Readings

Education and the Idea of Mankind*
Elliott W. Eisner *University of Chicago*

One of the paradoxes of our times is that in an age pervaded by the clash of conflicting ideologies so little effort is spent in the schools in enabling students to critically examine their values and beliefs. If ever this responsibility could lie outside the school it surely was in days past—the problems of mankind today loom too large to be ignored or to be left to others.

But what contributes to intelligent decision-making in the realm of values? What sources are relevant and how are they to be used? It seems that at least three domains might be examined for their relevance to the problem posed. These domains are those of the sciences, the arts, and value theory itself. This paper will deal with the kinds of contributions each of these domains makes to the formation of values and to the education of men who might be better able than we have been to resolve the problems that face us now.

In no era has science been held in higher esteem. Far from the image of a few decades ago, the modern scientist is no longer considered an absent-minded professor who could not remember whether he was coming from or going to lunch; he is now a man to be respected. Even mothers who once looked upon the scientist as an eccentric egghead are encouraging their sons to consider a career in science. And no wonder. The twentieth century has been a dazzling century for science. Although lay people tend to confuse technology with science, the technological achievements made possible through scientific inquiry have rubbed off on both the scientist and on science. The schools are catching up with the public's view of this domain. New programmes in science are now old hat and the modern secondary school that does

* This article is reproduced from *The School Review* (Spring 1965) by permission of the author and The University of Chicago Press.

not have elaborate facilities for study in one or more of the scientific disciplines is considered out of date. Even psychologists have become interested in finding out how scientists go about their work and how the 'strategies' they use can be most efficiently taught to the young student.

Modern philosophers too have paid homage to science. Scientific empiricists, logical positivists, and workers in linguistic analysis have emphasized the value of scientific inquiry and discourse. They have pointed to the fact that science is an important, for some an exclusive, road to knowledge. To enable students to inquire scientifically is to enable them to produce knowledge, and to have knowledge is to have power. The ability to anticipate the future, as Ayer points out, is an ability not to be taken lightly. Science, as a way of describing, explaining, and, when possible, controlling phenomena is one of the most potent tools that man has created. It is one of man's most notable achievements.

Yet, notwithstanding the tremendous advances that scientific inquiries have produced and granted that the study of scientific methods and their products deserve a central place in any modern educational programme, the perplexities of establishing the normative ends toward which man ought to strive are still with us, and, unfortunately, these ends have not been and cannot be determined by science as it is now conceived. Scientific inquiry has gone beyond our wildest imagination in enabling us to obtain the desired, but it cannot determine the desirable. As David Hume suggested, one cannot logically proceed from a description of what is to a conception of what ought to be. How shall we, then, with the confidence we expect science to provide, determine those ends worth pursuing? How shall we determine the ends that we employ science to attain? On the one hand we have developed through science one of the most useful tools for attaining the ends we desire; we have created a most effective way of moving from ignorance to knowledge. Yet, on the other hand, the moral considerations that ought to guide the very inquiries that science undertakes are not logically derivable from its methods or its criteria.

If the logical dichotomy between fact and value, between the descriptive and the normative, holds, then to what source of knowledge can man turn in making decisions in the realm of values? Plato resolved this problem long ago by postulating a world of ideal forms which each soul glimpsed in heaven before its imprisonment in the human body.[1] Education, for Plato, was designed to draw out of the human soul the knowledge it already possessed but which in man's ignorance went unrealized. Plato believed that through the study of ideas as ideas— such as those found in mathematics, geometry, and astronomy—the individual would realize the rational powers that would enable him to recollect the ideal forms locked within his soul. Virtue, for Plato, was the child of knowledge, since he believed that no man who truly reached the exalted state of knowing would fail to act virtuously. Slavery and evil were both the consequences of ignorance. By treating the problem of knowing the good as a matter of rational unfolding, Plato placed in the hands of education the key to the good. In Plato's view the dichotomy between fact and value is false. To know is to be good.

The metaphysics that Plato constructed is not always acceptable to the modern man. Somehow the solution that he saw seems out of touch with our present view of reality. The soul, like the mental event, is looked upon by the hard-nosed student of human behaviour as a 'ghost in the machine.' And what modern day man wants to believe in ghosts!

When it is pointed out that science cannot formulate values scientifically, the arts are frequently looked upon as the obvious means of salvation. Study in the arts, it is believed, will provide the background that will enable men to make wise moral choices. If the study of science is to produce the architects of space, the study of the arts is supposed to produce the statesmen of values.

The question as to whether study of the arts can provide the kind of wisdom needed to make wise moral choices is seldom raised. The assumption seems to be that *since* the sciences deal with matters of fact, the arts *must* deal with matters of value. Yet many aestheticians have argued cogently that the justification for value positions is not the province of art. To be sure, the artist brings to his work values, but the value of his work, *qua* art, is not a function of his morality. The same principle holds for the scientist. Aristotle made this point clear when he held that the problem of moral choice exists in the domain of the practical rather than in the domain of the productive sciences where artistic activity takes place.[2] The arts, says Aristotle, concern themselves with making; the practical sciences, with doing. Moral choice, Aristotle holds further, cannot be made with the degree of confidence possible in the third realm of human activity, the theoretical. This is not to suggest that Aristotle dismisses the moral issue. He believes that the problem of determining wise moral choice is exceedingly important but that it is not likely to be made with certainty. 'We must be content, then,' says Aristotle, 'in speaking of such subjects and with such premises to indicate the truth roughly and in outline.' Aristotle not only excludes the arts as activities concerned with moral considerations but also tells us that we should be content with moral truth 'in outline.' 'For it is the mark of an educated man to look for precision in each class of things just so far as the nature of the subject admits.'

Roger Fry[3] and Clive Bell[4] have held that art is essentially the construction of significant form and that such form is derived from the qualities of the media that the artist uses. For the painter, these qualities are those of colour, line, and space; for the writer, words and plot; for the musician, tone and rhythm and tempo. In the views of those aestheticians who emphasize form, content or idea is at best a secondary consideration. For such men, the dominant, indeed the essential, consideration for determining the artistic value of the work is that of identifying the degree to which significance in form is achieved.

Formalistic aesthetic theorists hold further that since the defining characteristics of the work of art is the extent to which significance in form is achieved, the expectation that artistic works should contain moral values is untenable. Subject matter, they assert, has nothing to do with determining the quality of art; hence, the concept of 'artistic statement' in music or the visual arts is really a meaningless metaphor. At least one other strong and vocal philosophic position supports this view. Logical positivists and some scientific empiricists argue that meaning can be determined only if assertion is framed in a language capable of verification. Scientific procedures, they claim, are the only true source for determining meaning. The visual and the musical arts, poetry, all forms of metaphysics, and most types of literature contain 'statements' not capable of scientific verification; hence, they make no claim to knowledge. And, since, positivists argue, the arts do not provide knowledge, they cannot, to the extent that wise value choices are based on knowledge, be useful for making such choices, let alone for establishing a value base from which value decisions can be made.[5]

A leading positivist, Alfred Ayer, states:

As we have already said, our conclusions about the nature of ethics apply to aesthetics also. Aesthetic terms are used in eactly the same way as ethical terms. Such aesthetic words as 'beautiful' and 'hideous' are employed, as ethical words are employed, not to make statements of fact, but simply to express certain feelings and evoke a certain response. It follows, as in ethics, that there is no sense in attributing objective validity to aesthetic judgments, and no possibility of arguing about questions of value in aesthetics, but only questions of fact. A scientific treatment of aesthetics would show us what in general were the causes of aesthetic feeling, why various societies produced and admired the works of art they did, why taste varies as it does within a given society, and so forth. And these are ordinary psychological or sociological questions. They have, of course, little or nothing to do with aesthetic criticism as we understand it. But that is because the purpose of aesthetic criticism is not so much to give knowledge as to communicate emotion. The critic, by calling attention to certain features of the work under review, and expressing his own feelings about them endeavours to make us share his attitude towards the work as a whole. The only relevant propositions that he formulates are propositions describing the nature of the work. And these are plain records of fact. We conclude, therefore, that there is nothing in aesthetics, any more than there is in ethics, to justify the view that it embodies a unique type of knowledge.[6]

The separation of the arts from that sphere of activity which produces knowledge has not been universal among aestheticians. Some, like Ernest Cassirer, hold that the artist is very much concerned with knowing and that artistic knowing differs significantly from knowing through science.[7] While the scientist is concerned with the universal, the artist deals with the particular. While the scientist tries to formulate concepts that will be useful for comprehending the regular patterns of natural phenomena, the artist is concerned with experiencing and providing in symbolic form those ephemeral qualities which are no less real than those to which the man of science directs his attention. Knowledge, for Cassirer, is not the exclusive domain of science; the arts, too, provide knowledge. In concluding his celebrated chapter on 'Art' in his *Essay on Man*, Cassirer puts his case this way:

The two views of truth are in contrast with one another, but not in conflict or contradiction. Since art and science move in entirely different planes they cannot contradict or thwart one another. The conceptual interpretation of science does not preclude the intuitive interpretation of art. Each has its own perspective and, so to speak, its own angle of refraction. The psychology of sense perception has taught us that without the use of both eyes, without a binocular vision, there would be no awareness of the third dimension of space. The depth of human experience in the same sense depends on the fact that we are able to vary our modes of seeing that we can alternate our views of reality. *Rerum videre formas* is a no less important and indispensable task than *rerum cognoscere causas*. In ordinary experiences we connect phenomena according to the category of causality or finality. According as we are interested in the theoretical reasons for the practical effects of things, we think of them as causes or as means. Thus we habitually lose sight of their immediate appearance until we can no longer see them face to face. Art, on the other hand, teaches us to visualize, not merely to conceptualize or utilize, things. Art gives a richer, more vivid and colourful image of reality, and a more profound insight into its formal structure. It is characteristic of the nature of man that he is not limited to one specific and single approach to reality but can choose his point of view and so pass from one aspect of things to another.[8]

The task of determing whether the arts, like the sciences, provide man with knowledge is crucial if moral choices are affected by what men know. For, if moral choice is independent of knowledge, then clearly scientific and artistic knowing is of no relevance. If, however, moral considerations are functions in part, of man's knowing, then, to the degree to which art and science enable men to know, they are relevant.

It is clear that Ayer's criterion for warranting knowledge claims would exclude all spheres of human activity except science. If scientific criteria are the sole agents for warrant, obviously the arts must be rejected. But there is, to my mind, no convincing reason to believe that science is the exclusive source of knowledge. Men know much that contemporary methods in science are incapable of warranting. The history of science is ample testimony to the fact that scientific criteria change as scientific progress occurs. Furthermore, since knowledge, for the positivist, must be couched in some language system, thought not capable of being framed in language would have no status as knowledge; yet few would claim that language is the sole mediator of thought. Indeed, the activities of the poet and the visual artist are in large measure directed to those domains of human experience that are not capable of penetration by ordinary or scientific language. If ordinary language were an adequate substitute for artistic statement, the latter would hardly be necessary. To limit a concept of knowledge to the tentative criteria that science employs at the present is to exclude from man's knowing many of the unique ways in which he comes to understand reality.

Where does this leave us with respect to the contributions that the arts and sciences can make toward enabling students to make intelligent moral choices? Art and science do not formulate human valuations. Have they no contribution to make to the solution of moral problems? The sociologist may study the values held by members of various subcultures and social classes, but it is beyond his professional province to change those values. The historian may describe the values of ancient societies, but he has no responsibility for judging the values he describes. The anthropologist may study the values that determine the customs and mores in various cultures, but it is not his task to influence them.

The artist may reflect the pervasive values of his era through his paintings, the writer may penetrate the value core of the fictional characters he creates, the musician may employ certain values in selecting the type of music he chooses to write, but, like those working in science, artists may reflect or express values, but they do not formulate them. What then do the arts and the sciences, the two major areas from which content for the curriculum is drawn, have to contribute to the formation of moral values?

It is clear that value problems are neither framed nor resolved in a vacuum. The posing of a problem, the establishment of a premise, the formation of a solution are affected by what men bring to experience, by what men know. *The potential value of the arts and the sciences for enabling students to make wise moral choices is that art and science contribute to man's knowing.* But, although both spheres of activity provide knowledge, they do not deal with the formation of values, and it is in this area that men must be enabled to inquire, using in their inquiry the contributions the arts and sciences are capable of providing.

What are these contributions? What does science have to contribute to the making of intelligent moral choices?

Science, especially the social sciences, for example, deals with man, his relationship to others and to his self as an individual. By enabling the student to use the tools of scientific inquiry, the teacher of the social sciences can help him begin to understand the forces that affect human behaviour. History, for example, can provide the student with an understanding of the roots of his own culture. It can provide him with the data and with the methods necessary for identifying those concerns that have animated man since the beginning of recorded time. Through the study of history the student can be enabled to understand that, while the material conditions of life change through time, the aspirations, fears, and hopes of men have remained much the same. The anxiety that the astronauts must have felt as they manned the space ship that was to send them around the earth was probably felt no less keenly by the prisoners and sailors who boarded the 'Santa Maria' in the hope of finding a new travel route to the east. The study of history can provide a wealth of evidence that man's quest for peace has been and perhaps always will be continuous.

Sociology and anthropology have other contributions to make. Through these related disciplines, students can begin to understand the ways in which the environment and the culture affect their attitudes and outlook as adults. The concepts of social class, ethnocentrism, mores, custom, acculturation, and enculturation can serve as important tools with which students can come to recognize their observations of the world.

Benjamin L. Whorf, the noted linguist, has pointed out that the concepts employed in one's native language do much to determine the way in which the world is perceived.[9] Language is, in large measure, a tool that enables us to organize and handle experience. Indeed, one might say that it is largely through concepts that the world takes on comprehensible form. The concept of culture, for example, enables us to distinguish certain patterns of human organization from others. The concepts of personality, of role, of status, or of peer group provide students in the social sciences with the analytic tools necessary for differentiating and relating the data acquired through experience. Since the concepts one uses affect the ways in which one perceives the world, and since moral choices in the twentieth century need to be made within the context of mankind at large, there is no reason to assume that the introduction of the concept of mankind as a significant organizing element in the curriculum might also affect the student's world view.

If the concept of mankind were used as an organizing element in the curriculum, certain differences in school programmes might emerge. First, the scope of literary material to take one example, would broaden considerably. Instead of selecting books written almost exclusively by American- or English-speaking authors, a wide array of literature from a variety of nations would be considered. Instead of trying to understand the forces affecting American society, attention should also be focused toward trying to understand the forces that affect man and society more generally. Instead of developing a commitment to this nation 'right or wrong,' students would be encouraged to reflect upon national relationships within the context of mankind at large rather than upon a single and often narrow-minded nationalism. In short, if the problems and contributions of man were seen from the perspective of mankind, the student's concerns, the materials encountered, and the problems investigated would be placed within a frame of reference that goes well beyond his own national boundaries. The world at large, and mankind in particular, would become the context for reflecting upon human problems and potentialities. Education would serve to bring students to a type of intellectual and social maturity that rises above a narrow nationalism. An educational programme that devoted some of its time to mankind's larger problems might better prepare students to cope with the difficult world that seems to be their inheritance.

The contributions that the arts might make to the idea of mankind may be found in two of their most important functions: the way they enlarge man's knowing and their ability to penetrate the barriers of discursive language.

If one sets aside the notion that scientific knowledge is the *only* reliable or valid way in which men come to know, then one can begin to look to the arts to determine how they contribute to man's knowing. It has been said that, while science deals with the regular patterns of pehnomena, the arts deal with unique occurrences; the arts deal with the ephemeral and evanescent happenings that are no less real than the regularities that science describes. The artist, as it were, is able to perceive qualities that ordinary individuals overlook. His sensitivity to human emotion, to tonal quality, and to visual nuance combined with his technical skills and creative powers allows him to transform his responses to these qualities into physical form and thus to enable others who are less gifted to share in them.

Modern painting and sculpture are testimony enough to the power of the artistic eye. Subject matter that in previous years would have been considered unworthy of artistic attention now commands important positions in major exhibitions. Materials that once were considered unfit for serious artistic work are now used with ingenuity and skill by hundreds of accomplished artists. Thus, contemporary work in the visual arts, to take only one example, has opened our eyes to objects once considered mundane. DeKooning provides us with a fresh view

of men engaged in excavation, Sheeler helps us see industry as geo-
metric form, Westermann titillates our imagination in the way he
combines toys, old hardware, and machinery. Others working in the
visual arts have gone even further. The non-objectivists have forsaken
subject matter altogether and have shown us that by freeing ourselves
from slogans and labels that stand for the conventional we may be
able to experience objects as pure form. Mondrian, Albers, Rothko,
and Kline have, through their work, shown us how to experience the
visually qualitative as ends in themselves. By their perceptive eyes and
skilled hands, they have captured and shared with us the passing
moment of visual experience.

In another sense, the arts do not limit their attention to the ephemeral.
One may argue that the artist uses the particular and the passing only
to help man know the universal. The artist who reaches into the depths
of human experience and who creates from this depth a moving
artistic form gives us a glimpse of what is significant about the world.
The pain, trials, and finally the death of Jean Valjean can be understood
and appreciated precisely because his trials are not unique or remote
from those of mankind. The old man who alone in his boat at sea
rowed painfully on to beach the prize he had won can be experienced
in its depth because we have all struggled at some time in our lives to
achieve difficult and distant ends. Andrew Wyeth's painting 'Christina's
World,' can be understood because each of us has, to some degree,
experienced the mystic expanse of open land. The artist uses his
qualitative intelligence to control the qualitative dimensions of his
artistic problem—to deal with what is significant in human experience
in order to give it material and public form.[10]

Knowing through the arts is not limited to knowing about art. The
development of human sensitivity through art may make an important
contribution to the progress of science. Science, like art, begins in
observation. The man of science, if he is to raise questions about natural
phenomena, if he is to conceptualize the facts of experience, must
first be able to see at least in the initial stages of investigation or in
his 'mind's eye,' those aspects of the problem he chooses to investigate.
To the extent that study in the arts heightens human sensitivity to
the qualitative phenomena of reality and to the extent that it enhances
and nurtures human imagination, it plays an important role in furthering
scientific inquiry. The ability to construct models and formulate
relationships, to envisage networks of variables in interaction, is due,
in part, to the ability to iconize these relationships in a pictorial imagina-

tion. This ability may be furthered by the heightened aesthetic sensitivity that intensive artistic experience provides.

The second contribution of the arts, the contribution they make to communication, is no less important than their ability to heighten man's awareness of nature. Ordinary and scientific languages are both framed in conventional systems. By becoming familiar with the vocabulary and the syntax in which words are used, individuals sharing a common language are able to share common meanings. The limitation of linguistic systems upon communication is to be found in the fact that discursive language is rule bound. To understand a discursive language one must learn the rules of that language. The arts, however, are much less rule bound and provide a vehicle for communication across cultures that use different linguistic rules. Thus, the appreciation of Hokusai's 'The Great Wave at Kanagawa' is not dependent upon an understanding of the Japanese language. Divertimentos by Mozart, sonatas by Beethoven, and tone poems by Respighi are artistic forms that may be appreciated by people who have never seen Europe and who understand no foreign language. If the artist couches his statement significantly through the formal qualities he creates and if the individual has developed the qualitative intelligence necessary to respond to these qualities, a mode of communication takes place that is not possible in discursive language. The artistic work, in this case, assumes a function similar to that of the printed page; it acts as a mediator of the thoughts and feelings of one human being to another. John Dewey made this point quite eloquently when he wrote:

Expression strikes below the barriers that separate human beings from one another. Since art is the most universal form of language, since it is constituted, even apart from literature, by the common qualities of the public world, it is the most universal and freest form of communication. Every intense experience of friendship and affection completes itself artistically. The sense of communion generated by a work of art may take on a definitely religious quality. The union of men with one another is the source of the rites that from the time of archaic man to the present have commemorated the crises of birth, death and marriage.

Art is the extension of the power of rites and ceremonies to unite men, through a shared celebration, to all incidents and scenes of life. This office is the reward and seal of art. That art weds man and nature is a familiar fact. Art also renders men aware of their union with one another in origin and destiny.[11]

Dewey's conception of the power of art to 'render men aware of their union with one another in origin and destiny' has its analogue in the common observation that art not only communicates a very intimate and personal kind of knowledge but that the cultural exchange of art among politically antagonistic nations may make some small contribution to the amelioration of such antagonisms, that in the arts we have an important vehicle for promoting a better and deeper understanding and respect among peoples. That such a view of the power of art should be held is not surprising. It has long been observed that art reaches to the deepest levels of human experience. Artistic products, not unlike projective psychological data, reveal clues to the personality that are somehow obscured by ordinary or scientific language. Thus, that the products of artistic inquiry provide for a communion among men as Dewey observed has been attested to by almost all who have come to cherish the arts and who have developed the type of intelligence needed to understand them.

It is probably clear from what I have said that I believe that the arts and sciences *are* relevant to the formation of values. Since what men know and feel affect what they believe and how they behave, the arts and sciences as shapers of feeling and knowing are relevant to the problem of making moral choices. Yet, these fields affect values tangentially, changes in value are an ancillary consequence of their major aim. It is axiology, the study of values, that students need to confront. If students in school are not enabled to consider the range of value choices that exist among the problems they confront, where will they be enabled to do so? The controversies stirred by opposing values in social and political issues do not lie outside of education; they are the heart of it.

While few knowledgeable people would deny that problems of value underlie much of the difficulty mankind now faces, those same individuals would be hard pressed to find schools offering systematic programmes dealing with questions of value, let alone with the idea of mankind. At best, discussion of value is brought in *ad hoc* in the social studies programme or is treated descriptively as merely another aspect of social science.

The dichotomy of fact and value in American public education is not especially old. When laws were first passed requiring instruction for the young in the Massachusetts Bay Colonies in 1642, justification for their passage was made on the basis that the ability to read was necessary to know the Scriptures and that knowledge of the Scriptures was necessary in order to live in accordance with God's ways and, hence, necessary to obtain salvation.[12] The major feature of the laws that were passed in these colonies in 1642, 1647, and 1648 was that they enabled man to become a moral agent and to obtain divine deliverance. Instruction was instrumental to religious salvation. With the separation of church and state and with the growth of industrialization in the last half of the nineteenth century and immigration around the turn of this century, secularization increased and the schools took on different roles. Preparation for vocational skills, acculturation of the foreign born, and concern with the development of worthy leisure-time activities became important concerns of the school. With the growth of technology, experimental psychology, and other practices and movements committed to science, the schools moved more and more toward the separation of fact and value in education.

This chasm has grown so wide that it is not rare to hear educators and parents alike saying, 'The schools should concern themselves with helping the student acquire knowledge; the home will take care of his morals.' This position is not tenable. The school, for better or worse, is an ethically committed institution. It cannot be morally neutral. The selection of *significant* subject matter, the selection of *appropriate* modes of instruction, the determination of *good* educational objectives, the identification and reward of *outstanding* teachers all rest on some value base. The situation that must be faced is whether these values will continue to be implicit and covert or whether they will be objects of intelligent deliberation by both students and teachers alike.[13]

It is also significant, I think, that, while mankind is confronted with the most explosive situation it has ever faced, the schools avoid, by commission or by omission, discussion of the values issues that have made these problems so great. By and large, critical discussion and debate of politics, religion and, indeed, democracy itself is absent in the schools. The suggestion that students may ask whether democracy is a viable form of government in the twentieth century is seldom made. The suggestion that communism or socialism as alternative systems of economic organization are worthy of serious examination is rarely advanced. Recent overtures to teach about communism in the schools are often quickly followed by the suggestion that, of course, its vices should be made apparent to students. One may wonder about an educational programme in which so little confidence is placed in the critical powers of the students who are supposedly being educated.

The examination of contemporary social problems in American schools is yet another rare phenomenon. Certainly in the elementary schools and, in large measure in the secondary schools, history *is* the social studies. Although sociological, psychological, and anthropological theorists have created concepts that would enable students to organize and systematize their thinking on contemporary human problems, their theories, too, are omitted or underemphasized in the social studies curriculum. Many argue that theory from these disciplines is too difficult for the adolescent student, yet theory is produced by man to simplify and to organize; it functions to facilitate comprehension of the 'booming, buzzing confusion' of human experience. The most uneconomical and most difficult material to learn is material in which no pattern is recognizable. The most complex material to commit to memory in the social sciences and in the other studies is an unorganized description of isolated events. Theory at any educational level is perhaps the most efficient structure for learning. Yet history textbooks, to take only one example, are frequently crammed page after page with facts isolated from a larger conceptual structure that would enable the student to retain these facts and perhaps even to apply them as instruments of reflective thought.

What I argue for may be summed up as follows:

1. It seems of paramount importance to me that, if students are to make value choices intelligently, they understand the nature of the resources they are using. This means that it is important to help students to understand the characteristics of scientific inquiry, its tentative nature, and its relationship to value questions. Understanding the nature of the intellectual resources means also that students understand the nature of artistic statement and recognize the diverse ways in which art has been conceived as well as the unique ways in which it enables men to know.

2. I argue that, if students are to be able to cope intelligently with the economic, social, and political problems, they will need to think about such problems within the context of mankind at large. If the idea of mankind were introduced into the social studies curriculum, students might have the type of conceptual thread to which such problems might be attached. Their view of economic, social, and political problems when related to the idea of mankind might be

cast in a more comprehensive perspective and thereby provide greater promise for the future.

3. Finally, placing contemporary problems in the perspective of mankind will not, by itself, solve the moral dilemmas of man; another important mode of inquiry must be added. As the schools should attempt to develop the student's ability to engage in scientific and artistic inquiry, so should they spend time and effort to enable the student to engage in axiological inquiry. The tendency for the secondary schools to avoid the value questions involved in segregation, urban renewal, birth control, mental health, and national security is an abrogation of the school's responsibility to prepare individuals who will be able to deal intelligently with these problems. The suggestion that the study of values be made a significant part of the school curriculum should not be taken to mean that value problems should be discussed in the abstract or that doctrine should be incalculated. Quite the contrary. If students are to think with clarity about the concept of mankind, the value questions with which they cope should be related, as far as possible, to those issues that touch their lives. More meaningful ethical theory, sociology, and psychology can be taught in analysis of James Meredith's entrance into the University of Mississippi than in any long-range series of obtuse discussions on the nature of the good. The important point in dealing with such issues is that the students examine them from a variety of ethical, sociological, and psychological viewpoints. It is the recognition of the complexity of human life that students may begin to appreciate the enormity and significance of the problems they confront. It is through a concern with human problems *as they relate to mankind at large* that it may be possible to create the type of understanding that will enable man to use with wisdom those tools which have made this century the most promising and the most perilous he has ever known.

Notes

1. PLATO, *The Republic* trans. B. Jowett (New York: Random House, 1936).
2. *The Basic Works of Aristotle*, ed. Richard McKeon (New York: Random House 1941).
3. ROGER FRY, *Vision and Design* (London: Chatto & Windas, Ltd., 1920).
4. CLIVE BELL, *Art* (London: Chatto & Windas, Ltd., 1931).
5. ALFRED AYER, *Language, Truth and Logic* (New York: Dover Publications, 1946).
6. *Ibid.*, p. 113–14.

7. ERNST CASSIRER, *Essay on Man* (New Haven, Conn.: Yale University Press, 1944).
8. *Ibid.*, p. 170.
9. *Language, Thought and Reality—Selected Writings* (Cambridge, Mass.: Technology Press of Massachusetts Institute of Technology, 1956).
10. The concept of qualitative intelligence was to my knowledge first developed by John Dewey and developed later by Francis Villeman, Nathaniel Champlin and David Ecker. For a description of some aspects of this concept see my papers, 'Qualitative Intelligence and the Art of Teaching' (*The Elementary School Journal*, LXIII [March 1963] pp. 299–305), and 'Knowledge, Knowing and the Visual Arts' (*Harvard Educational Review*, XXX [Spring, 1963], pp. 208–18).
11. JOHN DEWEY, *Art as Experience* (New York: Minton, Balch & Co., 1934), pp. 270–71.
12. ADOLPH MEYER, *An Educational History of the American People* (New York: McGraw-Hill Book Co., 1957).
13. For an excellent discussion of the relationship of values to public education see HAROLD B. DUNKEL'S paper, 'Value Decisions and the Public Schools' (*School Review*, LXX [Summer 1962]).

Power and the Integrated Curriculum*

Frank Musgrove *University of Manchester*

The odd fact about modern mass society is that it is ever less 'massified'. It is ever more pluralistic, decentralized, differentiated, heterogeneous—fragmented, if you will: varied, contrastive, and infinitely interesting. Its solidarity is not, in Durkheim's terms, mechanical, segmentary, based on sameness and linearity; it is organic, multidimensional, based on specialization and the division of labour. We need to look carefully and critically at all countervailing proposals for unification, homogeneity, synthesis and integration: whether political, ideological, organizational, cultural or intellectual. It is not simply that they tend to be boring: they are also dangerous. They are the foundation of monopolies and of undue concentrations of power. I am doubtful of unified and integrated curricula and corresponding organizational structures. I believe that they are as dangerous as they are finally inefficient. My plea is for pluralism in the world of organization and in the province of the mind.

* This article has been reproduced from the *Journal of Curriculum Studies* (5, 1, 1973) by permission of the author and Wm. Collins Sons and Company Ltd.

The roots of specialization

The argument for subject specialization in the first half of this century was powerful, and it prevailed. It was not an argument about status and power—although we can see that these were involved; it was not even an argument about effective intellectual functioning. At root the argument was aesthetic: it was an argument about good taste. And good taste is a matter of selection, exclusion, constraint, discrimination. In 1946 Sir Richard Livingstone wrote: 'Any good education must be narrow . . . Education prospers by economy, by exclusion.'[1] Anything less restricted would be offensive to finer sensibilities. 'Overcrowding, in education as in housing,' wrote Livingstone, 'means ill-health, and turns the school into an intellectual slum.'[2] The good teacher is known by the number of subjects he refuses to teach. A. N. Whitehead had said much the same and for similar reasons. In his famous and influential *Aims of Education* (1932) he maintained: 'Mankind is naturally specialist . . . I am certain that in education, wherever you exclude specialism you destroy life.' Of course he made a famous attack on 'inert ideas', and this involved seeing ideas in different contexts, throwing them into new combinations. But his first educational commandment was this: 'Do not teach too many subjects.' And the final aim was aesthetic—it was an intellectual *style*, defined in terms of economy and restraint. Style, maintained Whitehead, is the 'peculiar contribution of specialism to culture'. And, indeed, more than that: 'Style is the ultimate morality of the mind.'

Neither the Spens *Report on Secondary Education* nor the Norwood *Report on Curriculum and Examinations* diverged significantly from these views. (The former was published in 1939, the latter in 1944.) The Spens Report maintained that each subject had its distinctive individuality and represented a unique intellectual tradition: they should not be 'unified' or otherwise 'fused'. The Norwood Report examined the concepts of an 'integrated' and a 'balanced' curriculum but found them largely meaningless. But both Reports were really counter-attacks: they were answering a case. The case had been presented by Dewey and largely accepted in the Hadow *Report on the Primary School* in 1931. It was in this Report, of course, that we have the famous pronouncement:

The curriculum is to be thought of in terms of activity and experience rather than of knowledge to be acquired and facts to be stored.

At least with children of primary school age, traditional subjects had no place. I would not dissent from this view. But I believe it is closely connected with the remarkable power that a number of studies have shown primary school heads to wield over their staff. It is the head who makes the decisions and staff meetings are virtually unknown.[3] In the absence of an intellectual and organizational pluralism, I would expect no less.

Specialization and the division of labour were of interest to 17th and 18th century jurists and political theorists; they were of interest to 18th and 19th century economists, and to 19th and 20th century sociologists. Eighteenth-century political theorists were concerned to separate the judiciary, the executive and the legislature in the interest of efficiency and justice; 19th-century economists were concerned with the division of labour and productivity and profits; 20th-century sociologists have been concerned with problems of social cohesion and divisiveness. (Psychiatrists have been interested, too, seeing fragmented, repetitive work as a source of 'alienation' and mental ill-health.[4]) But the philosophers of fourth-century Athens and contemporary Britain were also interested in specialization in a way which has some relevance to my theme. Their interests have been in labelling and the classification of phenomena as an aid—indeed a prerequisite—of efficient and systematic thought.

It is often said that life and its problems are not neatly divided into nicely bounded subjects: they are multidisciplinary, even inter-disciplinary. The curriculum should reflect this reality. But life is a bad teacher, for the simple reason that it *is* interdisciplinary and confusing. It needs sorting out. Of course, the language we learn in infancy helps us to do a lot of preliminary sorting out; and when a language is adjectivally rich a great deal of subtle sorting and re-sorting is possible. We do not need to regard black cows as a wholly different category from white cows. But language is not enough. In spite of Illich and the de-schoolers, we also need schools. Their job, essentially, is to bring some sort of order out of the bombardment of impression and experience to which real life exposes us.

The Sumerians erected one of the earliest civilizations on lists. In a rather crude way they wrote down on their tablets lists of things that seemed to belong together.[5] The Greeks made better lists, based on more subtle and rational criteria. Both the natural and the social sciences have important, even fundamental, classificatory functions. The first social science was law, and it was quite properly a matter of codes. Efficient codification lies at the heart of efficient intellectual activity; and I would not think it demeaning to speak of teaching and learning as 'decoding'.

Our contemporary philosophers have also been busy sorting things out, putting together things that belong together. Paul Hirst distinguishes between 'forms' and 'fields' of knowledge. 'Forms'—like Mathematics, Science and History—have unique conceptual schemes and tests of truth and falsehood: they can be discovered and isolated by logical analysis; 'fields'—like Geography and Engineering—are in some sense 'artificial', drawing on different forms of knowledge to illuminate a particular class of phenomena. The boundaries of fields and forms are differently drawn, but they are boundaries nonetheless. And Hirst is very cautious about lowering, removing or re-drawing these boundaries in the interest of some greater synthesis. Forms of knowledge have boundaries and are autonomous. Hirst concludes,

It is not at all clear what is meant by synthesizing knowledge achieved through the use of logically quite different conceptual schemes.[6]

Our contemporary zeal for synthesis and curriculum integration has many souces: Bloom's famous taxonomy of educational objectives is now perhaps more influential than Dewey's pragmatism.[7] Objectives rise hierarchically, as you know, from a humble 'knowledge of facts' to the pinnacle of 'synthesis'. I would not regard really knowing a fact as a humble accomplishment; but Bloom's allegedly ascending order of intellectual operations suggests that all our endeavours should aspire to the condition of synthesis. This famous taxonomy has been used to legitimize the most unlikely hybrid degree courses in our newer universities. It is assumed that Bloom's taxonomy applies universally to all subjects of study. I have doubts about the ordering of Bloom's objectives; I have graver doubts about their general applicability.

Boundaries and the division of labour

Formerly a hybrid was something of a bastard; today it is received in the most polite circles. I have phrased this in socio-moral terms, because at bottom the issue we are dealing with is moral. It is about the immorality of boundaries. The concept of a boundary is one of the most discreditable in contemporary consciousness. The immorality of boundaries is central to the complex of values which we call the counter-culture. It finds its supreme expression in encounter groups, and similar social exercises in boundary removal. The counter-culture is essentially tactile: touch has replaced death as the Great Leveller and academic hierarchies are stroked to extinction. Drugs remove the boundaries of normal experience. The first injunction of the counter-culture is to 'blow your mind'.

Now in a general way I strongly support the counter-culture and the complex of values which it promotes. This is the curriculum of the future: essentially expressive rather than rational-instrumental, tactile rather than verbal, contemplative rather than active, sensationalist and psychedelic rather than cerebral and devoted to restrained good taste. But this is for the future: appropriate to the social order we may have by the end of the century. In 1972 it is an exploratory curriculum for a highly gifted minority. At this point in time we must have some concern for system-maintenance. It is, regrettably, as a system-maintenance man that I talk today. I am talking about schools and academic systems as we know them; but by the end of the decade this may be a complete irrelevance.

Boundaries are of interest not only to philosophers and moralists but also to sociologists. Indeed, fashionable role theory is essentially about boundaries (and in the counter-culture the notion of a defined social or occupational role is as discreditable as the notion of a boundary[8] —for the same reason). But boundaries have interested sociologists as sources of social solidarity or division. And this is precisely the issue in discussion of the curriculum: the alleged 'fragmentation of knowledge'. I shall argue that respect for the autonomy of subjects is neither intellectually nor socially divisive; and that it is a vital defence against centralized autocracy. The division of labour does not divide; it cements.

Subject specialization is simply one instance of the division of labour. Emile Durkheim wrote about the general problem and the specific instance in 1893. He was discussing the question of social solidarity— the basic problem of sociology, the nature of the social bond. He distinguished between mechanical solidarity based on sameness, 'a system of segments homogeneous and similar to each other'; and organic solidarity based on differentiation and the division of labour. There was no doubt in Durkheim's mind that organic solidarity was superior: the more developed, advanced, even the more moral, form of social bonding. Mechanical solidarity was like an earthworm: its rings, all alike, juxtaposed in simple, linear array. By contrast, organic societies, are constituted, not by a repetition of similar homogeneous segments, but by a system of different organs each of which has a special role, and which are themselves formed of differentiated parts.[9]

Durkheim's prime example of the efficacy of organic solidarity was modern marriage: conjugal solidarity based on the sexual division of labour. Here was no advocacy of unisex or even Women's Lib (as I understand it). Marriage is strong and stable when there is a marked division of labour between men and women.

> Permit the sexual division of labour to recede below a certain level and conjugal society would eventually subsist in sexual relations pre-eminently ephemeral.[10]

(Of course this begs the question whether we actually want stronger and stable marriage: the counter-culture would deny this. But one thing that will be extremely problematical when the counter-culture prevails is the nature of the social bond.)

More than a century before Durkheim Rousseau had attacked (in the *Social Contract*) the division of labour and the money economy that made it possible. It was the certain way to servitude in the sense of the dependence of everyman upon everyman. Durkheim also noted the interdependence, and applauded it. The division of labour, he maintained,

> passes far beyond purely economic interests, for it consists in the establishment of a social and moral order *sui generis*. Through it, individuals are linked to one another. . . . Instead of developing independently they pool their efforts.[11]

Rousseau's prescription was for individual self-sufficiency and social anarchy. So too, in the last resort, is the integrated curriculum.

Durkheim recognized that the division of labour had certain pathological forms—in the world of industrial production, and in the world of learning. Extreme forms of academic specialization led to an 'anomic' condition of the division of labour. Different specialists, said Durkheim in 1890, proceed with their investigations as if the different orders of fact they study constituted so many independent worlds. In reality, however, they penetrate one another from all sides. . . .

I am sure that Durkheim was correct to call this condition 'anomic' and to deplore it as a pathological state. The division of labour normally had a contrary effect: it pulls people together. What I think we need to know much more about are the stages and levels of an academic subject at which interpenetration with others naturally occurs. Interpenetration is probably maximal in the very early and the very advanced stages of study: in the primary school and the postgraduate department. We see the relevance of other subjects when we have reached the boundaries of our own and push through them. It is true that the most exciting and creative work is occurring today on the boundaries between subject areas; but this is very advanced work that we are talking about. At lower levels, interdisciplinary work is more likely to lead to naive and inappropriate transfer of concepts. Terms like 'feedback' and 'programming' are today ubiquitous. When we transfer concepts we are usually inventing metaphors. Metaphors have their uses; but we delude ourselves and our students if we think they correspond precisely with reality. (Sociology is largely a gigantic metaphor; but I am sure Durkheim knew—and I hope we do, too—that society, however 'solidaire', is neither a machine nor an organism.)

Durkheim certainly knew the difficulty of curing the pathological condition he had diagnosed. He had no faith in adding liberal to specialist studies; and he did not see intellectual unity and synthesis as an individual achievement, something occurring in any one mind. The answer lay in sensitizing students and scholars to what was being done by others and their dependence on others' work. I will quote him on this crucial matter:

For science to be unitary, it is not necessary for it to be contained within the field of one and the same conscience—an impossible feat anyhow—but it is sufficient for all those who cultivate it to feel they are collaborating in the same work.

Social solidarity does not mean the disappearance of specialists and the rise of the generalists (as championed by the Swann Report):[12] it means interaction among specialists. Durkheim said,

The division of labour presumes that the worker, far from being hemmed in by his task, does not lose sight of his collaborators, that he acts upon them, and reacts to them.

The power base of the curriculum

Specialization means neither intellectual fragmentation nor organizational anarchy. In other words, teachers can cooperate without losing their subject identities and without being denied a strong departmental base. Whenever subjects are to be integrated, the departmental base is threatened. I am a very strong Department man both through intellectual conviction and bitter experience. Only one man wins when you integrate subjects and dissolve departments—the man at the top. Everyone else—pupils and students as well as staff—is exposed, vulnerable. I would not willingly work for the headmaster or vice-chancellor who thought that 'subjects' were dead.

We see the close connection between organizational power and subject boundaries in Sloman's Reith Lectures (1963). Subjects are not only intellectual systems; they are social systems: they confer not only a sense of identity on their members, they confer authority and they confer power. Sloman's strategy as the new Vice-Chancellor of Essex was to promote more integrated courses and reduce the power of departments. These are really two sides of the same coin. He said,

> Students . . will be admitted to schools, not to departments and they will follow in their first year a scheme of study common to the school. Staff will collaborate with other members of the same school in providing integrated courses. . . .[13]

Throughout the lectures we have approval of integrated courses and a corresponding attack on departments and the power of professors at their head. Academic subjects, departments and departmental heads have become wholly immoral in the last decade.

I have dealt elsewhere with the interplay between subject specialization and organizational power.[14] Within the loose boundaries of pre-bureaucratic schools and universities, academic entrepreneurs were often remarkable for their vigour, dash and enterprise—one thinks of Hawtrey at Eton and Hope at the University of Edinburgh in the early decades of the 19th century. It was possible for virtually autonomous, private enterprise departments to be established within the framework of a school's general organization. Stephen Hawtrey established a private enterprise mathematics department at Eton in 1837. He obtained a 40-year lease on a site in the college, built his own mathematical school in the form of a rotunda, a lecture-theatre which would accommodate 350 pupils, and recruited his own assistant mathematical masters. In 1851, after 14 years in this endeavour, he persuaded the college authorities to make mathematics a compulsory subject (three hours a week). But he had been at Eton for 19 years before he was officially recognized as a member of staff. His assistant mathematical masters never were.

I have no particular nostalgia for pre-bureaucratic forms of educational organization: they could spell servility at one extreme, or deadlock at the other (as commonly occurred in conflicts between the headmaster and the usher). Bureaucracy has provided the mechanisms for co-ordinating the work of different centres of power. But these power centres are essential to educational vitality. It is nowadays customary to attack departmental heads as 'robber barons'. Those who make the attack in these terms have profoundly misconceived the character of the medieval world. But much nearer to our own day, I think we can see in the intellectual history of 19th- and 20th-century Europe that great universities have arisen when professors have been given their head: when departments have been strong and unassailed by centralizing influences. Centralization commonly entails standardization and servility. Vitality lies in a vigorous, even defiant, pluralism.

Models for the future

Open-plan architecture and integrated curricula are part of the process of homogenization which social analysts see as the dominant trend of our times. I believe that the opposite is the case: that post-industrial societies are not characteristically homogenized and 'massified'; they are ever more segmented, differentiated, diversified. Differences are not removed but accentuated. And the trend is *not* toward more bureaucracy, if by bureaucracy we mean highly centralized forms of organizational control. Contemporary curriculum development and its organizational corollaries are a curious throwback: a retrogression which has no enduring place in post-industrial societies. In more homely terms, they take us back to all-age classes with class teachers all working in an unpartitioned hall. Both teachers and pupils work under conditions of maximum visibility. No one is more vulnerable. We are back to headmasters who enjoy undisputed sway partly because they can see everything, but chiefly because there are no firm centres of subject power and authority.

I believe that our schools, colleges and universities must be very loose confederations of diverse centres of academic power. This is the organizational style of the future: fluid, flexible, improvisational, with the centre de-emphasized and power on the periphery. The French sociologist, Crozier, has given us a sketch of this process of debureau-cratization. He maintains that the broad historical trend is for large-scale bureaucracies to become less bureaucratic in the severity of their control over members.[15] But in school we still demand loyalty (and conformity) of the order required by the great bureaucracies of history: the banking houses of Augsburg and Florence, the Jesuits, the Janissaries of the Ottoman Empire, the Prussian Grenadiers. Leaving was equivalent to treason—as it was at Oundle when the headmaster, Atkinson, was asked, not so very long ago, to resign because it became known that he was looking for another job.

Schon, in his recent Reith lectures, gave us a still more kaleidescopic picture when he talked of 'the loss of the stable state'. One of his major themes was the irrelevance and decline of the centre-to-periphery organizational model under conditions of rapid communication and widespread innovation.[16] (Toffler similarly talks of the rise of 'ad-hocracy' in which managers lose their monopoly of decision-making.[17]) The classical centre-to-periphery model is unable in times of rapid change to handle information centrally and provide the feedback that is essential. A network is now the appropriate model, rather than the wheel. Centres on the perimeter must assume responsibility and autonomy and make their own decisions. This is a far cry indeed from the contemporary school where effective innovation occurs only if the head says so.

I would support, then, unabated subject pluralism and a corres-ponding network or loose confederation of subject departments: not in order to prevent change, but to promote it. And I would accentuate distinctions and diversity in the curriculum, because the world is ever more differentiated and diverse. We have ever more structural differentiation in society, based upon age-grading and job specialization; it would be remarkable if this led to a 'mass society' of cultural standardization. And it does not, except to a very superficial view.[18] Social structure and culture do not vary so independently. What we have, in fact, is a surfeit of subcults, a bewildering diversity of life-styles available to us.[19] And future generations will have genuine choices available to them. This fact should be central to all thinking about the curriculum. As Toffler says: 'How we choose a life style, and what it means to us . . . looms as one of the central issues of the psychology of tomorrow.'[20]

In conclusion I will come back to the argument of Durkheim: that the division of labour does not divide or fragment society, but holds it together. It promotes interdependence and strengthens the bonds which unite men in societies. But the division of labour may become anomic or pathological; and in these circumstances it has the opposite effect. There have certainly been signs of 'anomie' in the academic division of labour. What is necessary is that all subject specialists should come together to decide on their common objectives and how each will make his distinctive contribution. 'Output goals' should be constantly under review and the interlocking contributions of different subject areas evaluated. But a centrally-directed master-plan is inadequate in a situation of rapid change and adaptation. Co-ordination will occur through the interaction of relatively autonomous subject specialists in more diffuse networks.

It has been feared that the headmaster may have no place in the operation of an integrated curriculum.[21] I have argued, on the contrary, that he is likely to have unprecedented primacy, as he busies himself more directly and personally in everyone's affairs and encounters none of the traditional centres of academic power. It is in the network that he will finally be lost, an archaic irrelevance, and subject teachers actually take the important decisions that are properly theirs.

Notes

1. R. LIVINGSTONE, *Some Tasks for Education*, OUP, 1946, p. 17.
2. *Ibid.*, p. 9.
3. For evidence on the decision-making habits of primary school head teachers compared with secondary school head teachers, see C. L. SHARMA, 'A Comparative Study of the Process of Making and Taking Decisions within Schools in the UK and USA', unpublished PhD thesis, University of London, 1963. For evidence regarding primary school head teachers as initiators of change and convenors of infrequent staff meetings, see MOIRA BROWN, 'Some Strategies Used in Primary Schools for Initiating and Implementing Change'; unpublished MEd thesis, University of Manchester, 1971.
4. E.g. ERICH FROMM, *The Sane Society*, Routledge and Kegan Paul, 1956.
5. GORDON CHILDE, *What Happened in History*, Pelican Books, 1942, pp. 12, 95, 119, 121 and 199.
6. PAUL H. HIRST, 'Educational Theory'. In: TIBBLE, J. W. (ed.) *The Study of Education*. London: Routledge and Kegan Paul, 1966.
7. B. S. BLOOM (1956) *Taxonomy of Educational Objectives : Cognitive Domain*. New York: David McKay.

8. See CHARLES A. REICH (1971) *The Greening of America*. Allen Lane, the Penguin Press, p. 168.
9. EMILE DURKHEIM (1933) *The Division of Labour in Society*, trans. by GEORGE SIMPSON. New York: The Free Press, p. 181.
10. *Ibid.*, p. 61.
11. *Ibid.*, p. 61.
12. *The Flow into Employment of Scientists, Engineers and Technologists*. London: HMSO, 1968.
13. A. E. SLOMAN (1964) *A University in the Making*. London: BBC, pp. 27–28.
14. FRANK MUSGROVE (1971) *Patterns of Power and Authority in English Education*. London: Methuen.
15. See M. CROZIER (1964) *The Bureaucratic Phenomenon*. Tavistock Publications, p. 85.
16. DONALD A. SCHON (1971) *Beyond the Stable State*. Temple Smith.
17. ALVIN TOFFLER (1970) *Future Shock*. The Bodley Head, p. 126.
18. C.f. H. J. WILENSKY 'Mass Society and Mass Culture: Interdependence or Independence', *American Sociological Review*, April 1, 1964.
19. See TOFFLER, *op. cit.*, pp. 233–285.
20. *Ibid.*, p. 271.
21. See D. N. HUBBARD and J. SALT (eds.) (1969) *Integrated Studies in the Primary School*. University of Sheffield Institute of Education.

Summary Appraisal

Both authors in the preceding papers identify the importance of basing curriculum decisions in the realities and values of the society served by the schools. However, it is interesting to note how they infer different courses of action for curriculum development from these realities and values. Eisner's concern is substantive—what students should be taught. His answer is that students should experience scientific inquiry, the arts, and values within a mankind perspective. Musgrove's concern is for procedure. He calls for subject specialization and the debureaucratization of formal schooling with power invested in the subject specialists. In considering these provocative papers, one should recognize the complexity and importance of questions related to the role of values in curriculum development. The question remains, 'What should be taught in our schools and by whom and how should such decisions be made?'

Suggested Readings

BROUDY, HARRY S. (1971). 'Democratic Values and Educational Goals.' In: *The Curriculum: Retrospect and Prospect*, The Seventieth Yearbook of The National Society for the Study of Education, Part I, University of Chicago Press, Illinois.

Two major questions are dealt with in this chapter of the Yearbook: What are democratic values and how are they to be construed in the present? Broudy makes the point that the goals of education must make their peace with the constraints of a modern mass society on the one hand, and the demands of democracy on the other. The chapter is important to anyone concerned with the many apparent anachronisms which exist in our social reality and with what these anachronisms mean for the curriculum of the schools.

FRANKENA, WILLIAM K. (1966). 'Philosophical Inquiry.' In: *The Changing American School*, The Sixty-fifth Yearbook of The National Society for the Study of Education, Part II, University of Chicago Press, Illinois.

This article sets forth five ways in which post World War II philosophy might have a bearing on the theory and practice of the schools: (1) by providing normative premises; (2) by providing premises of other sorts; (3) by providing conceptual or linguistic analyses and methodological elucidations; (4) by being made a part of the curriculum; and (5) by being included in the training of teachers and administrators. Utilizing such a framework, curriculum theorists and practitioners might well be in a better position to grapple with the question of the relationships between values and decision-making in education.

GOODLAD, JOHN I. and Others. (1974). *Toward a Mankind Curriculum: Adventures in Humanistic Education*. New York: McGraw-Hill Book Company.

This book proposes a curriculum which reaches across parochial, national boundaries and which promotes a wide-scale acceptance and understanding of the idea of mankind to guide all of man's activities. The book develops a four-part framework to guide the creation of mankind-oriented schools. The four are: study of the idea of mankind; teaching of conventional subject matter from a mankind perspective; emphasis on person-to-person relationships; and developing the total culture of the school as a true microcosm of mankind itself. Finally, the book describes one effort to implement the mankind curriculum in an experimental school setting.

TYE, KENNETH A. (1971). 'Educational Accountability in An Era of Change.' In: LESLEY H. BROWDER, JR. (ed.), *Emerging Patterns of Administrative Accountability*. Berkeley, California: McCutchen Press.

This paper builds on a conceptual framework of educational decision making set forth by John Goodlad (see Chapter 4) and describes the role of the various actors in the educational decision-making drama. In so doing, it shows how and by whom value decisions, policy-decisions, institutional decisions, and instructional decisions are made. Also, it discusses methods of evaluating such decisions and how such evaluation is related to 'accountability.'

Chapter 2

Aims and Objectives

Introduction

Curriculum as intentions, involves bridging the gap between the socio-political system which the school serves and the substance of schooling itself. It involves translating societal values into educational aims, as in statements such as, schools should develop the potentialities of all individuals, should develop in individuals the skills which will contribute to a productive life. While such statements may not tell us what to do, they serve as a basis for the statement of more specific instructional objectives.

'An educational objective is a statement of what students are to know, be able to do, prefer or believe as a consequence of being in a programme' (Goodlad and Richter, *op. cit.*). Since the emergence of the scientific movement in education around the turn of the century, there has been interest in the statement of educational objectives. Of late, that interest has focused upon the formulation of behavioural objectives. The cry of the neo-behaviourists has become, 'Help stamp out non-behavioural objectives.' Their position is that objectives should clearly set forth the behaviour to be acquired by the learner as a result of some instructional strategy. They reject statements which utilize ambiguous terms such as 'understand' or 'appreciate' to describe expected student outcomes. The crux of the matter, according to the neo-behaviourist, is that objectives must be stated in such a way as to be measurable.

Not everyone agrees with this position. There are those who believe that an insistence upon behavioural specificity in stating educational objectives can cause a kind of 'blindness' to important outcomes of schooling which are not yet 'measurable.' In addition, there are those neo-humanists who totally reject the need for stated objectives on a number of grounds: (1) preconceived objectives tend to preclude student involvement in decisions about their learning, (2) our measurement capabilities should not dictate what we do in our schools, (3) there is still a great deal of value in thinking of intentions in terms of what teachers do with learners rather than what behaviours are desired of students, and (4) a general rejection of the notion that human behaviour can be 'scientificized'—teaching is an art. These issues and related philosophical ones are dealt with by the papers in this section. These same issues will be dealt with for some time to come by those who are interested in translating curriculum intentions into transactional curriculum.

Gribble raises philosophical concerns about the behavioural objectives movement. He does not question the procedure of specifying objectives. Rather, he questions whether teachers ought to attempt to achieve many of the objectives which are thus specified. Gribble carries his argument further through an analysis of the *Taxonomy of Educational Objectives, Handbook II, Affective Domain.* (Krathwohl *et al.,* 1964). He suggests that the Taxonomy's attempt to clarify educational objectives in the affective domain is undermined because of its failure to distinguish between education and indoctrination in the parceling out of values and attitudes. The author states that such a distinction must be made in order to establish the criteria for determining whether a particular attitude or value in a particular field is warranted. This argument is based upon the assumption that a cognitive component is essential to the analysis of an affective state, and that component is the one which must satisfy the criteria of the subject being taught.

In his paper, Eisner gives a brief history of the development of the objectives movement in American education. He identifies four limitations of curriculum theory regarding the functions of educational objectives. First, the dynamic and complex process of instruction yields outcomes far too numerous to be specified in advance in behavioural and content terms. Second, in some subject areas, especially the arts, the specification of terminal behaviours is frequently impossible and/or undesirable. Third, curriculum theory which views educational objectives as standards by which to measure educational achievement overlooks those modes of achievement which are not measurable. Finally, classroom activities can be identified that seem useful and appropriate, from which objectives or consequences can be derived. Eisner's paper clearly points out that curriculum theory needs to allow for a variety of processes to be employed in the construction of curriculum.

Reference

KRATHWOHL, D. R., BLOOM, B. S. and MASIA, B. (1964). *The Taxonomy of Educational Objectives, Handbook II. Affective Domain.* London: Longmans, Green & Co.

Readings

Educational Objectives: Help or Hindrance?[1]*

Elliot W. Eisner *Stanford University*

If one were to rank the various beliefs or assumptions in the field of curriculum that are thought most secure, the belief in the need for clarity and specificity in stating educational objectives would surely rank among the highest. Educational objectives, it is argued, need to be clearly specified for at least three reasons: first, because they provide the goals toward which the curriculum is aimed; second, because once clearly stated they facilitate the selection and organization of content; third, because when specified in both behavioural and content terms they make it possible to evaluate the outcomes of the curriculum.

It is difficult to argue with a rational approach to curriculum development— who would choose irrationality? And, if one is to build curriculum in a rational way, the clarity of premise, end or starting point, would appear paramount. But I want to argue in this paper that educational objectives clearly and specifically stated can hamper as well as help the ends of instruction and that an unexamined belief in curriculum as in other domains of human activity can easily become dogma which in fact may hinder the very functions the concept was originally designed to serve.

When and where did beliefs concerning the importance of educational objectives in curriculum development emerge? Who has formulated and argued their importance? What effect has this belief had upon curriculum construction? If we examine the past briefly for data necessary for answering these questions, it appears that the belief in the usefulness of clear and specific educational objectives emerged around the turn of the century with the birth of the scientific movement in education.

Before this movement gained strength, faculty psychologists viewed

---

* This article has been reproduced from *The School Review* (Autumn 1967) by permission of the author and the University of Chicago Press.

the brain as consisting of a variety of intellectual faculties. These faculties, they held, could be strengthened if exercised in appropriate ways with particular subject matters. Once strengthened, the faculties could be used in any area of human activity to which they were applicable. Thus, if the important faculties could be identified and if methods of strengthening them developed, the school could concentrate on this task and expect general intellectual excellence as a result.

This general theoretical view of mind had been accepted for several decades by the time Thorndike, Judd, and later Watson began, through their work, to chip away the foundations upon which it rested. Thorndike's work especially demonstrated the specificity of transfer. He argued theoretically that transfer of learning occurred if and only if elements in one situation were identical with elements in the other. His empirical work supported his theoretical views, and the enormous stature he enjoyed in education as well as in psychology influenced educators to approach curriculum development in ways consonant with his views. One of those who was caught up in the scientific movement in education was Franklin Bobbitt, often thought of as the father of curriculum theory. In 1918 Bobbitt published a signal work titled simply, *The Curriculum*.[2] In it he argued that educational theory is not so difficult to construct as commonly held and that curriculum theory is logically derivable from educational theory. Bobbitt wrote in 1918:

> The central theory is simple. Human life, however varied, consists in its performance of specific activities. Education that prepares for life is one that prepares definitely and adequately for these specific activities. However numerous and diverse they may be for any social class, they can be discovered. This requires that one go out into the world of affairs and discover the particulars of which these affairs consist. These will show the abilities, habits, appreciations, and forms of knowledge that men need. These will be the objectives of the curriculum. They will be numerous, definite, and particularized. The curriculum will then be that series of experiences which childhood and youth must have by way of attaining those objectives.[3]

In *The Curriculum*, Bobbitt approached curriculum development scientifically and theoretically: study life carefully to identify needed skills, divide these skills into specific units, organize these units into experiences, and provide these experiences to children. Six years later, in his second book, *How To Make a Curriculum,*[4] Bobbitt operationalized his theoretical assertions and demonstrated how curriculum components —especially educational objectives—were to be formulated. In this book Bobbitt listed nine areas in which educational objectives are to be specified. In these nine areas he listed 160 major educational objectives which run the gamut from 'Ability to use language in all ways required for proper and effective participation in community life' to 'Ability to entertain one's friends, and to respond to entertainment by one's friends.'[5]

Bobbitt was not alone in his belief in the importance of formulating objectives clearly and specifically. Pendleton, for example, listed 1,581 social objectives for English, Guiler listed more than 300 for arithmetic in grades 1–6, and Billings prescribed 888 generalizations which were important for the social studies.

If Thorndike was right, if transfer was limited, it seemed reasonable to encourage the teacher to teach for particular outcomes and to construct curriculums only after specific objectives had been identified.

In retrospect it is not difficult to understand why this movement in curriculum collapsed under its own weight by the early 1930s. Teachers could not manage fifty highly specified objects, let alone hundreds. And, in addition, the new view of the child, not as a complex machine but as a growing organism who ought to participate in planning his own educational prgramme, did not mesh well with the theoretical views held earlier.[6]

But, as we all know, the Progressive movement too began its decline in the forties, and by the middle fifties, as a formal organization at least, it was dead.

By the late forties and during the fifties, curriculum specialists again began to remind us of the importance of specific educational objectives and began to lay down guidelines for their formulation. Rationales for constructing curriculums developed by Ralph Tyler[7] and Virgil Herrick[8] again placed great importance on the specificity of objectives. George Barton[9] identified philosophic domains which could be used to select objectives. Benjamin Bloom and his colleagues[10] operationalized theoretical assertions by building a taxonomy of educational objectives in the cognitive domain; and in 1964, Krathwohl, Bloom, and Masia[11] did the same for the affective domain. Many able people for many years have spent a great deal of time and effort in identifying methods and providing prescriptions for the formulation of educational objectives, so much so that the statement 'Educational objectives should be stated in behavioural terms' has been elevated—or lowered—to almost slogan status in curriculum circles. Yet, despite these efforts, teachers seem not to take educational objectives seriously—at least as they are prescribed from above. And when teachers plan curriculum guides, their efforts first to identify over-all educational aims, then specify school objectives, then identify educational objectives for specific subject matters, appear to be more like exercises to be gone through than serious efforts to build tools for curriculum planning. If educational objectives were really useful tools, teachers, I submit, would use them. If they do not, perhaps it is not because there is something wrong with the teachers but because there might be something wrong with the theory.

As I view the situation, there are several limitations to theory in curriculum regarding the functions educational objectives are to perform. These limitations I would like to identify.

Educational objectives are typically derived from curriculum theory, which assumes that it is possible to predict with a fair degree of accuracy what the outcomes of instruction will be. In a general way this is possible. If you set about to teach a student algebra, there is no reason to assume he will learn to construct sonnets instead. Yet, the outcomes of instruction are far more numerous and complex for educational objectives to encompass. The amount, type, and quality of learning that occurs in a classroom, especially when there is interaction among students, are only in small part predictable. The changes in pace, tempo, and goals that experienced teachers employ when necessary and appropriate for maintaining classroom organization are dynamic rather than mechanistic in character. Elementary school teachers, for example, are often sensitive to the changing interest of the children they teach, and frequently attempt to capitalize on these interests, 'milking them' as it were for what is educationally valuable.[12] The teacher uses the moment in a situation that is better described as kaleidoscopic than stable. In the very process of teaching and discussing, unexpected opportunities emerge for making a valuable point, for demonstrating an interesting idea, and for teaching a significant concept. The first point I wish to make, therefore, is that the dynamic and complex process of instruction yields outcomes far too numerous to be specified in behavioural and content terms in advance.

A second limitation of theory concerning educational objectives is its failure to recognize the constraints various subject matters place upon objectives. The point here is brief. In some subject areas, such as mathematics, languages, and the sciences, it is possible to specify with great precision the particular operation or behaviour the student is to perform after instruction. In other subject areas, especially the arts, such specification is frequently not possible, and when possible may not be desirable. In a class in mathematics or spelling, uniformity in response is desirable, at least insofar as it indicates that students are able to perform a particular operation adequately, that is, in accordance with accepted procedures. Effective instruction in such areas enable students to function with minimum error in these fields. In the arts and in subject matters where, for example, novel or creative responses are desired, the particular behaviours to be developed cannot easily be identified. Here curriculum and instruction should yield behaviours and products which are unpredictable. The end achieved ought to be something of a surprise to both teacher and pupil. While it could be argued that one might formulate an educational objective which specified novelty, originality, or creativeness as the desired outcome, the particular referents for these terms cannot be specified in advance; one must judge after the fact whether the product produced or the behaviour displayed belongs in the 'novel' class. This is a much different procedure than is determining whether or not a particular word has been spelled correctly or a specific performance, that is, jumping a 3-foot hurdle, has been attained. Thus, the second point is that theory concerning educational objectives has not taken into account the particular relationship that holds between the subject matter being taught and the degree to which educational objectives can be predicted and specified. This, I suppose, is in part due to the fact that few curriculum specialists have high degrees of intimacy with a wide variety of subject matters and thus are unable to alter their general theoretical views to suit the demands that particular subject matters make.

The third point I wish to make deals with the belief that objectives stated in behavioural and content terms can be used as criteria by which to measure the outcomes of curriculum and instruction. Educational objectives provide, it is argued, the standard against which achievement is to be measured. Both taxonomies are built upon this assumption since their primary function is to demonstrate how objectives can be used to frame test items appropriate for evaluation. The assumption that objectives can be used as standards by which to measure achievement fails, I think, to distinguish adequately between the application of a standard and the making of a judgment. Not all—perhaps not even most—outcomes of curriculum and instruction are amenable to measurement. The application of a standard requires that some arbitrary and socially defined quantity be designated by which other qualities can be compared. By virtue of socially defined rules of grammar, syntax, and logic, for example, it is possible to quantitatively compare and measure error in discursive or mathematical statement. Some fields of activity, especially those which are qualitative in character, have no comparable rules and hence are less amenable to quantitative assessment. It is here that evaluation must be made, not primarily by applying a socially defined standard, but by making a human qualitative judgment. One can specify, for example, that a student shall be expected to know how to extract a square root correctly and in an unambiguous way, through the application of a standard, determine whether this end has been achieved. But it is only in a metaphoric sense that once can measure the extent to which a student has been able to produce an aesthetic object or an expressive narrative. Here standards are un-applicable; here judgment is required. The making of a judgment in distinction to the application of a standard implies that valued qualities are not merely socially defined and arbitrary in character. The judgment by which a critic determines the value of a poem, novel, or play is not achieved merely by applying standards already known to the particular product being judged; it requires that the critic—or teacher— view the product with respect to the unique properties it displays and then, in relation to his experience and sensibilities, judge its value in terms which are incapable of being reduced to quantity or rule.

This point was aptly discussed by John Dewey in his chapter on 'Perception and Criticism' in *Art as Experience*.[13] Dewey was concerned with the problem of identifying the means and ends of criticism and has this to say about its proper function:

> The function of criticism is the re-education of perception of works of art; it is an auxiliary process, a difficult process, of learning to see and hear. The conception that its business is to appraise, to judge in the legal and moral sense, arrests the perception of those who are influenced by the criticism that assumes this task.[14]

Of the distinction that Dewey makes between the application of a standard and the making of a critical judgment, he writes:

> There are three characteristics of a standard. It is a particular physical thing existing under specifiable conditions; it is *not* a value. The yard is a yard-stick, and the meter is a bar deposited

in Paris. In the second place, standards are measures of things, of lengths, weights, capacities. The things measured are not values, although it is of great social value to be able to measure them, since the properties of things in the way of size, volume, weight, are important for commercial exchange. Finally, as standards of measure, standards define things with respect to *quantity*. To be able to measure quantities is a great aid to further judgments, but it is not a mode of judgment. The standard, being an external and public thing, is applied *physically*. The yard-stick is physically laid down upon things to determine their length.[16]

And I would add that what is most educationally valuable is the development of that mode of curiosity, inventiveness, and insight that is capable of being described only in metaphoric or poetic terms. Indeed, the image of the educated man that has been held in highest esteem for the longest period of time in Western civilization is one which is not amenable to standard measurement. Thus, the third point I wish to make is that curriculum theory which views educational objectives as standards by which to measure educational achievement overlooks those modes of achievement incapable of measurement.

The final point I wish to make deals with the function of educational objectives in curriculum construction.

The rational approach to curriculum development not only emphasizes the importance of specificity in the formulation of educational objectives but also implies when not stated explicitly that educational objectives be stated prior to the formulation of curriculum activities. At first view, this seems to be a reasonable way to proceed with curriculum construction: one should know where he is headed before embarking on a trip. Yet, while the procedure of first identifying objectives before proceeding to identify activities is logically defensible, it is not necessarily the most psychologically efficient way to proceed. One can, and teachers often do, identify activities that seem useful, appropriate, or rich in educational opportunities, and from a consideration of what can be done in class, identify the objectives or possible consequences of using these activities. MacDonald argues this point cogently when he writes:

> Let us look, for example, at the problem of objectives. Objectives are viewed as directives in the rational approach. They are identified prior to the instruction or action and used to provide a basis for a screen for appropriate activities.

There is another view, however, which has both scholarly and experiential referents. This view would state that our objectives are only known to us in any complete sense after the completion of our act of instruction. No matter what we thought we were attempting to do, we can only know what we wanted to accomplish after the fact. Objectives by this rationale are heuristic devices which provide initiating consequences which become altered in the flow of instruction.

In the final analysis, it could be argued, the teacher in actuality asks a fundamentally different question from 'What am I trying to accomplish?' The teacher asks 'What am I going to do?' and out of the doing comes accomplishment.[16]

Theory in curriculum has not adequately distinguished between logical adequacy in determining the relationship of means to ends when examining the curriculum as a *product* and the psychological processes that may usefully be employed in building curriculums. The method of forming creative insights in curriculum development, as in the sciences and arts, is as yet not logically prescribable. The ways in which curriculums can be usefully and efficiently developed constitute an empirical problem; imposing logical requirements upon the process because they are desirable for assessing the product is, to my mind, an error. Thus, the final point I wish to make is that educational objectives need not precede the selection and organization of content. The means through which imaginative curriculums can be built is as open-ended as the means through which scientific and artistic inventions occur. Curriculum theory needs to allow for a variety of processes to be employed in the construction of curriculums.

I have argued in this paper that curriculum theory as it pertains to educational objectives has had four significant limitations. First, it has not sufficiently emphasized the extent to which the prediction of educational outcomes cannot be made with accuracy. Second, it has not discussed the ways in which the subject matter affects precision in stating educational objectives. Third, it has confused the use of educational objectives as a standard for measurment when in some areas it can be used only as a criterion for judgment. Fourth, it has not distinguished between the logical requirement of relating means to ends in the curriculum as a product and the psychological conditions useful for constructing curriculums.

If the arguments I have formulated about the limitations of curriculum theory concerning educational objectives have merit, one might ask: What are their educational consequences? First, it seems to me that they suggest that in large measure the construction of curriculums and the judgment of its consequences are artful tasks. The methods of curriculum development are, in principle if not in practice, no different from the making of art—be it the art of painting or the art of science. The identification of the factors in the potentially useful educational activity and the organization or construction of sequence in curriculum are in principle amenable to an infinite number of combinations. The variable teacher, student, class group, require artful blending for the educationally valuable to result.

Second, I am impressed with Dewey's view of the functions of criticism—to heighten one's perception of the art object—and believe it has implications for curriculum theory. If the child is viewed as an art product and the teacher as a critic, one task of the teacher would be to reveal the qualities of the child to himself and to others. In addition, the teacher as critic would appraise the changes occurring in the child. But because the teacher's task includes more than criticism, he would also be responsible, in part, for the improvement of the work of art. In short, in both the construction of educational means (the curriculum) and the appraisal of its consequences, the teacher would become an artist, for criticism itself when carried to its height is an art. This, it seems to me, is a dimension to which curriculum theory will someday have to speak.

Notes

1. This is a slightly expanded version of a paper presented at the fiftieth annual meeting of the American Educational Research Association, Chicago, February, 1966.
2. FRANKLIN BOBBITT (1918), *The Curriculum*. Boston: Houghton Mifflin.
3. *Ibid.*, p. 42.
4. FRANKLIN BOBBITT (1924), *How To Make a Curriculum*. Boston: Houghton Mifflin.
5. *Ibid.*, pp. 11–29.
6. For a good example of this view of the child and curriculum development, see *The Changing Curriculum, Tenth Yearbook*, Department of Supervisors and Directors of Instruction, National Education Association and Society for Curriculum Study (New York: Appleton-Century Crofts Co., 1937).
7. RALPH W. TYLER (1951), *Basic Principles of Curriculum and Instruction*. Chicago: University of Chicago Press.

8. VIRGIL E. HERRICK (1950), 'The Concept of Curriculum Design.' In: VIRGIL E. HERRICK and RALPH W. TYLER (1950) *Toward Improved Curriculum Theory*, (Supplementary Educational Monographs, No. 71 [Chicago: University of Chicago Press, 1950]), pp. 37–50.

9. GEORGE E. BARTON, JR. (1950), 'Educational Objectives: Improvement of Curriculum Theory about Their Determination,' *ibid.*, pp. 26–35.

10. BENJAMIN BLOOM *et al.* (ed.) (1956), *Taxonomy of Educational Objectives, Handbook I: The Cognitive Domain.* New York: Longmans, Green & Co.

11. DAVID KRATHWOHL, BENJAMIN BLOOM and BETRAM MASIA (1964), *Taxonomy of Educational Objectives, Handbook II: The Affective Domain.* New York: David McKay, Inc.

12. For an excellent paper describing educational objectives as they are viewed and used by elementary school teachers, see PHILIP W. JACKSON and ELIZABETH BELFORD (1965), 'Educational Objectives and the Joys of Teaching,' *School Review*, LXXIII, 267–91.

13. JOHN DEWEY (1934), *Art as Experience.* New York: Minton, Balch & Co.

14. *Ibid.*, p. 324.

15. *Ibid.*, p. 307.

16. JAMES B. MACDONALD (1965), 'Myths about Instruction,' *Educational Leadership*, XXII, No. 7 (May), 613–14.

Pandora's box: The Affective Domain of Educational Objectives*

J. H. Gribble *Department of Education, University of Melbourne*

I hold that education should concern itself with the emotions and leave the intellect to look after itself. But what chance have the emotions in a system that makes school subjects of importance?

A. S. Neill, *Times Educational Supplement*,
17th July, 1966.

I. Philosophy and the analysis of educational objectives

B. S. Bloom's taxonomies of educational objectives[1] raise important questions about the role of philosophical analysis in curriculum theory. Philosophers of education characteristically claim that one of their major concerns is with conceptual clarification—with analysis of 'the language

---

* This article has been reproduced from the *Journal of Curriculum Studies* (2, 1, 1970) by permission of the author and Wm. Collins Sons and Company Ltd.

of education'. An apparently similar preoccupation is acknowledged by Bloom and his colleagues:

> We envisioned several major values arising from the attempt to order these desired outcomes. In the first instance, the actual sharing in the process of classifying educational objectives would help the member of the group *clarify* and tighten the 'language of educational objectives'. We were aware that all too frequently educational objectives are stated as meaningless platitudes and cliches. Some view them as an opportunity to use a type of prose found frequently in the superlatives employed by advertising men and the builders of political platforms. If, however, educational objectives are to give direction to the learning process and to determine the nature of the evidence to be used in appraising the effects of learning experiences, the terminology must become clear and meaningful.[2]

By breaking down vaguely generalized statements of objectives into components which can be specified behaviourally Bloom has undoubtedly performed a useful service. *If* teachers and educational committees wish to achieve the educational objectives they set up then it is essential that they specify the behavioural outcomes which would indicate failure of success in the achievement of the objectives.

The question which I want to raise about many of the objectives which are thus specified by Bloom and his colleagues is whether teachers *ought* to attempt to achieve the objectives. My thesis is that clarification and behavioural specification of the platitudes and cliches which are frequently offered as 'educational objectives' is often a necessary step towards exposing their inappropriateness as *educational* objectives. Bloom asks,

> If we obscure the objectives in the affective domain and bury them in platitudes, how can we examine them, determine their meaning, or do anything constructive about them?[3]

The examination of such platitudes, the determination of their meaning must certainly be prior to our doing anything about them. But frequently such analysis leads us to decide to do nothing about them on the grounds that they are not, properly, educational objectives at all. Once we allow that any old objective of any old teacher or committee is to count as an educational objective and must be 'taxonomized' as such, then we find ourselves fighting a much more difficult battle against the undesirable and inappropriate activities which sometimes go on in schools.

Bloom concludes the introduction to the second handbook of the taxonomy by issuing a challenge to educational philosophers:

> . . . back of all the more operational and psychological problems is the basic question of what changes are desirable and appropriate. Here is what the philosopher, as well as the behavioural scientist must find ways of determining what changes are desirable and what changes are necessary.[4]

The main contention of this paper is that no satisfactory account of educational objectives in either the cognitive or the affective domain can be made unless it has reference throughout to what are desirable and appropriate changes. These are not considerations which arise only when a classification of educational objectives is completed for such a classification must discriminate between *educational* objectives and those which are not educational objectives.

II. Logical considerations in the analysis of educational objectives

In the first handbook, *The Cognitive Domain*, Bloom accepts the assumption of the teachers and curriculum makers who provide the raw material of the *Taxonomy* that the development of mind through knowledge is a desirable and necessary part of education. This has, in fact, been ably argued by educational philosophers[5] but Bloom gives no indication that he is aware that this is a position which requires argument. What would Bloom say about possible objectives such as, 'getting children to use alchemical techniques in effecting changes in metals' or 'analysing personality traits by using phrenology' or 'predicting future events astrologically'? Presumably his response would be that he did not come across such objectives in the literature. But it is important to ask why such objectives do not appear, for unless the grounds for excluding such objectives are made clear we run the risk of failing to make clear the conceptual connection between 'education' and the development of cognition through rational knowledge.[6] It is tacitly assumed, in the first handbook, that 'cognitive' objectives in education are tied to standards of truth and procedures for arriving at truth. Astrological and alchemical procedures cannot be included among the forms of analysis and synthesis which are to be developed in education because astrology and alchemy are not forms of knowledge. This point tends to be obscured by Bloom's distinction between 'knowledge' and 'skills and abilities'.[7] We might be led to think that such skills as analysis and synthesis are 'general abilities' rather than skills which are logically differentiated with reference to the particular form of knowledge in which the analysis or the synthesis is performed. We might even be led to think that a training in alchemical analysis and synthesis could be part of 'education' on the grounds that it strengthened one's 'analytical powers' or 'synthesizing powers' even though it involves the adoption of false beliefs. However, although the distinction between 'knowledge' and 'skills and abilities' could be misleading in these ways, the danger is largely circumvented by Bloom's specification of what the skills and abilities are in relation to the distinctive operations involved in the formation of judgements in the various forms of knowledge. His illustrative test items provide the answer to such questions as 'analysis of what?', 'synthesis of what?', for they make it plain that what is meant is historical analysis and synthesis, scientific analysis and synthesis and so on.

The consequences of separating the domain of affective objectives in education from knowledge are far more serious. We can no longer assume, in the second handbook, that 'affective objectives' such as 'satisfaction in response' or 'commitment' relate to the development of desirable states of mind. I have argued above that in the cognitive domain the guarantee that the abilities and skills are educationally desirable is provided by the close connection in the illustrative test items between the development of 'analysis' and 'synthesis' and so on and the standards of truth and the procedures for establishing truth in the various forms of knowledge. So that although Bloom claims in the first handbook that every effort was made to avoid value judgements about objectives and behaviours, to 'permit the inclusion of objectives from all educational orientations',[8] the decision to discriminate *educational* objectives necessitates a fundamental value judgement—that education is concerned with the development of mind through knowledge. In the second handbook, however, 'affective objectives' in education are described as if they were separable from the development of mind through knowledge and the illustrative test items reinforce this impression. When we ask, 'satisfaction in response to what?' or 'commitment to what?' the answers we are given through the examples in the test items do not refer us to standards of what is valuable and desirable, presumably because Bloom sees it as his task to be 'neutral' with respect to these 'value questions'.

When Bloom explains the 'neutrality' of the taxonomy he says that what is meant is that it 'should be broad enough to include objectives from any philosophic orientation and thus from any culture'.[9]

It seems unlikely that the publicly avowed objectives of most schools, in western society, would differ markedly from ours in America even when the political orientation is markedly more authoritarian. On the other hand, the scheme does provide levels for the extreme inculcation of a prescribed set of values if this is the philosophy of a culture.[10]

Two points become apparent here:

(i) The taxonomy is referred to as a classification of 'school' objectives; the distinction between these and educational objectives is ignored.

(ii) The consequences of a failure to observe this distinction are apparent in the second sentence where Bloom's 'neutrality' leads him to accept what appears to be a form of indoctrination as embodying objectives for which the taxonomy ought to make room. This would be inappropriate in a taxonomy of *educational* objectives. While there will be wide differences as to whether a particular set of beliefs does constitute a 'doctrine', the 'extreme inculcation of a prescribed set of values' exhibits a lack of concern for whether the values are defensible or not. Without such a concern we would be unable to distinguish education from indoctrination.[11]

In the first handbook Bloom tells us that

We recognize the point of view that truth and knowledge are only relative and that there are no hard and fast truths which exist for all time and all places.[12]

As I have explained, there was no need to challenge the epistemological assumptions which are implied by this remark. For this 'recognition' does not lead Bloom to allow the passing on of false beliefs and specious procedures as legitimate educational objectives, at least in the first handbook. Bloom is not 'neutral' with regard to knowledge and truth. His view that they are 'relative' does not lead him to make room, in *The Cognitive Domain*, for the development of false beliefs and specious procedures if *these* are part of the 'philosophy of a culture'. But no restrictions are placed, even tacitly, on the 'values' which may be passed on in education. I shall argue that this crucial divorce between the two domains (which are logically indivisible) is disastrous for the second handbook. But first, let us try to see how and where the divorce came about.

The crucial point in the separation between the 'logical' considerations of the first handbook and the 'psychological' considerations of the second comes in Bloom's discussion of category 6.00, Evaluation, in *The Cognitive Domain*. This category is presented as 'a major link with the affective behaviours where values, liking, and enjoying (and their absence or their contraries) are the central processes involved'.[13] '*Evaluation*' involves the use of criteria and standards for making value judgements and Bloom resolves to consider 'only those evaluations (as distinct from what he calls 'opinions') which are or can be made with distinct criteria in mind'.[14] This resolution is made on the grounds that 'educational procedures are intended to develop the more desirable rather than the more customary types of behaviour'.[15]

It is at this point that Bloom misses the opportunity to introduce the necessary 'logical' considerations into his classification of objectives in the affective domain—necessary if the second handbook is to be part of a classification of *educational* objectives. He acknowledges frequently enough that 'at all levels of the affective domain, affective objectives have a cognitive component'[16] but he fails to see that this cognitive component (the 'judgement' or 'the way someone "sees" the object of feeling') is the crucial factor in determining whether an affective response is desirable or not and thus whether it is an appropriate educational objective. He misses the opportunity because his distinction between 'judgements' (which he sees as belonging to the cognitive domain) and 'opinions' (which he sees as belonging to the affective domain) is misconstrued as a merely psychological distinction—a matter of how *consciously* the criteria are 'in mind'.[17] Whereas there is nothing necessarily 'desirable' (and thus potentially 'educational') about using the criteria for one's evaluations 'consciously'. The important consideration in education is that the judgements and evaluations which children make can be seen to relate to the publicly acceptable criteria for making judgements and evaluations in the various forms of knowledge. It is this which distinguishes them from arbitrary or biased 'opinions', the passing on of which cannot constitute an educational objective. It is quite beside the point to ask how 'consciously' someone has the criteria 'in mind' when he makes a judgement or evaluation. The degree of 'internalization' of criteria for making evaluations has nothing to do with the appropriateness or inappropriateness of the criteria.

I am arguing that the criteria for making evaluations (in morals or music or literary criticism or whatever) are the only criteria for estimating the desirability of an affective response in such areas and thus for determining whether or not a particular affective objective is an educational objective. An 'internalization' continuum, of the sort which Bloom describes, may have some interest to psychologists but it is useless as a means of classifying or ordering educational objectives unless it is closely related to the cognitive core of affective responses. The business of education in the affective domain is to get children feeling positively toward what is valuable or true or right in so far as there are publicly acceptable criteria for determining goodness or truth or rightness. These criteria are not contingently related to the specification of educational objectives in the affective domain—they are a necessary part of such a specification.

In many cases, particularly in the aesthetic and moral realms, the criteria are obscure and contested. Bloom notes this when he refers to the objective 'responds emotionally to a work of art'. He remarks,

> While we could recognize a cognitive component in such an objective we should clearly be less certain to secure agreement among educators about the most appropriate cognitive behaviour to accompany the affective behaviour.[18]

But the difficulty here and throughout most of the second handbook is at least partly of Bloom's own making. For 'responds emotionally to a work of art' should never have been admitted as an educational objective. If the objective were to be properly stated it would read, 'responds with the appropriate emotion to particular works of art'.[19] Affective responses such as this require for the elucidation very close attention to the way a child *sees* a particular work of art. This 'cognitive' behaviour does not merely 'accompany' the affective behaviour—it is an essential part of the analysis of the affective behaviour. C. A. Mace sums up a conclusion common to preceding philosophical discussions of 'emotions' which can be extended to all 'affective' responses:

Every emotional or affective state involves a 'judgement', an appraisal of a situation, a perception of some feature of the situation, some kind of cognition . . .[20]

But, Mace adds, the 'cognitive' component can take the form of a grossly mistaken belief. Similarly Peters argues that the 'standard uses' of 'emotion' and other 'affective' terms refer to something which 'comes over people when they consider a situation in a certain kind of light'[21]— and this consideration frequently involves a misapprehension of the situation or phenomenon.

This point is important when we consider what is involved in achieving educational objectives in the affective domain. In the analysis of a child's affective response to a work of art, for example, it is crucial to get at the way the child sees the work. The only way we can get him to feel differently about it is to get him to see it differently. And the only way we can decide whether or not the child's response is appropriate or inappropriate is by referring to whatever criteria are available for making judgements about works in the particular art form.

It does occur to Bloom on one occasion that the 'cognitive' analysis of a work of art may be necessary for 'truly' appreciating a work of art:

In some instances teachers use cognitive behaviour not just as a means to affective behaviour but as a kind of prerequisite. Thus appreciation objectives are often approached cognitively by having the student analyse a work of art so that he will come to understand the way in which certain effects are produced—the nuances of shading to produce depth, colour to produce emotional tone etc. Such analysis on a cognitive level, when mastered, may be seen as learning necessary for 'truly' appreciating a work of art.[22]

Bloom fails to see the sense in which an appropriate cognitive core to the 'appreciation' *is* necessary. In so far as the student is responding to irrelevant features of the work then he is not truly appreciating the work. This is not a psychological point—it is not that a student has to go through a certain order of 'psychological steps' in order to 'truly' appreciate a work of art. He may even be unable to articulate the reasons for his response. For example, confronted with Turner's *The Slave Ship* he may say 'It's something to do with the light in the painting that I appreciate most'. Such an appreciation must be distinguished from another which is appreciative of the painting on the ground that it is very big. In *both* cases, of course, the affective response relates to 'a perception of some feature of the situation, some kind of cognition'. It would be educationally insignificant if both children said merely that they 'liked' the painting. The achievement of educational objectives in the affective domain is necessarily related to the cognitive core of the affective responses, to the appropriateness or inappropriateness of the way the object of the affective response is perceived. Bloom notes that there may be a variety of 'correct' responses.[23] But he nowhere emphasizes the corollary of this, that there is a distinction between correct and incorrect responses. Once this is admitted then the achievement of educational objectives in the affective domain become governed by 'logical' considerations.

As an example of a standard 'affective objective' sought by teachers of literary appreciation we could take one which Bloom cites: 'Increased appetite and taste for what is good in literature'.[24] Such an objective may be found in many statements of objectives for courses in literary appreciation. It is a genuine educational objective, connected as it is with the development of desirable states of mind and related, as it seems to be, to the 'logic' of literary appreciation. The important word in the statement is '. . . what is *good* in literature', for this presupposes criteria and procedures for making and evaluating responses to literature.[25] But stated as it is the objective is platitudinous and we look to the test illustrations to find the clarification and specification of the objective in terms of behaviours which would show that a child not only discriminated successfully between good and bad works of literature but also preferred or 'appreciated' those which are good. Bloom's test illustration is adapted from the Chicago Eight-Year Study.

QUESTIONNAIRE ON VOLUNTARY READING

Directions: The purpose of this questionnaire is to discover what you really think about the reading which you do in your leisure time. . . . Consider each question carefully and answer it as *honestly* and *frankly* as you possibly can. There are no 'right' answers as such. It is not expected that your own thoughts or feelings or activities relating to books should be like those of anyone else. There are three ways to mark the Answer Sheet:

Y means that your answer to the question is Yes.
U means that your answer to the question is Uncertain.
N means that your answer to the question is No.
30. Do you read essays, apart from school requirements? (**N**)

53. Do you ordinarily read fewer books during the summer vacation period than you do during a similar period of time when school is in session? (Y)

55. Have you ever done further reading or consulted other people in an attempt to learn more about the period, the events, or the places presented in a book which you have read? (N)

67. Do you read books chiefly because your parents or teachers urge you to do so? (Y)[26]

A student's responses to these items could reveal nothing about whether he is responding to what is good in literature.[27] What is most striking about the sample statements of the objectives of teaching literary appreciation at subsequent taxonomic levels is that this vital qualitative (and 'cognitive') component vanishes almost completely. At 2.2 we have

Objective: Engages in a variety of leisure time reading activites.[28]

Neither this objective nor its test illustrations have any reference to the student's discrimination between good and bad literature. At 2.3 Satisfaction in Response, the first test illustration, Example A[29] relates the affective response to the student's reading of particular examples of 'good' novels, but the *source* of the student's satisfaction remains obscure. Thus, the student may have derived satisfaction from reading *War and Peace* for the wrong reasons (e.g. 'because it is such a long novel'). Example B,[30] testing the objective, 'Finds pleasure in reading for recreation' asks the student to give his 'general reactions' to whatever fiction he has been reading. Some of the responses to the test items could be relevant indicators of the achievement of a relevant affective objective, e.g., 'Feeling the beauty of the author's style', but only if it were related to particular works in which the style *is* beautiful. But since the test items do not ask the student to discriminate *True Confessions* trash from the good fiction they have read, answers to the test questions are quite useless as indicators of the achievement of any objective of teaching literary appreciation. In fact the student who 'enjoys a good cry' over *Nancy's Broken Date,* if she has ever been taught literary appreciation, reveals the failure of the teaching. Even Example C, 'Has satisfaction in reading the plays covered in a drama course',[31] which presumably involves 'good' plays, bears no reference in the test questions to the *source* of the satisfaction. And in Example D the students are asked numerous questions about their response to the books they take from the school library without reference to *which* books they have taken.

It is not until we get to taxonomic level 3.2, Example E, that we find another genuine example of an educational objective in the domain of aesthetic judgements, with

Objective: Preference for artistically appropriate choice.[32]

But how hopelessly general and intellectually poverty-stricken are the test questions! How could anyone have an opinion as to whether 'A still life does not convey any definite mood'? The testers are quite confident that a still life—*any* still life—does convey a definite mood; if the student disagrees with the statement then this is an indication of a preference for an artistically appropriate choice. This is a case not merely of disregard for the qualitative and cognitive component in affective responses, it is a case of a profound ignorance of their nature.

From this point in the taxonomy the objectives in the literary domain take on a highly instrumental flavour. At level 3.2, Example F, 'Wants to develop insight about people through the reading of novels'[33] is an objective which may imply some regard for qualitative considerations but it is hardly an objective which is intrinsic to the study or appreciation of literature. It is difficult to know what to make of 3.3, Example C, 'Devotion to reading as an avenue for self-improvement', but 4.1, Example B, 'Uses reading to derive ideas about the conduct of life'[34] lacks any qualitative component and is highly instrumental into the bargain.

Except for the occasional use of the words 'good literature' there is no reason why answers to the tests which Bloom offers as indicating failure or success in achieving each of these objectives could not be just as satisfactory from someone who had never attempted a course in literary appreciation. What Bloom offers us through most of the second handbook are not educational objectives nor does he offer us tests for the attainment of educational objectives, for such objectives are inseparably tied to the attainment of a great variety of highly particular cognitive skills which are disregarded throughout most of the second handbook.

I argued earlier that this fatal separation between the 'logical' considerations of the first handbook and the 'psychological' considerations of the second handbook occurs during Bloom's discussion of taxonomic level 6.00, Evaluation, in *The Cognitive Domain*. This point is amply demonstrated when we contrast the test illustration from the context of literary appreciation which appears at this level in the first handbook with those we have been examining from the second handbook.

Given a poem, determine criteria of evaluation which
are appropriate and apply them.

Since there's no help, come let us kiss and part;
Nay, I have done, you get no more of me,
And I am glad, yea glad with all my heart
That thus so cleanly I myself can free;
Shake hands forever, cancel all our vows,
And when we meet at any time again,
Be it not seen in either of our brows
That we one jot of former love retain.
Now at the last gasp of love's latest breath,
When, his pulse failing, passion speechless lies,
When faith is kneeling by his bed of death,
And innocence is closing up his eyes,
Now if thou wouldst, when all have given him over,
From death to life though mightst him yet recover.

Write an essay of from 250–500 words, describing and evaluating
the foregoing poem. In your description you should employ such
terms as will reveal your recognition of formal characteristics of
the poem. Your principles of evaluation should be made clear—
although they should not be elaborately described or defended.[35]

Bloom rightly takes it for granted that 'truly evaluating' this poem
requires the exercise of a number of cognitive skills. But as we have
seen he is not willing to assume that 'truly appreciating' a poem will
also require familiarity with the procedures and criteria for making
judgements in literary criticism. In Bloom's account this is but one
route among many to the achievement of 'affective objectives' in education and, in general, cognitive behaviour is portrayed by Bloom as
being a merely contingent 'accompaniment' to behaviour which reveals
the attainment of affective objectives. Whereas part of what is *meant*
by 'appreciating' a poem is that the reader is responding to those
aspects of the poem which make it a good poem and this is part of what
is involved in evaluation of the poem. In this sense, evaluation, with
all the 'cognitive' operations and logical considerations it may involve,
is not just a psychological 'pre-requisite' to the attainment of educational
objectives in the affective domain—it is a logically necessary part of
the analysis of what constitutes an educational objective in the affective
domain

III. Are there criteria for evaluating affective responses in morals and the arts?

I have tried to show that the 'clarification of the language of educational objectives' undertaken by Bloom suffers from deficiencies which are largely a result of his inattention to difficulties which require philosophic analysis. While Bloom's behavioural specification of otherwise vague objectives in education is often valuable, his concept of 'education' is either unanalysed or confused and this undermines his attempt to clarify educational objectives in the affective domain. This is most apparent in his failure to distinguish between education and indoctrination in the passing on of values and attitudes. This distinction must be made with reference to the criteria for determining whether a particular attitude or value in a particular field is warranted. Reference to a cognitive component is essential to the analysis of any affective state, and in education the cognitive component which is appropriate to the achievement of an affective objective is that which satisfies the criteria which are operative in the particular subject being taught.

I want to conclude by considering a counter-argument which might be advanced by Bloom which would focus attention on an issue which I have dealt with in a rather high-handed fashion. Bloom might argue that I fit his description of the 'shameless indoctrinator'. As he remarks,

Cognitive behaviour may be used to indoctrinate points of view and to build attitudes and values. Indeed, we do this shamelessly in the aesthetic fields, where we want our students to learn to recognize 'good' poetry, painting, architecture, sculpture, music and so on. But in most areas of the curriculum we have a horror of indoctrinating the students with any but our most basic core values (we cannot always agree on the nature of these core values, the court cases on religion in the schools are an example). In most instances where indoctrination is avoided we seek to have the student take his own position with respect to the issue. Thus a discussion may result in the development of a variety of 'correct' positions and attitudes with respect to the area of concern, rather than in a single type of behavioural outcome as where a cognitive objective has been achieved. This also occurs where there are conflicts in values within our own culture. For example, the problems of honesty vs. dishonesty vs. 'white lies' or of competition vs. co-operation usually result in a variety of acceptable solutions, each a function of the situation in which such conflict arises.[36]

I think the important issue which is being raised here is whether or not there *are* publicly acceptable criteria for making moral or aesthetic evaluations. Perhaps I have been too freely assuming the existence of such criteria. If 'attitudes', 'values', 'appreciations', 'commitments' in these areas are arbitrary or private matters of opinion then teachers who try to get students to recognize what is 'good' in the arts or in morals may well be 'shamelessly indoctrinating'. This can be avoided, according to Bloom, if we allow the student to 'take his own position' with respect to such issues. Value judgements would thus seem to be characterized as Hume does, as statements of emotional preferences, mere consequences of our differing psychological makeups. As Hume puts it,

> Morality consists . . . not in any *matter of fact* . . . morality is not an object of reason. Take any action allowed to be vicious: Wilful murder, for instance. Examine it in all lights, and see if you can find that matter of fact, or real existence, which you call *vice*. In whichever way you take it, you find only certain passions, motives, volitions, and thoughts. There is no other matter of fact in the case. The vice entirely escapes you, as long as you consider the object. You never can find it, till you turn your reflexion into your own breast, and find a sentiment of dissapprobation, which arises in you, towards this action. Here is a matter of fact; but 'tis the object of feeling, not of reason. It lies in yourself, not in the object. So that when you pronounce any action or character to be vicious, you mean nothing, but that from the constitution of your nature you have a feeling or sentiment of blame from the contemplation of it.[37]

If Bloom does view value judgements as being 'arbitrary' statements of emotional preferences it would help to explain why, in the example of evaluating the poem on p. 72, the student is asked to 'determine criteria of evaluation'. He is told that 'Your principles of evaluation must be made clear', presumably because a wide variety of 'correct' principles could be expected and must be accepted by the examiner. On the other hand the student is expected to be able to 'defend' his principles. This is surely a paradoxical position, which is widespread in moral philosophy. The paradox is incisively exposed by Phillipa Foot:

Those who are influenced by the emotivist theory of ethics (see the quotation from Hume above) and yet wish to defend what Hare has called 'the rationality of moral discourse' generally talk a lot about 'giving reasons' for saying that one thing is right and another wrong. The fact that moral judgements need defence seems to distinguish the impact of one man's moral views upon others from mere persuasion or coercion, and the judgements themselves from mere expressions of likes and dislikes. Yet the version of argument in morals currently accepted seems to say that, while reasons must be given, no one need accept them . . . How 'x is good' can be a well founded moral judgement when 'x is bad' can be equally well founded it is not easy to see.[38]

Bloom does seem unwilling to allow that value judgements in morals or the arts are distinct from mere likes and dislikes for he sees the teacher's impact on children when he attempts to pass on attitudes and values as a form of persuasion or coercion or indoctrination. But in so far as *some* attitudes and positions in these fields are 'correct' and capable of defence then there must surely be criteria for making the judgements.

It is outside the scope of this paper to offer an account of the nature of such criteria. I have maintained elsewhere[39] that the moral procedural principles of impartiality and respect for persons and the considerations of the harm or benefit which the adoption of moral rules might have are very general criteria which distinguish moral judgements from mere expressions of likes and dislikes. It is much more difficult to make out a case for there being analogous principles in the realm of aesthetic judgements and any attempt to do so would require another paper. But if we consider for a moment the very extensive literature of literary criticism, for example, it would be extraordinary if the elaborate argumentation which we find here is being carried on without reference to criteria which are tacitly acknowledged by literary critics. Unlike morals, however, there has been very little work by philosophers on the 'logic' of arguments in art criticism.

It would be a just criticism of this paper to complain that it fails to give a description of the logical considerations which, it argues, are a necessary part of clarifying educational objectives in the domain of values and attitude formation. The main point I have tried to make is of a much more general kind, to the effect that an attempt to clarify such objectives without attending to their crucial 'logical' component must be unsatisfactory. Philosophers of education have already done useful work in the more logically 'clearcut' areas of the curriculum, and Bloom's work on the 'affective domain' does, as he suggests, open a 'Pandora's box' of concepts which should keep philosophers who are interested in curriculum theory busy for a long time.

Notes

1. B. S. BLOOM, *et al.*, *Taxonomy of Educational Objectives*. The Classification of Educational Goals, *Handbook I Cognitive Domain*, 1956, *Handbook II Affective Domain*, 1964 (Longmans, Green and Co. Ltd., London). For ease of reference I refer to Bloom without mentioning the names of his colleagues. In the notes I refer to each of these books as *Handbook I* and *Handbook II*.
2. *Handbook II*, p. 4.
3. *Ibid.*, p. 91.
4. *Ibid.*, p. 90.
5. P. H. HIRST (1965), 'Liberal Education and the Nature of Knowledge', *Philosophical Analysis and Education*, (ed.) R. D. Archambault. London: Routledge and Kegan Paul Ltd.
6. See HIRST, *ibid.*
7. I have indicated the dangers of this distinction in more detail in my *Introduction to Philosophy of Education*. Boston: Allyn and Bacon Inc., 1969, pp. 57–8.
8. *Handbook I*, pp. 6–7.
9. *Handbook II*, p. 43.
10. *Ibid.*, p. 43.
11. The distinction between education and indoctrination is discussed at some length in my *Introduction to Philosophy of Education*, *op. cit.*, pp. 29–40. See also the concluding part of this paper.
12. *Handbook I*, p. 32.
13. *Ibid.*, p. 185.
14. *Ibid.*, p. 186.
15. *Ibid.*, p. 186.
16. *Handbook II*, p. 53.
17. *Handbook I*, p. 186 (also, p. 19).
18. *Handbook II*, p. 53.
19. It may, of course, be denied that 'emotional' responses to works of art are necessary or appropriate. Certainly the emotion which is appropriate to seeing a performance of *King Lear* would be quite different from observing real events of the kind which occur in the play. When teachers expect children to be 'moved' by plays and poems, *what* do they expect? And what could they legitimately expect?
20. R. S. PETERS and C. A. MACE, 'Emotions and the Category of Passivity', *Proceedings of the Aristotelian Society*, January, 1962, p. 139.
21. *Ibid.*, p. 119.
22. *Handbook II*, p. 55–6.
23. *Ibid.*, p. 56.
24. *Ibid.*, p. 124.

25. In these ways the objective is quite distinct from other objectives which Bloom includes, such as 'Willingness to comply with health regulations', the achievement of which is to be tested by such items as whether or not the student wears overshoes or rubbers during wet cold weather or goes to bed about the same time each night. The formation of such habits is characteristic of training them, not educating them.
26. *Handbook II*, p. 124.
27. Teachers of literary appreciation might be surprised, at first, to see that the responses which most obviously indicate achievement of the objective are inappropriate, i.e. if a child never reads essays apart from school requirements, reads fewer books in the vacation than at school, never tries to find out anything about what he reads and who reads books under external constraint is alleged to have shown that the objective, 'Increased appetite and taste for what is good in literature', has in some measure been achieved. But we find in a footnote on p. 124 that this objective is not a 2.1 objective. In fact it is a 3.1 objective—'Acceptance of a value'. The answers are said to be illustrative of a 2.1 response to a 3.1 objective. If the objective were to be stated at the 2.1 level it would take a form similar to 'Completion of assigned readings'. And as Bloom remarks, 'educational objectives in reading are rarely, if ever, stated at the 2.1 level.' As with objectives at level 1.00 these are really statements of the *conditions* for achieving educational objectives. Unless the student attends to his teacher or to his books and carries out some relevant tasks the achievement of affective objectives would not be possible for he would have no relevant *cognitive* experience to which he could give an affective response. So that the test under discussion does not indicate achievement of an educational objective—all it does is to indicate that responses at higher taxonomic levels are not being made. But even if responses at a 3.1 level were given they would still not indicate that an educational objective had been achieved since they do not reveal whether a student is responding to what is *good* in literature.
28. *Handbook II*, p. 129.
29. *Ibid.*, p. 134.
30. *Ibid.*, p. 134.
31. *Ibid.*, p. 135.
32. *Ibid.*, p. 148.
33. *Ibid.*, p. 148.
34. *Ibid.*, p. 158.
35. *Handbook I*, p. 198.
36. *Handbook II*, p. 56.
37. 'A Treatise of Human Nature', *Hume's Ethical Writings*, (ed.) Alisdair MacIntyre (New York and London: Collier Books, The MacMillan Co., 1965), p. 196.
38. PHILLIPA FOOT, 'Moral Arguments', *Mind*, 1958, p. 502.
39. *Introduction to Philosophy of Education*, *op. cit.*, Chapter 5.

Summary Appraisal

Neither of the papers in this section rejects a 'scientific' approach to curriculum planning, one which calls for the selection of aims and objectives to guide instruction and evaluation. What they do is to raise serious philosophic questions which need to be answered in order to avoid a totally dogmatic position which eliminates the possibility of alternative routes to the development of curriculum theory (intentions) and practice (transactions). Eisner calls upon theory to allow for a variety of processes for developing curriculum and instruction and Gribble raises a somewhat more specific but even more basic question about the relationship between values and objectives. These are serious questions which cannot be avoided by the student of curriculum. But while these papers raise many important questions, it is obvious that they are not collectively comprehensive enough to build an adequate perspective for those concerned with the role of aims and objectives in curriculum development. Several additional papers are set forth below as suggested readings.

Suggested Readings

HOGBEN, D. (1970). 'Are Behavioural Objectives Really Necessary?' *The Australian Journal of Education*, 14, 3, 330–35.
This articles sets forth some of the difficulties for curriculum development and evaluation involved in the demand that outcomes be identified as specific behavioural objectives to be achieved. The author strongly rejects the subordination of creative teachers to experts in measurement. Further, he suggests that objectives must be questioned on philosophic grounds. A good bibliography is provided.

JACKSON, PHILIP W. and ELIZABETH BELFORD (1965). 'Educational Objectives and the Joys of Teaching,' *School Review*, 73, 3, 267–91.
The authors report research on 'artist' teachers who somehow escape 'scientific' definition. They note that such teachers derive little satisfaction from accomplishing pre-selected objectives. While the size of the sample is questionable, the findings of the study are provocative.

MACDONALD, JAMES B. and BERNICE WOLFSON (1970). 'A Case Against Behavioural Objectives,' *The Elementary School Journal*, 71, 3, 119–27.
Macdonald and Wolfson reject the behavioural objectives model for determining instruction because they set it as inadequate and restrictive. They

recommend the study of other approaches, namely the idea of planned activity from which students select their own learning experiences.

POPHAM, JANES (1972). 'Objectives '72,' *Phi Delta Kappan*, 53, 7, 432–35.
Popham, a recognized advocate of behavioural objectives, modifies his position somewhat but still presents a strong case for the specification of behavioural objectives. This article should be read by students of curriculum if they wish a balanced view of the issues surrounding the current behavioural movement. The bibliography is also valuable. In the same issue, an article by PHILIP G. SMITH ('On the Logic of Behavioural Objectives') takes a position similar to that of Eisner's article in this chapter.

TYLER, RALPH W. (1973). 'The Father of Behavioural Objectives Criticizes Them: An Interview with Ralph Tyler, *'Phi Delta Kappan*, 55, 1, 55–57. Tyler, often called the 'father of educational objectives' in the United States, is interviewed and states 'An educational objective does not need to be specific in order to be clear, attainable, and capable of assessment.'

Chapter 3

Curriculum Evaluation

Evaluation is an important and yet frequently neglected aspect of curriculum decision-making. The curriculum developer needs to make judgements about the adequacy of his principles and materials in achieving the goals he has set for student learning. Evaluation in this context is intended to influence the finished product of a curriculum project and is termed 'formative' evaluation (Scriven, 1967). What Scriven calls 'summative' evaluation on the other hand is of more importance to the potential adopter of the new curriculum, the teacher or administrator, since it provides a description of the strengths and weaknesses of a curriculum, indicating what may or may not be accomplished by it.

Both forms of evaluation should be distinguished from assessment, for the purpose of the latter is to provide information about the capabilities, achievements, and attitudes of individual students while the former is intended to say something about the effectiveness of the curriculum materials and ideas in giving rise to desired student learning. Assessment of student performance in general is one but only one of the relevant pieces of evidence which enter into a thorough curriculum evaluation. Other more important forms of evidence are identified in the articles which follow and in the suggested readings.

The importance of curriculum evaluation is increasing as a result of the increased rate of curriculum change and the increasing variety of curricula available to schools and colleges. In times when curricula changed slowly if at all, when they were sanctioned by tradition and accepted as having 'stood the test of time', the need for evaluation was much less obtrusive than when, as at present, curricula are changing rapidly and, as a result, generating a far greater variety of curricular possibilities.

Introduction

The existance of variety suggests that the area of choice to the teacher or administrator is much enlarged. However, for choice to be exercised in any meaningful sense, teachers and administrators must be aware of their own objectives (whether these are determined *by* them or *for* them) and also aware of the characteristics of particular curricula, an awareness that can only come about as a result of thorough, dependable and open evaluation studies.

Each author whose article appears below makes a different contribution to our thinking about curriculum evaluation. White, from the standpoint of philosophy, presents a thoughtful analysis of the concept of curriculum evaluation—a prerequisite for clear thinking and adequate decision making—and makes a number of useful, indeed essential distinctions. Eisner from the insights which derive particularly from the fields of the expressive and creative arts identifies ways in which traditional models of evaluation seem to be lacking and to require supplementation.

Reference

SCRIVEN, M. (1967). *The Methodology of Evaluation* in *Perspectives on Curriculum Evaluation*, AERA. Monog. No. 1. Chicago: Rand McNally.

Readings

The Concept of Curriculum Evaluation*

J. P. White *Lecturer in Philosophy of Education, University of London Institute of Education*

'Curriculum evaluation' is a term used more and more in educational discussion. New curricula are being developed on every hand. These curricula have to be 'evaluated'. 'Curriculum evaluators' are being appointed to current research projects. It is important, in the early days of a new large-scale educational venture such as the present curriculum reform movement, to make sure that the conceptual framework within which it is being undertaken is as clear as may be. This paper is a rough-hewn attempt at clarifying the concept of curriculum evaluation.

How does one find out what curriculum evaluation is? One way would be to go to a book like D. K. Wheeler's on *Curriculum Process*, for instance, and see what he has to say in his chapter on the topic.[1] Here it seems that evaluation is a phase in the process of constructing and reconstructing curricula. Its purpose is to see whether curriculum objectives are being, or have been, achieved[2]—so that modifications in them can be made if necessary. Evaluating is here, then, a part of *making* a curriculum.

But the word 'evaluation' may have other meanings, besides this semi-technical one. The people who work for *Which?* are, I suppose, evaluating products. What they are doing is seeing if they are worth while buying, seeing how good they are in comparison with others. Evaluating something is assessing its value—or, to leave Latin altogether for Anglo-Saxon—it is seeing whether it is any *good*. Now things can be good in many different ways: people and actions may be morally good; paintings and poems can be aesthetically good; a knife or a car can be instrumentally good, i.e. as an efficient means to an end—and so forth.

---

* This article has been reproduced from the *Journal of Curriculum Studies* (5, 1973) by permission of the author and Wm. Collins Sons and Company Ltd.

When we evaluate something, therefore, we can assess its worth from many points of view; a painting, for instance can be evaluated financially —as a possible good investment—or aesthetically—as a possible candidate for a National Gallery.

Like anything else, a new curriculum can be evaluated in all sorts of ways. Some of these we can clearly leave out of the picture. A dictator might evaluate a history curriculum as better than its rivals as a means of inculcating obedience to the Party. A mercenary educational publisher might see a curriculum as likely to catch on and as a good means of increasing his profits. I take it we can eliminate points of view like these. For I assume that when educationists evaluate new curricula they are assessing their value largely from an educational point of view, rather than from a political or a financial one. I say '*largely* from an educational point of view', because there do seem to be situations when non-educational evaluations are required. If, for instance, curriculum A is being compared with curriculum B to see which is the better, and if there is no difference between A and B in the time in which children tend to complete either or the degree to which they remember what they have learnt, etc., but curriculum A requires materials five times as costly as those in B, then, all in all, B may be said to be a better buy than A. Again one might compare *this* sort of curriculum-evaluation with a *Which?* report on, say, record-players. The prime consideration in buying a record-player is whether it does its job well—i.e. if it faithfully produces the sounds on the record; but a very important subsidiary consideration is how much it costs. Curriculum evaluation, similarly, must have educational criteria largely in mind, but cost and perhaps other factors cannot be omitted.

It might be worth following this analogy with *Which?* evaluations a little further. Just as private individuals want to know the overall best buy in record-players or hair-dryers, so teachers, teacher-trainers, inspectors, etc., want to know what is the overall best buy in methods and curricula. Warburton and Southgate's recently published evaluation of I.T.A. as against traditional orthography is precisely the sort of thing required.[3] Of course, Warburton and Southgate were concerned with a reading scheme rather than with a new curriculum. *Their* evaluation problems were complex enough. No doubt comparisons between whole curricula will be even more complicated. But they will have to be made if the recent upsurge of interest in developing new curricula is not to be fruitless: we cannot just assume that 'new' means 'better'.

The kind of evaluation I have just been describing—where one curriculum is compared with another against certain criteria—economy in time or money, etc., is largely empirical. It is not the only kind of empirical evaluation. There is also that described earlier by Wheeler, whose purpose is to see whether a curriculum under construction is achieving its objectives—to see, for instance, whether one designed in theory to teach such and such concepts to 11-year-olds succeeds in practice in engaging with their interests and abilities and is not, say, too abstract or boring. Evaluation of the latter sort is sometimes called 'formative' or 'on-going'; it is a part of *making* a curriculum, not of putting it through a *Which?*-type test. The latter is an example of what is sometimes called 'summative' or 'final evaluation'. Problems arise about where one draws the line between 'formative' and 'summative' evaluation—and perhaps there is no hard-and-fast line to draw. But all I want to stress here is that these both proceed by empirical observation.

I bring them together in this way to distinguish them from other forms of evaluation which are *not empirical*. Both the empirical types mentioned presuppose that the curriculum under investigation has clear objectives and that criteria can be laid down in terms of pupil behaviour for when these objectives have been attained. But suppose that curriculum A has been evaluated both in a Wheeler-type way and in a *Which?*-type way and has turned out to be more economical in time and money etc., than curricula B and C. Would this show that it was a good buy? Not necessarily. For nothing has been said yet to show that its *objectives* are any good. One curriculum may be better than another in getting children to learn off all the 'capes and bays' of Europe. It may be good instrumentally as a means to this objective, but whether it is good *educationally*—i.e. whether its objectives are worthwhile—is another matter. We are back with the extreme generality and many-sidedness of the word 'good'—And in reaching this point, we see that the term 'curriculum evaluation' can be taken in quite another sense, where now it is the objectives themselves which are being evaluated, to see if they are educationally any good.

How does one do this? What methods can the curriculum evaluator use? Wheeler has little doubt that these are empirical. He writes (p. 284): 'The answer to the question "What in our rapidly-changing society, is of most worth to children and youth?" is still too often given in terms of "philosophical" orientation and traditional practice. As more becomes known about human growth and social interaction, objectives must more and more be derived from facts, principles and theories which relate to these areas. Behaviour, learning process, social and individual needs, all give rise to theoretical models . . .' As often, it is not always clear quite what Wheeler has in mind in this passage, but it is at least clear that he thinks that further research in the human sciences, in psychology and sociology, will provide the criteria of curricular worthwhileness that we are looking for. But how can empirical research alone determine what should be taught? No empirical fact can alone justify a conclusion that something is right or ought to be done (in this case, that the objectives of curriculum x are educationally all right). For how do you pass from an empirical statement, about something which is the case (and contains no value-term) to a statement which *does* contain a 'right' or an 'ought'? There is just no argument here: it simply cannot be done.

This fact is often obscured, as in Wheeler's case, by a reference to 'social' or 'individual needs'. This appeal to needs is a favourite among curriculum-makers: children must learn such and such because they have a need to earn a living, to develop a sense of responsibility, etc.— or because society needs an adaptable labour force etc. etc. There is no logical objection to defending objectives by reference to needs, as long as it is clear that individual needs cannot be discovered by psychology, or social needs by sociology. Needs are not observable features of individuals or of societies. The term 'need' is necessarily value-laden. To say that a hungry man needs food is not only to say that without food he will die: it is also to imply that dying would be a bad thing, that he ought to keep alive. If we say that society needs an adaptable labour force, this is to assume that whatever this adaptable labour force is needed for—e.g. high productivity or a higher standard of living—is a good thing. So while we may agree with Wheeler that curriculum objectives may be justified by reference to needs, this is not to accept his belief that everything can now be left to empirical science; for we are still left with value statements which themselves have to be justified.[4]

Statements about individual and social needs are easily translatable into statements about what is good for individuals or societies, or, if you like, about what is in their interests. We are now clearly in the realm of values. And at this point some curriculum theorists see the red light. Wheeler, again, for instance. Contradicting rather what he says elsewhere, he writes that 'this (evaluation) process itself, because it involves value-judgements, must necessarily be more subjective than objective'. (p. 273) Value-judgements, it seems, are largely subjective matters. If so, it is understandable that some curriculum theorists tend to shy away from evaluating objectives. For any evaluation—in terms, say, of whether the stated objectives are in the pupils' or society's interests—will necessarily reflect the evaluator's own subjective beliefs about these interests; and what right has any man to impose his personal preferences in this way, especially when the social consequences of such imposition might be so immense?

While this stance is admirable in its liberalism, one should not overlook its unfortunate consequences. For curriculum objectives themselves imply value-judgements—that it is *good*, from some point of view or other, for children to learn such and such. But if all value-judgements are subjective, the curriculum objectives must simply express *someone's* personal preferences, whether those of the development team themselves, or, if already existing objectives are being used, those of others who have managed to influence curricula in their own preferred directions. *Someone* is going to have to decide what things shall be taught; and if there can be no independent, objective evaluation of such decisions, it seems that it will be the strongest pressure groups which will do this.

This is an unwelcome conclusion, but it seems the only one open. We cannot hope to find the objectivity we are looking for by making the evaluation of objectives empirical; and given that such evaluation is value-laden, it seems to be necessarily subjective and therefore not worth doing. *Laissezfaire* seems the only alternative. If a pressure group is strong enough to get the Schools Council to promote a new curriculum to teach Spanish from the age of six or housecraft for less able 13-year-old girls, so be it: we can only pray that, *per impossibile*, some Invisible Hand will regulate what happens for the pupils' and the common good.

But there is no reason for such despair. There is no reason to assume *a priori* that any evaluation of curricular objectives must reflect mere personal preferences. The general proposition on which this despair rests—that all value judgments are subjective, i.e. cannot, in the last analysis, be rationally defended—itself must be argued for: it cannot just be assumed to be true. To look into all the arguments pro and con would be a long job, and something I could not do here. But it is important, once again, to stress the great *variety* of kinds of value-judgment that can be made.[5] Whether one can say objectively whether something is a good knife is one question; whether Guinness is (truly) good for you is another; and whether one can determine on rational grounds the Good Life for Man is a third. Each type of goodness—and there are many more than these—must be separately examined.

Mention of the Good Life for Man raises a further point. I would be prepared to argue that value-judgments in this area are to a large extent subjective. Different individuals may have very different ideals of life: in saying that I prefer a life of comfort to a life of action or contemplation, I am expressing a personal preference: I am sceptical about how far individual ideals can be objectively rated, as better or worse. Now a curriculum theorist holding a similar view *might* conclude that value-judgments about curricular objectives are likewise subjective, on the following argument. Any curriculum ought to be at least in the interests of the child; but if one cannot say objectively—i.e. on the basis of reasons that any rational man would accept—what sort of life a child should lead when he grows up, how can one say what it is in his interests to learn at school? But a reply to this argument is that subjectivity about what life a person ought to lead does not entail subjectivity about what he ought to learn at school. Indeed, the clearer it becomes that we *cannot* predetermine the Good Life for others, the clearer it seems to become that we ought to ensure that by the time he grows up a child can understand the nature of all the different activities which *might*— or might not—form a part of the Good Life, as he sees it, so that he is is in a position to decide himself what life to lead. This, as I have argued elsewhere[6], would give one a good reason for insisting on the compulsory inclusion in every child's curriculum of those activities—mathematics, physics, the arts etc.—which, unlike playing football, or cooking, or speaking French, cannot be understood at all from the outside, i.e. without actually engaging in them. Being a subjectivist about the Good Life is thus compatible with being a rather tough-minded supporter of the compulsory teaching of the 'disciplines': indeed, one position leads pretty directly to the other. Subjectivism in this area does *not* imply, as some appear to think, leaving the child as free as possible to decide what things he wants to learn.

Whatever the rights and wrongs of these particular arguments, my main point here is that in assessing curricular objectives, one should not just *assume* that objectivity will be impossible. One must simply work through the arguments presented for the objectives, see if they are valid, and press for further arguments to support the premises on which they rest. It is only when people begin to discuss the rationale for curriculum objectives, only when they begin to press the argument back to more fundamental values and assumptions, that we shall be able to judge how objective or subjective the issues are. It is remarkable how little of this *fundamental* questioning there has been in the recent

movement for curriculum reform. Should less able children learn a
foreign language? Should anyone be made to learn one? Is one purpose
of RE to promote moral development? To what extent is 'integration'
of curriculum-areas a good thing? Should so-called 'Newsom' children
be given a non-acdemic curriculum? Are there any grounds for
assuming that the things one child has learnt by the time he leaves
school should be any different from what any other school-leaver has
learnt? Etc., etc. Curriculum developers may well discuss such
questions in private; but there has been very little public debate on
them, at least at a more than superficial level. There should be more.
Only then could one see how far *good* reasons can be given for different
curriculum proposals. I am willing to bet that the area in which rational,
objective assessment is possible is larger than is sometimes believed.
(This is assuming that the participants to the discussion are not tram-
melled by a vested interest, e.g. in a particular subject, but are prepared
to question the value of their own discipline (or whatever) in a serious
attempt to work out what the content of education should be.)

I have mentioned so far a number of different sorts of curriculum
evaluation: two empirical sorts—the on-going check on objectives and
the summative comparison of one curriculum with another; and one
non-empirical sort, the evaluation of objectives in terms of their
educational value. All these forms of evaluation presuppose one thing
in common: that the curriculum under investigation has clear objectives.
If it has not, then it makes no sense either to ask whether they are being
attained (or are attained, e.g. more quickly than by another curriculum)
or to ask whether they are educationally respectable.

All this indicates that there is room for another—another non-
empirical—form of evaluation. This will review the internal logic of
the new curriculum, presumably at a quite early stage in the development project. The questions asked will be: has the curriculum got
clear, behaviourally-testable objectives? If so, is the curriculum
internally organized, in its different parts, in such a way that it is likely
to achieve these objectives? As already indicated, this latter question is
partly empirical: one cannot tell simply from a blueprint whether
children will learn through it. But it is not wholly empirical: a historian
could tell without experiment, just by reflection, that a curriculum
which consisted, say, in rote-learning certain historical names and dates
could never succeed in its objective of getting children to understand
different historical interpretations of the causes of the Russian
Revolution. There is room, therefore, for experts in a discipline to

assess whether the material and the order in which it is presented are *prima facie* likely to promote the objectives.

What, now, of the other job just mentioned, of assessing whether or not the objectives themselves are clear? This is clearly a task of major importance. It is especially important, I would suggest, as far as many of the Schools Council's curriculum schemes are concerned. This applies particularly to some of the schemes produced for the Young School Leaver. Working Paper No. 11, 'Society and the Young School Leaver', is one example. I have described elsewhere[7] how difficult it is to see just what it is aiming at; that one moment it looks like a new-fangled means to promote the oldfangled end of producing an obedient and contented proletariat and the next it seems like a rather muddled attempt to get some sociology on to the curriculum. It would not be difficult to take other such curricula to pieces in this way, the one entitled *An Approach through Religious Education,* for instance.[8] I am aware that these are only working papers, not fully elaborated curricula. Perhaps it is unfair to make these charges when one is very much on the sidelines; but it does seem, at least to this outside observer, that some of the Schools Council's projects could well be improved in the clarity with which they explain what they are about. This is not unconnected with the earlier points I made, about the need to evaluate the objectives of particular curricula in the light of reflection on more general educational values. The Schools Council, as far as I am aware, has done very little fundamental thinking on what the curriculum as a whole should be like: if anything, it tended, in its early days, to take over a rather traditional framework of assumptions, dating back, through the Newsom Report, to the elementary tradition of prewar times.[9] It is not surprising, if fundamental value-issues are not thought through, that the objectives of specific curricula are so often blurred or woolly. Let us hope that things will not always be like this.

One reason why the objectives of many of the Young School Leaver projects are not clear is that it is uncertain quite who the Young School Leaver is. When I first looked at these schemes, I imagined they were short-term solutions to the problem of educating those 14- or 15-year-old children of low ability who are anxious to leave school as soon as possible. But it seems from the Foreword to Working Paper No. 14 that they are to be the bases of 'relevant and useful five year courses for pupils leaving school at 16'. The Young School Leaver is thus identified, I take it, at 11, not in his last year or so. It is crucially important to be clear who the Young School Leaver is meant to be. If he is the pupil in his last year or so, there is a short-term problem of knowing what to do with him. (Whether solutions to the problem should become *institutionalized* is another matter. It would be disastrous if last year curricula of this sort came to structure the whole of secondary education). If he is being selected at *11*, however, to follow curricula designed on the assumption that he will *not* be staying on beyond 16, this is just as educationally indefensible as the old elementary system: it is closing doors for the child, not opening them, shunting him off along the downhill track. I suggest that this ambiguity in the expression 'Young School Leaver' helps to account for the obscurity of purpose of several of these schemes.

The general point I wish to make here is that curricula, if they are to be evaluated in any way, must have clear objectives. *A fortiori,* they must have objectives. It might seem that this is a truism. But apparently it is not: some would wish to question it, Charity James, for instance, argues explicitly in her book *Young Lives at Stake* against planning curricula in terms of objectives.[10] Her main argument is that Bloom's 'Taxonomy', which she considers the 'subtlest enterprise in this field', is not very helpful and so, by implication, if this will not do, what will? But this is a poor argument. The 'Taxonomy' is an attempt to classify possible *sorts* of objectives, in a highly abstract, subject-neutral fashion. How could a mere classification possibly help one to select which objectives to go for in a new chemistry or history curriculum? If objectives cannot be derived from empirical investigation, neither can they be derived from a logical classification of objectives. But the fact that Bloom's 'Taxonomy' cannot be used for this purpose does not show that planning in terms of objectives is useless. How else, indeed, could one plan?

Charity James is not alone in her opposition to objectives. She keeps company in this with Lawrence Stenhouse. He wrote in a recent description of his Humanities Project in *Education Canada,*

The main interest of our design is the absence of behavioural objectives from the conceptualization and planning of our curriculum. Any sophisticated curriculum worker is bound to be aware of the limitations of a design directed towards specified terminal student behaviour. Objectives are merely a simplifying device to help us choose from the range of hypotheses we could put forward about the effects of a curriculum innovation in a school or system.[11]

This passage, in its apparent conflation of 'objective' with 'behavioural objective', provokes a question of relevance not only to the Humanities Project but to curriculum development in general: are all curriculum objectives behavioural? To answer it, let us look more closely at the phrase 'behavioural objectives'. This could mean one of two things: (i) objectives which themselves *consist in* pupils' behaving in certain ways; (ii) objectives whose attainment is *tested by* observing pupils behaving in certain ways. It is important to make this distinction. The objective of an elocution course may be to make one speak in such and such ways. Here the objective is 'behavioural' in both senses, (i) and (ii). Not only this: but the particular behaviour aimed at is also the behaviour observed in testing. This need not always be the case. One objective of a course in clear thinking, for instance, may be to get students to test the validity of arguments which people put to them. The objective here is likewise 'behavioural' in sense (i), but the behaviour here—the pupils' reflection on the validity of arguments—is not *observable*, as in the elocution case. On the other hand, any *testing* of whether this objective has been reached will necessarily go by what the pupil can be *observed* to do—e.g. his verbal or written accounts of fallacies. The clear-thinking course has thus a 'behavioural objective' in both senses, (i) and (ii), just like the elocution course; unlike the latter, however, the behaviour referred to in (i) differs from the behaviour in (ii). It would be wrong, however, to think that if a curriculum has 'behavioural objectives' in sense (ii), it must also have them in sense (i), either observably or non-observably. The objective of a course in poetry appreciation may be to get pupils to come to respond aesthetically to certain poems. It is doubtful how far aesthetic responses to works of art should be called forms of 'behaviour'. Behaviour is something active, intention-guided. This is equally true of observable behaviour, like walking down the street, as of unobservable, like solving a mathematics problem in one's head. But aesthetic response is, like other emotional reactions, a *passive* rather than an active phenomenon. If so, the objective in question is not 'behavioural' in sense (i). Neither are other likely curriculum objectives. Knowing that such and such is the case may well be a curriculum objective; but a person who knows something is not necessarily *doing* anything. But a curriculum can lack 'behavioural objectives' in sense (i), but have them in sense (ii). Aesthetic response may not be a form of behaviour, but whether someone has learnt to respond aesthetically in the way required can only be tested by what he can be observed to say or write, etc. The same is true of knowing.

Need a new curriculum have 'behavioural objectives'? It depends on the sense of the term. Objectives need not be 'behavioural' in sense (i), as we have seen. But it does not follow that there should be no 'behavioural objectives' in sense (ii). On the contrary. Any new curriculum must be aiming at changing pupils (not necessarily changing their *behaviour*) in some ways. Whether or not it succeeds in this aim can only be discovered by observing pupils' behaviour, to see, e.g., whether they have acquired such and such items of knowledge, capacities, responses, etc. Any curriculum should have objectives; though these need only be 'behavioural' in sense (ii).

It is thus easy to see how someone might come to believe that new curricula need not be planned in terms of objectives. The germ of truth in one's premises might be that objectives need not be 'behavioural' in sense (i). From this it would be easy to slide to the—false—proposition that they need not be 'behavioural' in sense (ii). If one then assumed that all objectives were behavioural, one could quickly end up holding that curricula need not have objectives of any sort. It would be unfortunate if this conclusion—however it was arrived at—became widely accepted in curriculum development circles: for, as stated earlier, a curriculum without (behaviourally testable) objectives cannot be evaluated in any of the ways discussed so far.

I have described a number of different forms of curriculum evaluation, and it might be thought that the few examples we have seen to date of evaluation projects in this country would fit under one of these rubrics or another. But several of the projects described in J. D. Williams's article on evaluation in H. J. Butcher's book on *Educational Research*[12] do not fit. Clare Burstall's evaluation of French teaching in primary schools studies the *effects* of such teaching on other areas of learning, e.g. on pupils' attainment in English and arithmetic. Williams's own study of modern mathematics tests the hypothesis that learning modern mathematics at an early age will raise performance on intelligence tests. Both of these, then, examine certain *effects* of a new curriculum—which is a different form of evaluation from those mentioned.

It also raises new difficulties. By what criteria does one select the possible effects one wants to study, given that there are innumerable such effects? Why select performance in intelligence, English tests, etc. in evaluating new French and mathematics curricula? Some reason must be given for this beyond the obvious fact that it is relatively easy to do empirical research of this sort. The same goes for projects examining the effects of a curriculum on changes in children's attitudes or motivation, where these are not part of the curriculum's original objectives. What is from a research point of view a manageable study is not, for that reason alone, a useful one.

This is not necessarily to exclude all evaluation of effects. Some may be very valuable: one would have to look into a project's rationale to see this. But it is clear, at least, that it is *not enough* to evaluate a curriculum by its effects, however useful this evaluation is. This brings me back to the main point which I wish to underline in this paper, and with which I shall end. There is no single 'process' of curriculum evaluation: there are many different forms of it. All (or most) of them can and should play a part in assessing whether or not a new curriculum is any good, whether or not it is worth teachers' while adopting it. This, I take it, is the ultimate point of all curriculum evaluation. A curriculum has not been positively evaluated in this full sense until it has been shown to have clear objectives and appropriate means to achieve them; to have objectives which have been proved against all comers to be educationally respectable; to connect with the abilities of those pupils for whom it is designed; and to be more efficient than rivals in the field. Only then can it get its tick. There is a distinct danger that if one keeps the term 'evaluation' only for a particular *kind* of evaluation, e.g. for Wheeler's ongoing, feedback evaluation, or for evaluation of effects, the result may be confusion. People may confuse the broader with the restricted sense. It may then seem that as long as a curriculum has been evaluated (in one of the restricted senses) it has been shown to be worth adopting. But this simply is not so. Whether it is any good or not can only be seen when *all* the different kinds of evaluation just described have been carried out.

For many of the distinctions I have drawn in this paper I am indebted to Michael Scriven's recent article on 'The Methodology of Evaluation'[13]. And I would like to try to conclude by emphasizing, with Scriven, the importance and the complexity of curriculum evaluation. If all the different roles described are to be filled by the same person, he will have to be equipped not only with skills of empirical research, and a knowledge of relevant aspects of the economies of education, of costing, for instance, but also with a knowledge of the subject matter to be taught and some experience of teaching it. A philosophical training would also be useful, though not perhaps a *sine qua non*, for assessing the overall clarity of curriculum objectives and the arguments for or against their educational value. Also, if all these roles are to be filled by one person, he will be both—as an 'ongoing' evaluator—a part of the development team, and, in his other roles, an independent judge of its activities, the guardian of teachers' and pupils' interests, the man who sees that public money tied up in these schemes is well spent. It seems too much to expect one person to carry all these roles. How far is there a case for a division of labour here—into, say, (*a*) ongoing evaluators (*b*) non-empirical evaluators of the clarity and worthwhileness of objectives and (*c*) summative evaluators on the *Which?* model?

Notes

1. D. K. WHEELER (1967), *Curriculum Process*. University of London Press. Ch. 10, cf. also Ch. 2.
2. This definition of evaluation is common in recent discussions of the subject. See, e.g., J. F. KERR (1968), *Changing the Curriculum*. University of London Press, p. 21.
3. F. W. WARBURTON and VERA SOUTHGATE (1969), *ITA: an Independent Evaluation*. John Murray and W. & R. Chambers.
4. For a fuller analysis of 'need', see R. F. DEARDEN, ' "Needs" in Education', *British Journal of Educational Studies*, November, 1966.
5. C. H. VON WRIGHT (1963), *The Varieties of Goodness*. London: Routledge and Kegan Paul.
6. 'Learn as you Will', *New Society*, 4 December, 69.
7. 'Instruction in Obedience', *New Society*, 2 May, 68.
8. 'Humanities for the Young School Leaver. An approach through Religious Education', (Schools Council, 1969). Cf. also 'An approach through History', (Schools Council, 1969).
9. Cf. my 'Curriculum Mongers', *New Society*, 6 March, 69.
10. C. JAMES (1968), *Young Lives at Stake*. London: Collins.
11. L. STENHOUSE (1969), 'Handling Controversial Issues in the Classroom', *Education Canada*, December.
12. H. J. BUTCHER, *Educational Research in Britain*, (University of London Press, 1968).
13. M. SCRIVEN (1967), 'The Methodology of Evaluation', AERA *Monographs No. 1: Perspectives of Curriculum Evaluation*. Chicago: Rand McNally.

Emerging Models for Educational Evaluation[1]*

Elliott W. Eisner *Stanford University*

In this paper I will develop three ideas that seem to me to hold promise for improving the process of educational evaluation. These ideas deal with some of the issues surrounding the character and functions of

* This article has been reproduced from *School Review* (August 1972) by permission of the author and The University of Chicago Press.

educational objectives, the variety of outcomes that one might reasonably expect schooling to yield, and a set of methods that appear useful for evaluating the character and effects of school programmes. That the relationship between objectives and evaluation is, at least theoretically, an intimate one is clear. Almost all writers on education generally and curriculum theory particularly emphasize the point that evaluation procedures should be related to the objectives one has formulated. Thus, any modification in either the content or the form of objectives can have important implications for the method and goals of evaluation. This paper describes some ways in which objectives can be conceived and provides the conditions necessary for expanding modes of educational evaluation.

I would like to say at the outset that the ideas I will develop here are in their infancy. I have not written about them in detail in professional journals; they are glimmers that the task of writing this paper have brightened. They are collectively, as Joseph Schwab might say, an invitation to inquiry rather than a rhetoric of conclusions.[2]

In many ways, the development of new and better ways to evaluate is counter to at least one of the major developments on the educational scene. I am of course referring to the rash of books and articles that have recently appeared chastising the schools for being test ridden, impersonal, oppressive, indifferent to students as people, bureaucratic, and mindless. *How Children Fail, Compulsory Miseducation, The Open Classroom, The Lives of Children,* and *The Way It's Spozed to Be* are only a few of these books. And their diagnoses of the ills of schooling are antithetical to those found in the books published one and two decades ago, which in their own way also chasitised the schools. *Retreat from Learning, Quackery in the Public School, Why Swiss Schools Are Better than Ours, Educational Wastelands :* the titles tell their stories. The schools, those who run them, those who prepare teachers for them, and those who work in them have borne the brunt of the attacks.

Yet it is because of these attacks and the kind of passionate reform they urge that the need for more adequate methods of educational evaluation becomes even more important. The educational conservatives of the late forties and early fifties introduced the theme that was to herald the curriculum reform movement. That movement, developed with the help of the National Science Foundation and the US Office of Education, provided what some of the conservative critics wanted.[3] It provided a no-nonsense curriculum developed by scholars, implemented by teachers, and geared, at least initially, to the production of young scientists and mathematicians. Educational reform in the mid-fifties was seen primarily as curriculum reform.

That educational reform could be achieved merely through curriculum reform is a seductive aspiration. I wish it were that easy. If we have learned anything from the curriculum reform movement, it is that the problems that pervade our schools go well beyond problems of curriculum. This is not to say that the curriculum of a school, by which I mean the programme it provides to students, is unimportant. School programmes are important. But one must also realize, as the Holts, Friendenbergs, Dennisons, Goodmans, and Kohls have brought to our attention, that other aspects of the school are also important and, some claim, much more important than the formal curriculum.[4]

The radical critics have made salient the idea that the type of relationship existing between teacher and student is critical. They have pointed out that the organizational structure of the school teaches as surely as the lesson in a workbook or test. The reward system of the school—the covert, muted one—speaks loudly. In short, they have injected a dimension that was generally neglected in the cool, cognitive approach taken by curriculum reformers during the fifties and sixties.

The language and the perceptiveness of some of the reformers are persuasive and in many parts of the country are being heeded. In California, the free schools have become a movement. While their lives are short—their average tenure is about a year and a half—people continue to establish schools that are intended to provide radical alternatives to the public schools. New journals concerned with free schools are being published. And in Berkeley, California, free-school people have elected a candidate for the school board.

Yet it is precisely because the language of the radical reformers is persuasive and because the movement for alternative schools is growing that the need for sound and careful evaluation is important. There is no virtue climbing aboard alluring bandwagons only to find after some pain and dismay that we have indeed been taken for a ride. Rhetoric is not enough when the policies that such rhetoric yields can affect millions of students and teachers.

In calling attention to the growing dissatisfaction with American public schools and the alternatives that are being created, I do not wish to imply that my concern with developing more adequate models for evaluation rests solely upon the desire to assess the consequences of these so-called free schools. That task is important, but it is only a part of the problem. The school programmes to which 52 million children are exposed annually are the prime subject that warrants attention. The need for more adequate methods of evaluation is surely as great for this population as it is for that segment of the school population attending free schools.

There is no doubt in my mind that the evaluation movement in education, especially as fostered by the efforts of those who worked on school surveys during the period from 1910 to 1920 and in psychometrics and test development during the First World War, made important contributions to the scientific study of education.[5] At a time when there was a need for more precise and sophisticated conceptions of schooling and teacher training, statistics and other quantitative methods were appropriate and useful tools. One should not forget that the first department of education in an American university was established in 1873; in 1920, education as a formal field of study and practice was still in its childhood. Through the efforts of such men as E. L. Thorndike, John Watson, Harold Rugg, and Charles Hubbard Judd,[6] the tools of research and, more importantly, the conceptions underlying research became a part of the armamentarium of the evaluator. Education evaluation has grown up within the general field of educational research, and it is only recently that efforts have been made to distinguish between the two.

There was a period in the development of education when the family resemblance between educational research and educational evaluation was a virtue, but educational evaluation employing the premises and practices of educational research has some important limitations. I would like to identify a few of these limitations in order to provide a context for the ideas I will develop later.

First, in the efforts that are made to evaluate the effects of a new programme or method of teaching, inadequate attention is often given to distinguishing between findings that are statistically significant and those that are educationally significant. Differences between experimental and control groups can have no educational significance in spite of the fact that the differences are not random ones.[7]

Second, there has been a tendency to reduce educational problems into forms that fit research paradigms instead of finding research and evaluation procedures that fit the problems. The power of the ideas of correlation, analysis of variance, and random selection and assignment is enormous. But there is a tendency to conceive of research questions within the parameters such ideas provide instead of raising interesting questions and inventing fresh ways to answer them.

Third, there has been an overwhelming tendency to attempt to evaluate the effects of programmes on student behaviour, with very little attention paid to the the assessment and description of the environment which creates such effects. This observation has been made most cogently by Lee Shulman in a recent issue of the *Review of Educational Research*:

> The language of education and the behavioural sciences is in need of a set of terms for describing environments that is as articulated, specific and functional as those already possessed for characterizing individuals.
>
> An example that is familiar to all educators is the continued use of such gross terms as 'deprived' or 'disadvantaged' to characterize the environments of many minority-group children. Labelling the setting as 'disadvantaged', of course, communicates little that is meaningful about the characteristics of that environment. Educators seem unable to progress beyond such a simple dichotomy as 'advantaged-disadvantaged.' Reviewers and critics of research have long realized that even those few categories which attempt to describe environments, such as social class, have been remarkably ineffectual in pinpointing the educationally relevant differences in the backgrounds of individuals.[8]

Not only do I agree with Schulman's observations, but a review I did of the last two years of the *American Educational Research Association [AERA] Journal* indicated that experimental studies reported in those volumes provide about three and a half to four times as much space to reporting the findings of the studies as they do to describing the treatment. Somewhere between one and a half and two and a half inches of copy is devoted to describing what it was that the experimenter manipulated. How can one be expected to replicate experimental studies when such a paucity of information concerning the characteristics of the treatment is provided?

A fourth characteristic of many of the efforts to evaluate the effects of schooling is the failure to recognize the difference between what students will do and what they can do. For example, achievement tests are given in contexts in which students know they must perform well. The set that is induced by the test administrator, the form the test takes, and the setting in which it is administered tend to elicit not what students will do in typical situations in their lives but how they can perform under artificial circumstances. One revealing example of such a situation occurred annually during my years in elementary school. When I was a student at Lawson Elementary School during the 1940s I was expected, as were all of my classmates, to take a handwriting test on a yearly basis. Each year from grade 3 on the teacher would write on the blackboard in her finest cursive form the following: 'This is a sample of my handwriting on January 24, 1943. If it is not as good as it should be for a student of my age and grade, I will try with my teacher's help to improve by this time next year.'

I remember vividly sitting on the hard oak seat attached to a desk screwed into the floor, eight deep in rows of six. The white, slick, lined paper was before me with the blue-black watery ink at my right as I sat with scratchy pen in hand. Oh, how I worked! To copy those two sentences in my best hand was a venture as difficult as crossing the Niagara on a high wire. After twenty minutes of pain I was through— in my best hand. But what I turned in to the teacher was no more a sample of my handwriting than it was of the man in the moon's. If my teachers wanted to know how I wrote, all they had to do was to look at what I was writing on any school day.

All too many achievement tests have similar characteristics: concurrent or predictive validity is too often a neglected consideration. We ought to be concerned not only with immediate effects, but with long-term effects. What will the child be like a year after the course is over is a far more telling question than how he behaves on the final exam.

In this sense it might be more reasonable to conceive of dependent variables as independent variables. After all, what we want to predict is surely more than test performance. Test performance can be, and in my opinion ought to be, looked upon as a predictor of the future. Using the standard conception, the dependent measure tells you whether the treatment has been effective during the treatment period. *Now* the educational question emerges. Given that it has been effective during the treatment period, does it last? Is it used? Does it make a difference in how people function? There is no doubt in my mind that such questions will be difficult to answer, but there is also no doubt that these questions must be addressed if we are to know if schooling is more than a game.

A fifth characteristic of experimental research which filters into evaluation practices is the extreme brevity of the treatment that is provided. Making important and enduring differences in people requires either a great deal of time or a very powerful treatment, something in the form of a peak experience or one that is traumatic. Neither peak experiences nor traumas are typical of our experimental efforts: thus, time is required to bring about changes of a significant and enduring variety. Yet the average duration of experimental treatment time per subject in experimental studies reported in the last two volumes of the *AERA Journal* is about 40 minutes—40 minutes to bring about a change that is to have educational significance! (Everyone, I am sure, realizes that such changes require at least an hour!)

Now there is a good reason for the brevity of experimental treatments. Short treatments increase control, and control reduces confounding. When confounding occurs, the ability to explain is reduced. Yet paradoxically, the more controlled the experiment the more difficult it might be to generalize it to classroom practice, for it is precisely the lack of tight control that characterizes most classrooms. It seems to me we need longer treatment periods as well as more sensitive instruments with which to evaluate the programmes that are provided in schools.

Yet despite the caveats I have enumerated, there is interesting work taking place in the field of educational evaluation. The development of criterion-referenced testing is useful even though several of Professor Ebel's[9] reservations are well grounded. The aptitude-treatment-interaction work by Professors Cronbach and Snow[10] also holds promise even though consistent interactions have not been found. The idea of aptitude-treatment-interaction is persuasive and makes psychological sense. Daniel Stuffelbeam's[11] context, input, process, and product model is a more comprehensive conception of the loci for evaluation than has been previously articulated. Michael Scriven's[12] contributions are important new ideas in the evaluation field. In short, good work is being done. I would like now to contribute to that work by explicating the three ideas I identified at the beginning of this paper.

Many of you are familiar with prescriptions concerning the use of instructional objectives in curriculum planning and evaluation. The rationale for their use is straightforward: one must know what it is that a student is able to do in order to determine the effectiveness of the curriculum. This idea was developed in prototype by Franklin Bobbitt in 1924, refined by Henry Harap in the late twenties, rationalized by Ralph Tyler in his famous curriculum syllabus in the early fifties, exemplified in the cognitive domain by Benjamin Bloom in the middle fifties, extended into the affective domain by David Krathwohl, and given extremely precise meaning by Robert Mager in the early sixties. I will not reiterate the limitations that such a concept has as a comprehensive view of educational planning. Many readers are familiar with the views I have expressed in various journals and monographs on the subject.[13] My effort to conceptualize the expressive objective was intended to provide some balance to what I consider to be an extremely narrow vision of what education is and how planning for it should occur. The expressive objective is an outcome of an activity planned by the teacher or the student which is designed not to lead the student to a particular goal or form of behaviour but, rather, to forms of thinking-feeling-acting that are his own making. The expressive curriculum activity is evocative rather than prescriptive and is intended to yield outcomes which, although educationally valuable, are not prescribed or defined beforehand. The task of the teacher is to look back, as it were, to evaluate what happened to the student rather than to ask whether the student achieved '90 per cent mastery of a set of items placed before him during a 40-minute period.' The expressive activity is one in which the creative personalistic use of skills gained in instructional activities can be employed, developed, and refined. The expressive objective is the outcome of such activities.

These ideas are not new. I have written about them before. Why then do I reiterate them here? Only to refresh your memory so that the distinction between the instructional and the expressive objective can be seen more clearly as I describe a third type of objective that I believe to be logically distinct from the latter two.

As I thought about instructional and expressive objectives, it occurred to me that neither of these types adequately fits the kind of tasks given to designers, architects, engineers, and commercial artists. Product designers, for example, work for a client who generally has a problem—a specific problem—that he wants the designer to solve. He might say to the designer, 'I need a device that can be marketed for under 50 cents, which can be made on a vacuum press, and which ladies can use to carry cosmetics.' The problem that the designer has is to take the specifications that are provided by the client, specifications which define function but which do not provide a solution, and to invent an image that provides a solution within the parameters set by the client. In such a situation, the problem is highly delineated but the range of potential solutions is, in principle, infinite. Furthermore, there is generally little difficulty in determining the success of the solution. In this Type III objective—I do not have an appropriate name for it yet—

the designer, or architect, or engineer must bring his imaginative resources to bear upon a highly specific problem but one that makes possible a wide variety of solutions. In distinction, the instructional objective provides the solution; what the student is to be able to do is specified in advance, and the objective and the student's behaviour or product at the end of an instructional sequence are ideally isomorphic. In spelling or mathematics, for example, instructional objectives describe answers that are known in advance. In Type III objectives, although the problem is known the solutions are not. Ingenuity of solution, appraised on the basis of the parameters or specifications of the problem, is the ideal.

An example might make the use of Type III objectives clear in curriculum planning. Let us assume that a teacher or curriculum development group is working in the area of the social studies and is attempting to develop objectives and learning activities for children around 10 or 11 years of age. The topic being dealt with is the way in which the community handles the movement of people within its boundaries. The curriculum writers are interested in helping children understand that population density affects the type of controls imposed and that optimal solutions to movement need to be appraised by a variety of criteria, time, cost, aesthetic considerations, and so forth. To help children appreciate and understand the dimensions of such a problem, the curriculum writers decide to deal with problems of traffic control and traffic flow and formulate a Type III objective which asks children to improve the flow of traffic by modifying in some way the current traffic patterns near the school. These modifications should make auto traffic more efficient and time saving and should make it safer for students. No new streets can be built; changes must come about by modifying traffic flow on existing streets. A classroom teacher using such an objective would, if he desired, set up teams of students to study this problem and to formulate potential solutions. Each team's solution will be presented and considered by the class as a whole. What the teacher looks for in evaluating achievement is not a preconceived fit between a known objective and a known solution but an appraisal, after an inquiry of the relative merit of solution to the objective formulated, in this case solving problems of traffic control.

With the expressive objective, neither the parameters nor the specifications are given. The student can define his own problem or task and create his own solution. Thus, of the three, the expressive is the most open, the Type III objective is less open, and the instructional objective is least open. But the distinctions between the three types of objectives are not, I believe, matters of degree but matters of kind. Type III objectives encourage the teacher to provide high degrees of structure in setting the problem but also encourage him to leave the avenues for potential solutions wide open. Within the specifications provided, anything that works well, works.

One can legitimately ask whether the distinctions between the three types of objectives I have described are simply an exercise in analysis or whether they have any practical utility for educational planning. I believe these concepts are heuristic, that is, they lead one to view curriculum decision making and evaluation in unconventional ways. They lead to fresh questions. With the three types of objectives, we can now examine a curriculum, one developed either nationally or by the classroom teacher, to determine the extent to which objectives of each type are provided and the degree of emphasis devoted to each. We can compare curricula in different subject matters to determine their use of such objectives.

Furthermore, we can now begin to examine evaluation tools such as standardized tests to determine the extent to which they provide for items or tasks related to these objectives, and if they do not, we can build instruments appropriate for such objectives. Finally, we can consciously begin to design learning activities within the parameters suggested by these types of objectives.

In addition to these tasks, we can inquire whether there is an appropriate rhythm among the types of learning activities implied by the three types of objectives and whether principles can be formulated that teachers might use to decide when to emphasize each type. In short, the distinctions I have drawn indicate more acute directions than can be taken in the construction and evaluation of educational programmes. When we recognize that we do not need, indeed cannot successfully have, a single, monolithic conception of educational objectives, we are in a position to generate alternatives in curriculum development and educational evaluation that a single view will not permit. Type III objectives, for want of a better name, can, I believe, provide a wider scope for such inquires.

A second idea that I would like to discuss deals with an image of the types of outcomes that it seems reasonable to assume are the products of teaching. The dominant, if not exclusive, orientation toward evaluating the effects of instruction is one which is aimed at determining the extent to which objectives are attained. Objectives in turn are usually couched within some subject-matter field, especially when it comes to the evaluation of academic achievement. Such a vision or model of evaluation fails, I believe, to attend to other, perhaps equally important, consequences of instruction. For example, it is part of educational lore that a teacher not only teaches a subject matter, but he also teaches himself. Those of us who have had the good fortune to have studied under great teachers know this in acute terms, but even lesser teachers teach themselves. How teachers attack a problem, what their standards of excellence are, their sense of excitement or boredom when they encounter a new idea, their expectations for deportment, their tolerance for ambiguity, their need for precision: these are all teachable characteristics that teachers inevitably convey to students during the course of their work. These effects one might call teacher-specific outcomes. Outcomes dealing with subject-matter achievement are content specific.

Teacher-specific and content-specific outcomes are not the only ones that arise in the course of instruction. The student makes his own outcomes. As a result of his previous life history, his particular interests, his turn of mind, the angle at which he comes at things, the student, like all of us, makes his own meaning. Although a substantial portion of the meanings made during the course of a course will be common to virtually all students in that course, each student will develop meanings that are unique. Each is likely to construct from that course ideas which are peculiarly his own. These outcomes are student specific. Seen in the image of a triadically divided circle (see fig. 1), one-third of that cirle represents *content-specific outcomes,* a seond third represents *teacher-specific outcomes,* and a final third represents *student-specific outcomes.* Content-specific and teacher-specific outcomes are likely to be homogeneous in character across students. That is, the characteristics

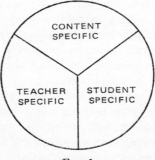

Fig. 1

and values that teachers teach by virtue of what they are, are in large measure common to most, if not all, students in class. Especially in mastery learning are such common outcomes desired.[14] But along with the common inevitably comes the unique. The way a student personalizes meanings—the ideas he creates that are spin-offs from the content of the course or from the musings of the teacher—is also important. Indeed, in the long run they might be among the most important contributions of schooling. This dimension as well as the contributions that the teacher makes to students because he is a particular type of human being have been neglected aspects of educational evaluation. Yet if we are to understand the effects of the programmes that are provided, surely these outcomes too must be examined. Thus, this triadic image of outcomes, bounded by a circle representing their unity, discloses the second idea of the three that I mentioned earlier.

Finally, I want to suggest a set of methods that I consider promising as a complement to the quantitative procedures now used so widely for educational evaluation. That set is the procedures and techniques of art criticism. The criticism of art is the use of methods designed to heighten one's perception of the qualities that constitute the work. The end of criticism as Dewey observed is the re-education of the perception of the work of art.[15] To achieve this end, the critic must bring two kinds of skills to his work. First, he must have developed highly refined visual sensibilities; that is, he must be able to see the elements that constitute a whole and their interplay. Second, he must be capable of rendering his perceptions into a language that makes it possible for others less perceptive than he to see qualities and aspects of the work that they would otherwise overlook. The critic, like a good teacher or book, directs attention to the subtle, he points out and articulates, he vivifies perception.

This vivification of perception which it is the critic's office to further is carried out by a particular use of language. It is quite clear that our discourse is not as differentiated as our sensibilities. We experience more than we can describe.[16] Thus, what the critic must do is not to attempt to replicate the visual, dramatic, or musical work verbally, but to provide a rendering of them through the use of poetic language. The vehicle the critic employs are suggestion, simile, and metaphor. These poetic vehicles carry the viewer to a heightened perception of the phenomena.

An example of the use of such linguistic resources can be found in art critic Max Kozloff's description of a painting by Robert Motherwell:

As an example, let me take a 1962 canvas, *Chi Ama, Crede* (Who Loves, Trusts), in which a recurring flaw, a disproportion of the generalized over the particular, is held at bay. It is a 12-foot frieze of wandering tan zones, surrounding two utterly eccentric, squirming turpentine blots of cool rusts, all this laid on in very close values. Basically the picture posits a contrast between restful, opaque fields that hold the surface and uneven strains that, with their shifting shadows, open up a translucent space and suggest a watery, organic agitation. But these rather hormonal blots are hemmed or even locked in by the ground at every stop of their fading perimeters. Here the artist reveals an overloaded liquidity that has dried up and been absorbed, and a mat, diffident facade that discloses an unsuspected strength. But suddenly, at one point, he withholds the paint tissue and, in an irregular glimpse of white canvas, flicks a whip of splatters that are almost electric under the murky circumstances. The whole thing glows as a vicarious pageant of his psyche.[17]

What Kozloff is doing here is using the connotative aspects of language to disclose the 'ineffable' content of visual-emotional experience. Kozloff writes of his efforts as a critic:

For this, the most appropriate devices at my disposal have been innuendo, nuance, and hypothesis, because what is peripheral to direct statement in language is often central to a pictorial encounter or its memory. The more willingly this condition is acknowledged, the more readily is it possible to avoid the imputation of fact to something which is not 'factual,' while remaining faithful to that catalyst of our aesthetic life—credulity.[18]

Much of what goes on in schools can be illuminated by the tools of criticism. As a generic method, criticism is especially suited to articulating the unique and the personalistic outcomes that are so highly prized by those who complain of the school's impersonality. The reason criticism is so suited is because it does not depend upon the conventional application of class concepts for description and because it does not restrict itself to the primary surface of a situation; the secondary surface, that is, the situation's expressive and underlying qualities, is also a candidate for description and interpretation. Such a mode of evaluation has not, as far as I know, been employed in its full-blown form (although one of my students is using such a method to examine teaching as an art form). There are in the literature examples that approximate such an approach to evaluation:

> I see again in mind my rickety raftered rocky prefab that split the melting frost in the spring. With Sammy Snail wandering down upon us from the rafters, the sun thick tangible bars across the rising dust from the bare floor boards, the loud ever-moving, ever-talking life of the New Race, from corner to corner, from wall to wall, both on the floor and upon the desks. Tall towers rocking precariously, fantastic shapes in colour leaping from the ten-child easel, Little Ones in eddying figures dancing, the clay-births, the sand turning into a graveyard under passionate brown fingers, the water through with one-pint building wharves, bombers zooming on the blackboards, outrageous statements in funnily spelt words on the low wall blackboards, children singing, quarrelling magnificently, laughing for nothing, infectiously crying for nothing infectiously, Waiwini's Little Brother wailing to me that somebodies they broked his castle for notheen. Bleeding Heart laughing his head off, the Tamatis' dog snuggling about for a cuddle, Pussy insinuating herself fastidiously, the Ginger Rooster scratching about ambitiously for culture, pictures of the meeting house and pa and the Ghost and of big-footed people kissing and words like shearing shed and beer and graveyard and wild piggy and lollies, tongues patrolling Maori lips over intensely personal writing, voices raised in exuberance, in argument, in reading, laughter, singing and crying and How-do-you-spell-Nanny. And our *floor!* You should see our floor! Round about the ten-child easel where the colour drips, it's prettier than the face of the countryside itself. You'd think Autumn himself had passed this way with his careless brush; slinging his paint about in his extravagant way. And noise . . . noise! And the whole show rocking like an overcrowded dinghy on high seas.[19]

Although autobigraphical, such an account of classroom life gives the reader a vivid picture of its qualities and of Sylvia Ashton-Warner's attitude toward it.

But one might ask, 'Isn't such a method merely subjective?' Can nonquantified description using poetic devices be anything more than the expression of taste and liable to the grossest forms of unreliability?

Not necessarily. In a very important sense, criticism is an empirical method. The adequacy of criticism is tested on the work itself. If what the critic describes cannot be seen in the work, his criticism fails to perform its function. In short, what he points out must be capable of being seen. Such a test is easier to apply to non-ephemeral works such as visual art and music than to the qualities that constitute classroom life, but such qualities are surely not so fugitive that their existence lasts only for a moment. Much of what is important in teaching and in learning is recurrent and regular. Criticism as a set of methods for analysis and disclosure can, I believe, make them vivid.

As a *complement* to the quantitative procedures we now use, such methods hold much promise. Their realization will require the creation of programmes designed to prepare individuals with such skills. In a venture of this kind, departments of art, English, drama, and anthropology might be called upon for assistance. The promise of such procedures for dealing incisively with educational programmes that might in the future become much more individualized than they are now is persuasive.

Notes

1. This paper was originally prepared for presentation at the Distinguished Visiting Scholars Programme, Department of Educational Psychology, Michigan State University. I wish to express my gratitude to the students and faculty of that institution for their incisive and stimulating comments and critique of this paper.
2. JOSEPH J. SCHWAB (1961), 'The Teaching of Science as Enquiry,' in *The Teaching of Science*. Cambridge, Mass.: Harvard University Press.
3. It is estimated that the National Science Foundation and the US Office of Education have allocated well over $100 million for teacher training and curriculum development in sciences and in mathematics over the past ten-year period.
4. See PHILIP W. JACKSON (1968), *Life in Classrooms*. New York: Holt, Rinehart & Winston.
5. For a lucid account of the psychometric work during the First World War, see GERALDINE JONCICH (1968), *The Sane Positivist: A Biography of Edward L. Thorndike*. Middletown, Conn.: Wesleyan University Press, pp. 356–82.
6. LAURENCE A. CREMIN (1961), *The Transformation of the School*. New York: Alfred A. Knopf, Inc., *passim*.
7. The notion that scientific inquiry is value neutral has been disputed by numerous students of science. For two cogent accounts of this problem, see JACOB BRONOWSKI'S *Science and Human Values* (New York: Harper & Row, 1959) and THOMAS KUHN'S *The Structure of Scientific Revolutions* (Chicago: University of Chicago Press, 1962).

8. LEE SHULMAN (1970), 'Reconstruction of Educational Research,' *Review of Educational Research*, 40, 3 (June), 374–75.
9. ROBERT EBEL (1971), 'Criterion-referenced Measurements: Limitations,' *School Review*, 79, 2 (February), 282–88.
10. LEE J. CRONBACH and RICHARD SNOW (1969), *Individual Differences in Learning Ability*. Washington: US Office of Education.
11. DANIEL STUFFELBEAM (1967), 'The Use and Abuse of Evaluation in Title III', *Theory into Practice*, 6, 3 (June), 126–33.
12. MICHAEL SCRIVEN, 'Education for Survival', Mimeographed, available from author. 57pp.
13. ELLIOT W. EISNER (1967), 'Educational Objectives: Help or Hinderance?' *School Review*, 75, 3 (Autumn), 250–60, and 'Instructional and Expressive Objectives: Their Formulation and Use in Curriculum.' In: W. JAMES POPHAM *et al.*, *Instructional Objectives*. American Educational Research Association Monograph no. 3. Chicago: Rand McNally & Co., 1969, pp. 1–18.
14. BENJAMIN BLOOM, 'Mastery Learning and Its Implications for Curriculum Development.' In: ELLIOT W. EISNER (ed.) (1971) *Confronting Curriculum Reform*. Boston: Little, Brown & Co., pp. 17–49.
15. JOHN DEWEY (1934), *Art as Experience*. New York: Minton, Balch & Co., p. 324.
16. For a brilliant discussion of the relationship of experience to discourse, see MICHAEL POLANYI, (1966) *The Tacit Dimension*. New York: Doubleday & Co.
17. MAX KOZLOFF (1969), *Renderings*. New York: Simon & Schuster, pp. 169–70.
18. *Ibid.*, p. 10.
19. SYLVIA ASHTON-WARNER (1963), *Teacher*. New York: Simon & Schuster, pp. 220–21.

Summary Appraisal

The standpoints of the authors are somewhat different and give rise to different insights and interpretations. White stands outside the process of curriculum development and curriculum decision-making and asks pertinent questions about our thinking in this area. He draws an analogy between curriculum evaluation and the work of consumers' associations, perhaps dwelling a little too much on the limitations of this analogy. There is an important sense in which teachers require just the sort of information about curriculum packages and ideas which consumers' reports provide for other goods and services. Eisner, in contrast, is very much on the inside of the process of curriculum development, in art and related fields. Both viewpoints, and indeed many others, are required to develop a complete picture of so multi-faceted an activity as curriculum evaluation.

Suggested Readings

TYLER, R. W. (Ed.) (1969). *Educational Evaluation: New Roles, New Means.* NSSE 68th Yearbook Pt. II. Chicago: University of Chicago Press.
This yearbook contains an impressive collection of essays on various aspects of evaluation. Of particular value for those intersted in curriculum evaluation are the following:

BLOOM, B. S., 'Some Theoretical Issues Relating to Educational Evaluation.'

FLANAGAN, J. C., 'The Uses of Educational Evaluation in the Development of Programmes, Courses, Instructional Materials and Equipment, Instructional and Learning Procedures and Administrative Arrangements.'

STAKE, R. E. and DENNY, I., 'Needed Concepts and Techniques for Utilizing more fully the Potential of Evaluation.'

Most of the essays, and particularly those mentioned above, are concerned with principles of evaluation. A more practical orientation, based on personal experience and amounting almost to a 'how-to-do-it' work is:

GROBMAN, H. (1968). *Evaluation Activities of Curriculum Projects* AERA. Monograph Series on Curriculum Evaluation 2. Chicago: Rand McNally and Company.

For case study material the following will be found useful:

GORDON, I. J., 'An Instructional Theory Approach to the Analysis of Selected Early Childhood Programs.'
SOAR, R. S. and SOAR, R. M., 'An Empirical Analysis of Selected Follow Through Programs: An Example of a Process Approach to Evaluation.'
Both can be found in *Early Childhood Education*, ed. by GORDON, I. J. (1972). NSSE 71st Yearbook Pt. II. Chicago: University of Chicago Press.

Finally some examples of English experience of, and approaches to, curriculum evaluation appear in:

SCHOOLS COUNCIL (1973). *Evaluation in Curriculum Development: Twelve Case Studies.* London: Macmillan Schools Council Research Studies.

Chapter 4

Curriculum Theory

Introduction

In many ways it can be said that the 'science' of curriculum has advanced little since the publication of the 26th National Society for the Study of Education Yearbook in 1927. In that Yearbook, issues were set forth which today remain critical to curriculum inquiry and which still remain unresolved. The Yearbook was concerned about the gap between school curriculum and American life, on the one hand, and about the gap between curriculum and the learner on the other. Also, there was a concern for curriculum decision-making based upon funded knowledge on the one hand and conventional wisdom on the other. Further, the question of the relationship between curriculum and instruction (intentions and transactions) was raised and discussed. Finally, the overreaching need for an empirical approach to solving the problems of curriculum was clearly stated.

To be sure, since the publication of the landmark Yearbook, there has been thoughtful and contemporary work done in the field which has contributed to the development of a 'science' of curriculum. One only has to review the works of Herrick, Tyler, Goodlad, and Bloom to recognize this fact. However, curriculum development remains by-and-large, as Macdonald (1971) declares in the Seventieth Yearbook of the Society, 'an historical accident.' Further, and perhaps more importantly, empirical as well as non-empirical inquiry into curriculum has been piecemeal.

What is needed more than ever in the field of curriculum is a renewed effort to search out solutions to curriculum problems through the building of curriculum theory or conceptual systems and models which lead to theory and through orderly research which tests such theories and/or conceptualizations.

Before proceeding, and for the sake of clarity, we can define curriculum theory as Beauchamp (1961) does:

> . . . Curriculum theory is a set of related statements that gives meaning to the school curriculum by pointing up the relationship among its elements and by directing its development, its use, and its evaluation.

The papers in this section deal with the question of theory building in curriculum. Schwab contends that, at worst, theory may be inappropriate and, at best, it may be inadequate as it is now being formulated. Johnson sets forth a curriculum model and suggests the need to distinguish between curriculum (intentions) and instruction (transactions) as a means toward the development of more adequate theoretical constructs.

Schwab makes three major points. First, he states that the field of curriculum needs new principles and methods. As evidence of this need he cites the fact that there is a growing tendency among those currently involved in theoretical curriculum inquiry to 'flee' in a variety of ways. Second, he indicates that the curriculum field has reached this position because of an unexamined reliance upon extant theory in an area when theory is partly inappropriate and where extant theories are inadequate. He cites various theories of knowledge, personality, and society which are often in conflict with one another and which are too frequently employed in a doctrinaire manner. Finally, he points out that adequate new principles, methods and theories will be developed only when we seriously look to what actually goes on in schools. Thus, Schwab's major argument is that while the 'stuff' of theory is abstract or idealized, curriculum in action treats real things—real acts, real teachers, real children—things richer and different from their theoretical representations.

Johnson explores the relationship between curriculum (intentions) and instruction (transactions). He assumes that if curriculum serves any purposes, they are to guide instruction and to furnish criteria for evaluation. Curriculum must be a statement of intention, not a report of occurrences or results. When curriculum is viewed as a structured series of intended learning outcomes, instruction becomes the means by which intentions are translated into realities. Thus, the formulation of instructional plans or the development of instructional 'programmes' or 'packages' is to be distinguished from the process of implementation. The author carefully builds these assumptions through the review of numerous contemporary models and discourses derived from the literature on curriculum and instruction. The result is a series of models of his own which clarify the relationship between curriculum and instruction.

References

BEAUCHAMP, G. (1961). *Curriculum Theory*. Illinois: Cagg Press. (see also Third Edition, 1975).

MACDONALD, J. B. (1971). 'Curriculum Development in Relation to Social and Intellectual Systems'. In: MCCLURE, R. M. *The Curriculum in Retrospect and Prospect*. 70th Yearbook. Chicago: NSSE.

Readings

The Practical: A Language for Curriculum[1]*

Joseph J. Schwab *University of Chicago*

I shall make three points. The first is this: that the field of curriculum is moribund, unable by its present methods and principles to continue its work and desperately in search of new and more effective principles and methods.

The second point: the curriculum field has reached this unhappy state by inveterate and unexamined reliance on theory in an area where theory is partly inappropriate in the first place and where the theories extant, even where appropriate, are inadequate to the tasks which the curriculum field sets them. There are honourable exceptions to this rule but too few (and too little honoured) to alter the state of affairs.

The third point, which constitutes my thesis: there will be a renaissance of the field of curriculum, a renewed capacity to contribute to the quality of American education, only if the bulk of curriculum energies are diverted from the theoretic to the practical, to the quasi-practical and to the eclectic. By 'eclectic' I mean the arts by which unsystematic, uneasy, but usable focus on a body of problems is effected among diverse theories, each relevant to the problems in a different way. By the 'practical' I do *not* mean the curbstone practicality of the mediocre administrator and the man on the street, for whom the practical means the easily achieved, familiar goals which can be reached by familiar means. I refer, rather, to a complex discipline, relatively unfamiliar to the academic and differing radically from the disciplines of the theoretic. It is the discipline concerned with choice

---

* This article has been reproduced from *School Review* (November 1969) by permission of the author and The University of Chicago Press.

and action, in contrast with the theoretic, which is concerned with knowledge. Its methods lead to defensible decisions, where the methods of the theoretic lead to warranted conclusions, and differ radically from the methods and competences entailed in the theoretic. I shall sketch some of the defining aspects of practical disciplines at the appropriate time.

A crisis of principle

The frustated state of the field of curriculum is not an idiopathology and not a condition which warrants guilt or shame on the part of its practitioners. All fields of systematic intellectual activity are liable to such crises. They are so because any intellectual discipline must begin its endeavours with untested principles. In its beginnings, its subject matter is relatively unknown, its problems unsolved, indeed, un-identified. It does not know what questions to ask, what other knowledge to rest upon, what data to seek or what to make of them once they are elicited. It requires a preliminary and necessarily untested guide to its inquiries. It finds this guide by borrowing, by invention, or by analogy, in the shape of a hazardous commitment to the character of its problems or its subject matter and a commitment to untried canons of evidence and rules of inquiry. What follows these commitments is years of their application, pursuit of the mode of inquiry demanded by the principles to which the field has committed itself. To the majority of practitioners of any field, these years of inquiry appear as pursuit of knowledge of its subject matter or solution of its problems. They take the guiding principles of the inquiry as givens. These years of inquiry, however, are something more than pursuit of knowledge or solution of problems. They are also tests, reflexive and pragmatic, of the principles which guide the inquiries. They determine whether, in fact, the data demanded by the principles can be elicited and whether, if elicited, they can be made to constitute knowledge adequate to the complexity of the subject matter, or solutions which, in fact, do solve the problems with which the inquiry began.

In the nature of the case, these reflexive tests of the principles of inquiry are, more often than not, partially or wholly negative, for, after all, the commitment to these principles was made before there was well-tested fruit of inquiry by which to guide the commitment. The inadequacies of principles begin to show, in the case of theoretical inquiries, by failures of the subject matter to respond to the questions put to it, by incoherencies and contradictions in data and in conclusions which cannot be resolved, or by clear disparities between the knowledge yielded by the inquiries and the behaviours of the subject matter which the knowledge purports to represent. In the case of practical inquiries, inadequacies begin to show by incapacity to arrive at solutions to the problems, by inability to realize the solutions proposed, by mutual frustrations and cancellings out as solutions are put into effect.

Although these exhaustions and failures of principles may go unnoted by practitioners in the field, at least at the conscious level, what may not be represented in consciousness is nevertheless evidenced by behaviour and appears in the literature and the activities of the field as signs of the onset of a crisis of principle. These signs consist of a large increase in the frequency of published papers and colloquia marked by *a flight from the subject of the field*. There are usually six signs of this flight or directions in which the flight occurs.

Signs of crisis

The first and most important, though often least conspicuous, sign is a flight of the field itself, a translocation of its problems and the solving of them from the nominal practitioners of the field to other men. Thus one crucial frustration of the science of genetics was resolved by a single contribution from an insurance actuary. The recent desuetude of academic physiology has been marked by a conspicuous increase in the frequency of published solutions to physiological problems by medical researchers. In similar fashion, the increasing depletion of psychoanalytic principles and methods in recent years was marked by the onset of contributions to its lore by internists, biochemists, and anthropologists.

A second flight is a flight upward, from discourse about the subject of the field to discourse about the discourse of the field, from *use* of principles and methods to *talk* about them, from grounded conclusions to the construction of models, from theory to metatheory and from metatheory to metametatheory.

A third flight is downward, an attempt by practitioners to return to the subject matter in a state of innocence, shorn not only of current principles but of all principles, in an effort to take a new, a pristine and unmediated look at the subject matter. For example, one conspicuous reaction to the warfare of numerous inadequate principles in experimental psychology has been the resurgence of ethology, which begins as an attempt to return to a pure natural history of behaviour, to intensive observation and recording of the behaviour of animals undisturbed in their natural habitat, by observers, equally undisturbed by mediating conceptions, attempting to record anything and everything they see before them.

A fourth flight is to the sidelines, to the role of observer, commentator, historian, and critic of the contributions of others to the field.

A fifth sign consists of marked perseveration, a repetition of old and familiar knowledge in new languages which add little or nothing to the old meanings as embodied in the older and familiar language, or repetition of old and familiar formulations by way of criticisms or minor additions and modifications.

The sixth is a marked increase in eristic, contentious, and *ad hominem* debate.

I hasten to remark that these signs of crises are not all or equally reprehensible. There is little excuse for the increase in contentiousness nor much value in the flight to the sidelines or in perseveration, but the others, in one way or another, can contribute to resolution of the crisis. The flight of the field itself is one of the more fruitful ways by which analogical principles are disclosed, modified, and adapted to the field in crises. The flight upward, to models and metatheory, if done responsibly, which means with a steady eye on the actual problems and conditions of the field for which the models are ostensibly constructed, becomes, in fact, the proposal and test of possible new principles for the field. The flight backward, to a state of innocence, is at least an effort to break the grip of old habits of thought and thus leave space for needed new ones, though it is clear that in the matter of inquiry, as elsewhere, virginity, once lost, cannot be regained.

In the present context, however, the virtue or vice of these various flights is beside the point. We are concerned with them as signs of collapse of principles in a field, and it is my contention, based on a study not yet complete, that most of these signs may now be seen in the field of curriculum. I shall only suggest, not cite, my evidence.

The case of curriculum

With respect to flight of the field itself, there can be little doubt. Of the five substantial high school science curricula, four of them—PSSC, BSCS, Chems and CBA—were instituted and managed by subject-matter specialists; the contribution of educators was small and that of curriculum specialists near vanishing point. Only Harvard Project Physics, at this writing not yet available, appears to be an exception.

To one of two elementary science projects, a psychologist appears to have made a substantial contribution but curriculum specialists very little. The other—the Elementary Science Study—appears to have been substantially affected (to its advantage) by educators with one or both feet in curriculum. The efforts of the Commission on Undergraduate Education in the Biological Sciences have been carried on almost entirely by subject-matter specialists. The English Curriculum Study Centres appear to be in much the same state as the high school science curricula: overwhelmingly centered on subject specialists. Educators contribute expertise only in the area of test construction and evaluation, with here and there a contribution by a psychologist. Educators, including curriculum specialists, were massively unprepared to cope with the problem of integrated education and only by little, and late, and by trial and error, put together the halting solutions currently known as Head Start. The problems posed by the current drives toward ethnicity in education find curriculum specialists even more massively oblivious and unprepared. And I so far find myself very much alone with respect to the curriculum problems immanent in the phenomena of student protest and student revolt. (Of the social studies curriculum efforts, I shall say nothing at this time.)

On the second flight—upward—I need hardly comment. The models, the metatheory, and the metametatheory are all over the place. Many of them, moreover, are irresponsible—concerned less with the barriers to continued productivity in the field of curriculum than with exploitation of the exotic and the fashionable among forms and models of theory and metatheory: systems theory, symbolic logic, language analysis. Many others, including responsible ones, are irreversible flights upward or sideways. That is, they are models or metatheories concerned not with the judgment, the reasoned construction, or reconstruction of curriculums but with other matters—for example, how curriculum changes occur or how changes can be managed.

The flight downward, the attempt at return to a pristine, unmediated look at the subject matter, is, for some reason, a missing symptom in the case of curriculum. There are returns—to the classroom, if not to other levels or aspects of curriculum—with a measure of effort to avoid preconceptions (e.g., Smith, Bellack, and studies of communication nets and lines), but the frequency of such studies has not markedly increased. The absence of this symptom may have significance. In general, however, it is characteristic of diseases that the whole syndrome does not appear in all cases. Hence, pending further study and thought,

I do not count this negative instance as weakening the diagnosis of a crisis of principle.

The fourth flight—to the sidelines—is again a marked symptom of the field of curriculum. Histories, anthologies, commentaries, criticisms, and proposals of curriculums multiply.

Perseveration is also marked. I recoil from counting the persons and books whose lives are made possible by continuing restatement of the Tyler rationale, of the character and case for behavioural objectives, of the virtues and vices of John Dewey.

The rise in frequency and intensity of the eristic and *ad hominem* is also marked. Thus one author climaxes a series of petulances by the remark that what he takes to be his own forte 'has always been rare— and shows up in proper perspective the happy breed of educational reformer who can concoct a brand new, rabble-rousing theory of educational reform while waiting for the water to fill the bathtub.'

There is little doubt, in short, that the field of curriculum is in a crisis of principle.

A crisis of principle arises, as I have suggested, when principles are exhausted—when the questions they permit have all been asked and answered—or when the efforts at inquiry instigated by the principles have at last exhibited their inadequacy to the subject matter and the problems which they were designed to attack. My second point is that the latter holds in the case of curriculum: the curriculum movement has been inveterately theoretic, and its theoretic bent has let it down. A brief conspectus of instances will suggest the extent of this theoretic bent and what is meant by 'theoretic.'

Characteristics of theory

Consider first the early, allegedly Herbartian efforts (recently revived by Bruner). These efforts took the view that ideas were formed by children out of received notions and experiences of things, and that these ideas functioned thereafter as discriminators and organizers of what was later learned. Given this view, the aim of curriculum was to discriminate the right ideas (by way of analysis of extant bodies of knowledge), determine the order in which they could be learned by children as they developed, and thereafter present these ideas at the right times with clarity, associations, organization, and application. A theory of mind and knowledge thus solves by one mighty coup the problem of what to teach, when, and how; and what is fatally theoretic here is not the presence of a theory of mind and a theory of knowledge, though their presence is part of the story, but the dispatch, the sweeping appearance of success, the vast simplicity which grounds this purported solution to the problem of curriculum. And lest we think that this faith in the possibility of successful neatness, dispatch, and sweeping generality is a mark of the past, consider the concern of the National Science Teachers Association only four years ago 'with identifying the broad principles that can apply to any and all curriculum development efforts in science,' a concern crystallized in just seven 'conceptual schemes' held to underlie all science. With less ambitious sweepingness but with the same steadfast concern for a single factor—in this case, a supposed fixed structure of knowledge—one finds similar efforts arising from the Association of College Teachers of Education, from historians, even from teachers of literature.

Consider, now, some of the numerous efforts to ground curriculum in derived objectives. One effort seeks the ground of its objectives in social need and finds its social needs in just those facts about its culture which are sought and found under the aegis of a single conception of culture. Another grounds its objectives in the social needs identified by a single theory of history and of political evolution.

A third group of searches for objectives are gounded in theories of personality. The persuasive coherence and plausibility of Freudianism persuaded its followers to aim to supply children with adequate channels of sublimation of surplus libido, appropriate objects and occasions for aggressions, a properly undemanding ego ideal, and an intelligent minimum of taboos. Interpersonal theories direct their adherents to aim for development of abilities to relate to peers, 'infeers,' and 'supeers,' in relations nurturant and receiving adaptive, vying, approving and disapproving. Theories of actualization instruct their adherents to determine the salient potentialities of each child and to see individually to the development of each.

Still other searches for objectives seek their aims in the knowledge needed to 'live in the modern world,' in the attitudes and habits which minimize dissonance with the prevailing mores of one's community or social class, in the skills required for success in a trade or vocation, in the ability to participate effectively as member of a group. Still others are grounded in some quasi-ethics, some view of the array of goods which are good for man.

Three features of these typical efforts at curriculum making are significant here, each of which has its own lesson to teach us. First, each is grounded in a theory as such. We shall return to this point in a moment. Second, each is grounded in a theory from the social or behavioural sciences: psychology, psychiatry, politics, sociology, history. Even the ethical bases and theories of 'mind' are behavioural. To this point, too, we shall return in a moment. Third, they are theories concerning *different* subject matters. One curriculum effort is grounded in concern for the individual, another in concern for groups, others in concern for cultures, communities, societies, minds, or the extant bodies of knowledge.[2]

Need for an eclectic

The significance of this third feature is patent to the point of embarrassment: no curriculum grounded in but one of these subjects can possibly be adequate, defensible. A curriculum based on theory about individual personality, which thrusts society, its demands and its structure, far into the background or ignores them entirely, can be nothing but incomplete and doctrinaire, for the individuals in question are in fact members of a society and must meet its demands to some minimum degree since their existence and prosperity as individuals depend on the functioning of their society. In the same way, a curriculum grounded only in a view of social need or social change must be equally doctrinaire and incomplete, for societies do not exist only for their own sakes but for the prosperity of their members as individuals as well. In the same way, learners are not only minds or knowers but bundles of affects, individuals, personalities, earners of livings. They are not only group interactors but possessors of private lives.

It is clear, I submit, that a defensible curriculum or plan of curriculum must be one which somehow takes account of all these sub-subjects which pertain to man. It cannot take only one and ignore the others; it cannot even take account of many of them and ignore one. Not only is each of them a constituent and a condition for decent human existence but each interpenetrates the others. That is, the character of human personalities is a determiner of human society and the behaviour of human groups. Conversely, the conditions of group behaviour and the character of societies determine in some large part the personalities which their members develop, the way their minds work, and what they can learn and use by way of knowledge and competence. These various 'things' (individuals, societies, cultures, patterns of inquiry, 'structures' of knowledge or of inquiries, apperceptive masses, problem solving), though discriminable as separate subjects of differing modes of inquiry, are nevertheless parts or affectors of one another, or coactors. (Their very separation for purposes of inquiry is what marks the outcomes of such inquiries as 'theoretic' and consequently incomplete.) In practice, they constitute one complex, organic agency. Hence, a focus on only one not only ignores the others but vitiates the quality and completeness with which the selected one is viewed.

It is equally clear, however, that there is not, and will not be in the foreseeable future, one theory of this complex whole which is other than a collection of unusable generalities. Nor is it true that the lack of a theory of the whole is due to the narrowness, stubbornness, or merely habitual specialism of social and behavioural scientists. Rather, their specialism and the restricted purview of their theories are functions of their subject, its enormous complexity, its vast capacity for difference and change. Man's competence at the construction of theoretical knowledge is so far most inadequate when applied to the subject of man. There have been efforts to conceive principles of inquiry which would encompass the whole variety and complexity of humanity, but they have fallen far short of adequacy to the subject matter or have demanded the acquisition of data and modes of interpretation of data beyond our capabilities. There *are* continuing efforts to find bridging terms which would relate the principles of inquiry of one subfield of the social sciences to another and thus begin to effect connections among our knowledges of each, but successful bridges are so far few and narrow and permit but a trickle of connection. As far, then, as theoretical knowledge is concerned, we must wrestle as best we can with numerous, largely unconnected separate theories of these many, artificially discriminated sub-subjects of man.

I remarked in the beginning that renewal of the field of curriculum would require diversion of the bulk of its energies from theory to the practical, the quasi-practical, and the eclectic. The state of affairs just described, the existence and the necessarily continuing existence of separate theories of separate sub-subjects distributed among the social sciences, constitutes the case for one of these modes, the necessity of an eclectic, of arts by which a usable focus on a common body of problems is effected among theories which lack theoretical connection. The argument can be simply summarized. A curriculum grounded in but one or a few sub-subjects of the social sciences is indefensible; contributions from all are required. There is no foreseeable hope of a unified theory in the immediate or middle future, nor of a metatheory which will tell us how to put those sub-subjects together or order them in a fixed hierarchy of importance to the problems of curriculum. What remains as a viable alternative is the unsystematic, uneasy, pragmatic, and uncertain unions and connections which can be effected in an eclectic. And I must add, anticipating our discussion of the practical, that *changing* connections and *differing* orderings at different times of these separate theories, will characterize a sound of eclectic.

The character of eclectic arts and procedures must be left for discussion on another occasion. Let it suffice for the moment that witness of the high effectiveness of eclectic methods and of their accessibility is borne by at least one field familiar to us all—Western medicine. It has been enormously effective, and the growth of its competence dates from its disavowal of a single doctrine and its turn to eclecticism.

The place of the practical

I turn now, from the fact that the theories which ground curriculum plans pertain to different sub-subjects of a common field, to the second of the three features which characterize our typical instances of curriculum planning—the fact that the ground of each plan is a theory, a theory as such.

The significance of the existence of theory as such at the base of curricular planning consists of what it is that theory does not and cannot encompass. All theories, even the best of them in the simplest sciences, necessarily neglect some aspects and facets of the facts of the case. A theory covers and formulates the *regularities* among the things and events it subsumes. It abstracts a general or ideal case. It leaves behind the non-uniformities, the particularities, which characterize each concrete instance of the facts subsumed. Moreover, in the process of idealization, theoretical inquiry may often leave out of consideration conspicuous facets of *all* cases because its substantive principles of inquiry or its methods cannot handle them. Thus the constantly accelerating body of classical mechanics was the acceleration of a body in 'free' fall, fall in a perfect vacuum, and the general or theoretical rule formulated in classical mechanics is far from describing the fall of actual bodies in actual mediums—the only kinds of fall then known. The force equation of classical dynamics applied to bodies of visible magnitudes ignores friction. The rule that light varies inversely as the square of the distance holds exactly only for an imaginary point source of light. For real light sources of increasing expanse, the so-called law holds more and more approximately, and for very large sources it affords little or no usable information. And what is true of the best of theories in the simplest sciences is true *a fortiori* in the social sciences. Their subject matters are apparently so much more variable, and clearly so much more complex, that their theories encompass much less of their subjects than do the theories of the physical and biological sciences.

Yet curriculum is brought to bear not on ideal or abstract representatives but on the real thing, on the concrete case in all its completeness and with all its differences from all other concrete cases on which the theoretic abstraction is silent. The materials of a concrete curriculum will not consist merely of portions of 'science,' of 'literature,' of 'process.' On the contrary, their constituents will be particular assertions about selected matters couched in a particular vocabulary, syntax, and rhetoric. They will be particular novels, short stories, or lyric poems, each, for better or for worse, with its won flavour. They will be particular acts upon particular matters in a given sequence. The curriculum will be brought to bear not in some archetypical classroom but in a particular locus in time and space with smells, shadows, seats, and conditions outside its walls which may have much to do with what is achieved inside. Above all, the supposed beneficiary is not the generic child, not even a class or kind of child out of the psychological or sociological literature pertaining to the child. The beneficiaries will consist of very local kinds of children and, within the local kinds, individual children. The same diversity holds with respect to teachers and what they do. The generalities about science, about literature, about children in general, about children or teachers of some specified class or kind, may be true. But they attain this status in virtue of what they leave out, and the omissions affect what remains. A Guernsey cow is not only something more than a cow, having specific features omitted from description of the genus; it is also cowy in ways differing from the cowiness of a Texas longhorn. The specific not only adds to the generic; it also modulates it.

These ineluctable characteristics of theory and the consequent ineluctable disparities between real things and their representation in theory constitute one argument from my thesis, that a large bulk of curriculum energies must be diverted from the theoretic, not only to the eclectic but to the practical and the quasi-practical. The argument, again, can be briefly summarized. The stuff of theory is abstract or idealized representations of real things. But curriculum in action treats real things: real acts, real teachers, real children, things richer and different from their theoretical representations. Curriculum will deal badly with its real things if it treats them merely as replicas of their theoretic representations. If, then, theory is to be used well in the determination of curricular practice, it requires a supplement. It requires arts which bring a theory to its application: first, arts which identify the disparities between real thing and theoretic representation; second, arts which modify the theory in the course of its application, in the light of the discrepancies; and, third, arts which devise ways of taking account of the many aspects of the real thing which the theory does not take into account. These are some of the arts of the practical.

Theories from social sciences

The significance of the third feature of our typical instances of curriculum work—that their theories are mainly theories from the social and behavioural sciences—will carry us to the remainder of the argument for the practical. Nearly all theories in all the behavioural sciences are marked by the coexistence of competing theories. There is not one theory of personality but 20, representing at least six radically different choices of what is relevant and important in human behaviour. There is not one theory of groups but several. There is not one theory of learning but half a dozen. All the social and behavioural sciences are marked by 'schools,' each distinguished by a different choice of principle of inquiry, each of which selects from the intimidating complexities of the subject matter the small fraction of the whole with which it can deal.

The theories which arise from inquiries so directed are, then, radically incomplete, each of them incomplete to the extent that competing theories take hold of different aspects of the subject of inquiry and treat it in a different way. Further, there is perennial invention of new principles which bring to light new facets of the subject matter, new relations among the facets and new ways of treating them. In short, there is every reason to suppose that any one of the extant theories of behaviour is a pale and incomplete representation of actual behaviour. There is similar reason to suppose that if all the diversities of fact, the different aspects of behaviour treated in each theory, were somehow to be brought within the bounds of a single theory, that theory would still fall short of comprehending the whole of human behaviour—in two respects. In the first place, it would not comprehend what there may be of human behaviour which we do not see by virtue of the restricted light by which we examine behaviour. In the second place, such a single theory will necessarily interpret its data in the light of its one set of principles, assigning to these data only one set of significances and establishing them only one set of relations. It will remain the case, then, that a diversity of theories may tell us more than a single one, even though the 'factual' scope of the many and the one are the same.

It follows, then, that such theories are not, and will not be, adequate by themselves to tell us what to do with human beings or how to do it. What they variously suggest and the contrary guidances they afford to choice and action must be mediated and combined by eclectic arts and must be massively supplemented, as well as mediated, by knowledge of some other kind derived from another source.

Some areas of choice and action with respect to human behaviour have long since learned this lesson. Government is made possible by a lore of politics derived from immediate experience of the viccissitudes and tangles of legislating and administering. Institution of economic guidances and controls owes as much to unmediated experience of the marketplace as it does to formulas and theories. Even psychotherapy has long since deserted its theories of personality as sole guides to therapy and relies as much or more on the accumulated, explicitly nontheoretic lore accumulated by practitioners, as it does on theory or eclectic combinations of theory. The law has systematized the accumulation of direct experience of actual cases in its machinery for the recording of cases and opinions as precedents which continuously monitor, supplement, and modify the meaning and application of its formal 'knowledge,' its statutes. It is this recourse to accumulated lore, to experience of actions and their consequences, to action and reaction at the level of the concrete case, which constitutes the heart of the practical. It is high time that curriculum do likewise.

The practical arts

The arts of the practical are onerous and complex; hence only a sampling must suffice to indicate the character of this discipline and the changes in education investigation which would ensue on adoption of the discipline. I shall deal briefly with four aspects of it.

The practical arts begin with the requirement that existing institutions and existing practices be preserved and altered piecemeal, not dismantled and replaced. It is further necessary that changes be so planned and so articulated with what remains unchanged that the functioning of the whole remain coherent and unimpaired. These necessities stem from the very nature of the practical—that it is concerned with the maintenance and improvement of patterns of purposed action, and especially concerned that the effects of the pattern through time shall retain coherence and relevance to one another.

This is well seen in the case of the law. Statutes are repealed or largely rewritten only as a last resort, since to do so creates confusion and diremption between old judgments under the law and judgments to come, confusion which must lead either to weakening of law through disrepute or a painful and costly process of repairing the effects of past judgments so as to bring them into conformity with the new. It is vastly more desirable that changes be instituted in small degrees and in immediate adjustment to the peculiarities of particular new cases which call forth the change.

The consequence, in the case of the law, of these demands of the practical is that the servants of the law must know the law through and through. They must know the statutes themselves, the progression of precedents and interpretations which have effected changes in them, and especially the present state of affairs—the most recent decisions under the law and the calendar of cases which will be most immediately affected by contemplated additions to precedent and interpretation.

The same requirements would hold for a practical programme of improvement of education. It, too, would effect its changes in small progressions, in coherence with what remains unchanged, and this would require that we know *what is and has been going on in American schools.*

At present, we do not know. My own incomplete investigations convince me that we have not the faintest reliable knowledge of how literature is taught in the high schools, or what actually goes on in science classrooms. There are a dozen different ways in which the novel can be read. Which ones are used by whom, with whom, and to what effect? What selections from the large accumulation of biological knowledge are made and taught in this school system and that, to what classes and kinds of children, to what effect? To what extent is science taught as verbal formulas, as congeries of unrelated facts, as so-called principles and conceptual structures, as outcomes of inquiry? In what degree and kind of simplification and falsification is scientific inquiry conveyed, if it is conveyed at all?

A count of textbook adoptions will not tell us, for teachers select from textbooks and alter their treatment (often quite properly) and can frustrate and negate the textbook's effort to alter the pattern of instruction. We cannot tell from lists of objectives, since they are usually so vastly ambiguous that almost anything can go on under their aegis or, if they are not ambiguous, reflect pious hopes as much as actual practice. We cannot tell from lists of 'principles' and 'conceptual structures,' since these, in their telegraphic brevity are also ambiguous and say nothing of the shape in which they are taught or the extent.

What is wanted is a totally new and extensive pattern of *empirical* study of classroom action and reaction; a study, not as basis for theoretical concerns about the nature of the teaching or learning process, but as a basis for beginning to know what we are doing, what we are not doing, and to what effect—what changes are needed, which needed changes can be instituted with what costs or economies, and how they can be effected with minimum tearing of the remaining fabric of educational effort.

This is an effort which will require new mechanisms of empirical investigation, new methods of reportage, a new class of educational researchers, and much money. It is an effort without which we will continue largely incapable of making defensible decisions about curricular changes, largely unable to put them into effect and ignorant of what real consequences, if any, our efforts have had.

A very large part of such a study would, I repeat, be direct and empirical study of action and reaction in the classroom itself, not merely the testing of student change. But one of the most interesting and visible alterations of present practice which might be involved is a radical change in our pattern of testing students. The common pattern tries to determine the extent to which *intended* changes have been brought about. This would be altered to an effort to find out what changes have occurred, to determine side effects as well as mainline consequences, since the distinction between these two is always in the eye of the intender and side effects may be as great in magnitude and as fatal or healthful for students as the intended effects.

A second facet of the practical: its actions are undertaken with respect to identified frictions and failures in the machine and inadequacies evidenced in felt shortcomings of its products. This origin of its actions leads to two marked differences in operation from that of theory. Under the control of theory, curricular changes have their origin in new notions of person, group or society, mind or knowledge, which give rise to suggestions of new things curriculum might be or do. This is an origin which, by its nature, takes little or no account of the existing effectiveness of the machine or the consequences to this effectiveness of the institution of novelty. If there is concern for what may be displaced by innovation or for the incoherences which may ensue on the insertion of novelty, the concern is gratuitous. It does not arise from the theoretical considerations which command the novelty. The practical, on the other hand, because it institutes changes to repair frictions and deficiencies, is commanded to determine the whole array of possible effects of proposed change, to determine what new frictions and deficiencies the proposed change may unintentionally produce.

The other effective difference between theoretical and practical origins of deliberate change is patent. Theory, by being concerned with new things to do, is unconcerned with the successes and failures of present doings. Hence present failures, unless they coincide with what is repaired by the proposed innovations, go unnoticed—as do present successes. The practical, on the other hand, is directly and deliberately concerned with the diagnosis of ills of the curriculum.

These concerns of the practical for frictions and failures of the curricular machine would, again, call for a new and extensive pattern of inquiry. The practical requires curriculum study to seek its problems where the problems lie—in the behaviours, misbehaviours, and non-behaviours of its students as they begin to evince the effects of the training they did and did not get. This means continuing assessment of students as they leave primary grades for the secondary school, leave secondary school for jobs and colleges. It means sensitive and sophisticated assessment by way of impressions, insights, and reactions of the community which sends its children to the school; employers of students, new echelons of teachers of students; the wives, husbands, and cronies of ex-students; the people with whom ex-students work; the people who work under them. Curriculum study will look into the questions of what games ex-students play; what, if anything, they do about politics and crime in the streets; what they read, if they do; what they watch on television and what they make of what they watch, again, if anything. Such studies would be undertaken, furthermore, not as mass study of products of the American school, taken *in toto,* but as studies of significantly separable school and school systems—suburban and inner city, Chicago and Los Angeles, South Bend and Michigan City.

I emphasize sensitive and sophisticated assessment because we are concerned here, as in the laying of background knowledge of what goes in schools, not merely with the degree to which avowed objectives are achieved but also with detecting the failures and frictions of the machine: what it has not done or thought of doing, and what side effects its doings have had. Nor are we concerned with successes and failures only as measured in test situations but also as evidenced in life and work. It is this sort of diagnosis which I have tried to exemplify in a recent treatment of curriculum and student protest.[3]

A third facet of the practical I shall call the anticipatory generation of alternatives. Intimate knowledge of the existing state of affairs, early identification of problem situations, and effective formulation of problems are necessary to effective practical decision but not sufficient. It requires also that there be available to practical deliberation the greatest possible number and fresh diversity of alternative solutions to the problem. The reason for this requirement, in one aspect, is obvious enough: the best choice among poor and shopworn alternatives will still be a poor solution to the problem. Another aspect is less obvious. The problems which arise in an institutional structure which has enjoyed good practical management will be novel problems, arising from changes in the times and circumstances and from the consequences of previous solutions to previous problems. Such problems, with their strong tincture of novelty, cannot be solved by familiar solutions. They cannot be well solved by apparently new solutions arising from old habits of mind and old ways of doing things.

A third aspect of the requirement for anticipatory generation of alternatives is still less obvious. It consists of the fact that practical problems do not present themselves wearing their labels around their necks. Problem situations, to use Dewey's old term, present themselves to consciousness, but the character of the problem, its formulation, does not. This depends on the eye of the beholder. And this eye, un-illuminated by possible fresh solutions to problems, new modes of attack, new recognitions of degrees of freedom for change among matters formerly taken to be unalterable, is very likely to miss the novel features of new problems or dismiss them as 'impractical.' Hence the require-ment that the generation of problems be anticipatory and not await the emergence of the problem itself.

To some extent, the *theoretical* bases of curricular change—such items as emphasis on inquiry, on discovery learning, and on structure of the disciplines—contribute to this need but not sufficiently or with the breadth which permits effective deliberation. That is, these theoretic proposals tend to arise in single file, out of connection with other proposals which constitute alternatives, or, more important, constitute desiderata or circumstances which affect the choice or rejection of proposals. Consider, in regard to the problem of the 'single file,' only one relation between the two recent proposals subsumed under 'creativity' and 'structure of knowledge.' If creativity implies some measure of invention, and 'structure of knowledge' implies (as it does in one version) the systematic induction of conceptions as soon as children are ready to grasp them, an issue is joined. To the extent that the latter is timely and well done, scope for the former is curtailed. To the extent that children can be identified as more or less creative, 'structure of knowledge' would be brought to bear on different children at different times and in different ways.

A single case, taken from possible academic resources of education, will suggest the new kind of inquiry entailed in the need for anticipatory generation of alternatives. Over the years, critical scholarship has generated, as remarked earlier, a dozen different conceptions of the novel, a dozen or more ways in which the novel can be read, each involving its own emphases and its own arts of recovery of meaning in the act of reading. Novels can be read, for example, as bearers of wisdom, insights into vicissitudes of human life and ways of enduring them. Novels can also be read as moral instructors, as sources of vicarious experience, as occasions for aesthetic experience. They can be read as models of human creativity, as displays of social problems, as political propaganda, as revelations of diverisites of manners and morals among different cultures and classes of people, or as symptoms of their age.

Now what, in fact, is the full parade of such possible uses of the novel? What is required by each in the way of competences of reading, discussion, and thought? What are the rewards, the desirable outcomes, which are likely to ensue for students from each kind of reading or combinations of them? For what kinds or classes of students is each desirable? There are further problems demanding anticipatory consideration. If novels are chosen and read as displays of social problems and depictions of social class, what effect will such instruction in literature have on instruction in the social studies? What will teachers need to know and be able to do in order to enable students to discriminate and appropriately connect the *aperçus* of artists, the accounts of historians, and the conclusions of social scientists on such matters? How will the mode of instruction in science (e.g., as verified truths) and in literature (as 'deep insights' or artistic constructions or matters of opinion) affect the effects of each?

The same kinds of questions could be addressed to history and to the social studies generally. Yet, nowhere, in the case of literature, have we been able to find cogent and energetic work addressed to them. The journals in the field of English teaching are nearly devoid of treatment of them. College and university courses, in English or education, which address such problems with a modicum of intellectual content are as scarce as hen's teeth. We cannot even find an unbiased conspectus of critical theory more complete than *The Pooh Perplex,* and treatments of problems of the second kind (pertaining to interaction of literature instruction with instruction in other fields) are also invisible.

Under a soundly practical dispensation in curriculum the address of such questions would be a high priority and require recruitment to education of philosophers and subject-matter specialists of a quality and critical sophistication which it has rarely, if ever, sought.

As the last sampling of the practical, consider its method. It falls under neither of the popular platitudes: it is neither deductive nor inductive. It is deliberative. It cannot be inductive because the target of the method is not a generalization or explanation but a decision about action in a concrete situation. It cannot be deductive because it deals with the concrete case, not abstractions from cases, and the concrete case cannot be settled by mere application of a principle. Almost every concrete case falls under two or more principles, and every concrete case will possess some cogent characteristics which are encompassed in no principle. The problem of selecting an appropriate man for an important post is a case in point. It is not a problem of selecting a representative of the appropriate personality type who exhibits the competences officially required for the job. The man we hire is more than a type and a bundle of competences. He is a multitude of probable behaviours which escape the net of personality theories and cognitive scales. He is endowed with prejudices, mannerisms, habits, tics, and relatives. And all of these manifold particulars will affect his work and the work of those who work for him. It is deliberation which operates in such cases to select the appropriate man.

Commitment to deliberation

Deliberation is complex and ardous. It treats both ends and means and must treat them as mutually determining one another. It must try to identify, with respect to both, what facts may be relevant. It must try to ascertain the relevant facts in the concrete case. It must try to identify the desiderata in the case. It must generate alternative solutions. It must make every effort to trace the branching pathways of consequences which may flow from each alternative and affect desiderata. It must then weigh alternatives and their costs and consequences against one another and choose, not the right alternative, for there *is* no such thing, but the best one.

I shall mention only one of the new kinds of activity which would ensue on commitment to deliberation. It will require the formation of a new public and new means of communication among its constituent members. Deliberation requires consideration of the widest possible variety of alternatives if it is to be most effective. Each alternative must be viewed in the widest variety of lights. Ramifying consequences must be traced to all parts of the curriculum. The desirability of each alternative must be felt out, 'rehearsed,' by a representative variety of all those who must live with the consequences of the chosen action. And a similar variety must deal with the identification of problems as well as with their solution.

This will require penetration of the curtains which now separate educational psychologist from philosopher, sociologist from test constructor, historian from administrator; it will require new channels connecting the series from teacher, supervisor, and school administrator at one end to research specialist at the other. Above all, it will require renunciation of the specious privileges and hegemonies by which we maintain the fiction that problems of science curriculum, for example, have no bearing on problems of English literature or the social studies. The aim here is *not* a dissolving of specialization and special responsibilities. Quite the contrary: if the variety of lights we need are to be obtained, the variety of specialized interests, competences, and habits of mind which characterize education must be cherished and nurtured. The aim, rather, is to bring the members of this variety to bear on curriculum problems by communication with one another.

Concretely, this means the establishment of new journals, and education of educators so that they can write for them and read them. The journals will be forums where possible problems of curriculum will be broached from many sources and their possible importance debated from many points of view. They will be the stage for display of anticipatory solutions to problems, from a similar variety of sources. They will constitute deliberative assemblies in which problems and alternative solutions will be argued by representatives of all for the consideration of all and for the shaping of intelligent consensus.

Needless to say, such journals are not alone sufficient. They stand as only one concrete model of the kind of forum which is required. Similar forums, operating *viva voce* and in the midst of curriculum operation and curriculum change, are required: of the teachers, supervisors, and administrators of a school; of the supervisors and administrators of a school system; of representatives of teachers, supervisors, and curriculum makers in subject areas and across subject areas; of the same representatives and specialists in curriculum, psychology, sociology, administration, and the subject-matter fields.[4]

The education of educators to participate in this deliberative process will be neither easy nor quickly achieved. The education of the present generation of specialist researchers to speak to the schools and to one another will doubtless be hardest of all, and on this hardest problem I have no suggestion to make. But we could begin within two years to initiate the preparation of teachers, supervisors, curriculum makers, and graduate students of education in the uses and arts of deliberation—and we should.

For graduate students, this should mean that their future inquiries in educational psychology, philosophy of education, educational sociology, and so on, will find more effective focus on enduring problems of education, as against the attractions of the current foci of the parent disciplines. It will begin to exhibit to graduate students what their duties are to the future schoolmen whom they will teach. For teachers, curriculum makers, and others close to the classroom, such training is of special importance. It will not only bring immediate experience of the classroom effectively to bear on problems of curriculum but enhance the quality of that experience, for almost every classroom episode is a stream of situations requiring discrimination of deliberative problems and decision thereon.

By means of such journals and such an education, the educational research establishment might at last find a means for channelling its discoveries into sustained improvement of the schools instead of into a procession of ephemeral bandwagons.

Notes

1. Copyright 1969 by Joseph J. Schwab. All rights reserved. A version of this paper was delivered to Section B of the American Educational Research Association, Los Angeles, February 1969. This paper has been prepared as part of a project supported by a grant from the Ford Foundation.
2. It should be clear by now that 'theory' as used in this paper does *not* refer only to grand schemes such as the general theory of relativity, kinetic-molecular theory, the Bohr atom, the French construction of a tripartite psyche. The attempt to give an account of human maturation by the discrimination of definite states (e.g., oral, anal, genital), an effort to

aggregate human competences into a small number of primary mental abilities—these too are theoretic. So also are efforts to discriminate a few large classes of persons and to attribute to them defining behaviours: e.g., the socially mobile, the culturally deprived, the creative.

3. *College Curriculum and Student Protest.* Chicago: University of Chicago Press, 1969.

4. It will be clear from these remarks that the conception of curricular method proposed here is immanent in the Tyler rationale. This rationale calls for a diversity of talents and insists on the practical and eclectic treatment of a variety of factors. Its effectiveness in practice is vitiated by two circumstances. Its focus on 'objectives', with their massive ambiguity and equivocation, provides far too little of the concrete matter required for deliberation and leads only to delusive consensus. Second, those who use it are not trained for the deliberative procedures it requires.

The Translation of Curriculum into Instruction*

Mauritz Johnson *Professor of Education, State University of New York at Albany*

On the centrality of curriculum and instruction in the total educational enterprise there is general agreement. Far less agreement exists as to what curriculum and instruction are and how they relate to each other. The purpose of this paper is to explore the relationship between curriculum and instruction, on the assumption that efforts to improve these two areas would be greatly facilitated by a clearer and more widely shared understanding of what they are and how they relate to each other.

In a previous paper[1] an effort was made to find a useful definition of curriculum, clarify the source of curriculum, and outline very generally its relation to instruction. It was assumed that if curriculum serves any purposes, they are to guide instruction and to furnish criteria for evaluation. Curriculum, therefore, must be a statement of intention, not a report of occurrences or results.

An examination of how curriculum guides instruction will require a brief review of the concept of curriculum and a fuller inquiry into the nature of instruction as a basis for explicating an intervening process,

* This article has been reproduced from the *Journal of Curriculum Studies* (1, 2, 1969) by permission of the author and Wm. Collins Sons and Company Ltd.

which will be called *instructional planning*. The term 'programming' might be preferable for this process, except that it, like so many other terms in education, has acquired a more specific, technical meaning.

Whatever else education may be with respect to individual development or societal perpetuation and progress, it is, in any consideration of curriculum and instruction, essentially the translation of cultural content into individual learnings. The curriculum consists in the items of cultural content to be translated, expressed in terms appropriate to learning. Learning is necessarily limited to existing cultural content; although an individual may, in the process of receiving instruction, invent something that did not exist or discover something that was not known previously, these results cannot be attributed to learning, hence not to instruction, and therefore cannot be curricular. Whatever simulation of inquiry or discovery may be incorporated into instruction, it is clearly one matter to say that one has *learned* something new and quite another to say one has *discovered* something new. As Skinner[2] observes, 'by definition we cannot teach original behaviour, since it would not be original if taught . . .'

The system for translating cultural content into individual learning can be visualized as in Figure 1. The discussion that follows will approach the instruction planning component first from the curriculum, or input side then from the instruction, or output, side.

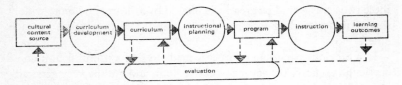

Fig. 1. Curriculum and instruction in the translation process

Cultural content as a source of curriculum

The language seems to lack a suitable term for the portion of a culture that is transmissible through instruction. When one has eliminated such cultural products as artifacts and institutions, the potentially teachable remainder consists of various kinds of meanings[3] or knowledge, if both of these terms can be used broadly enough to include attitudes and skills as well as cognitive understandings. Henderson[4] identified subject matter with knowledge, but limited it to cognitive knowledge in the form of analytic and contingent statements, prescriptions, and value statements. Roland[5] has pointed out, in a critique of Hartland-Swann's (1956) reduction of 'knowing that' to 'knowing how,' that a certain type of cognitive knowledge is reducible to 'knowing how' in the sense of ability to state the knowledge, but that human 'know dispositions,' in any event, are not limited to these two categories. If 'knowledge' is construed as the aggregation of all human 'know dispositions,' then, perhaps, knowledge can be said to subsume all teachable cultural content, everything man knows, believes, and can do.

Cultural knowledge is of two sorts, disciplined, and non-disciplined, the former derived from deliberate inquiry and formally structured, the latter derived from ordinary experience and structured informally, if at all. Goodlad and Richter[6] term these two curriculum sources 'funded knowledge' and 'conventional wisdom.' Both of these categories were encompassed by Aristotle's triad of theoretical, practical, and productive knowledge, roughly corresponding to cognitions, attitudes, and skills, respectively. Burke[7] used the Greek words *mathema, pathema,* and *poiema* with approximately the same meanings. It is necessary to recognize that attitudes, values, and other affective outcomes are important bases for the making of decisions and choices, the essence of Aristotle's 'practical' category. Indeed, the only time that attitudes and values (the latter being merely the objects of positive attitudes) come into play, other than to be verbalized, is in situations requiring choices.

Funded knowledge is organized into disciplines, not entirely discrete, but roughly classifiable as concerning fact, form, or norm at the singular, general, and comprehensive levels.[8] Internally, disciplines exhibit two components, which may be called content and process. These Schwab[9] refers to as the substantive and syntactic structures. Phenix[10] identifies the substantive with representative or key ideas, which may, he states, '. . . be understood fully only in relation to the process of inquiry.' This process, which corresponds to the syntactical element, differs from discipline to discipline, or at least among the six 'realms of meaning' which Phenix identified: the empiric, aesthetic, ethic, and synoetic, all undergirded by the symbolic and overarched by the synoptic disciplines.

While much remains to be done in defining the structure of disciplined knowledge, much less is known about the structure of non-disciplined

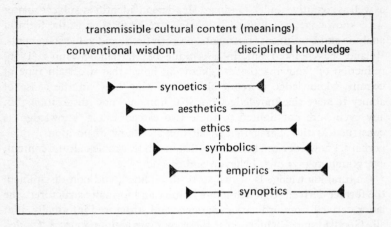

Fig. 2. The transmissible or knowledge component of cultural content, which is the source of curriculum, consists of six realms[11] **with varying proportions of disciplined and non-disciplined content**

knowledge. Figure 2, depicting cultural content, suggests that the realms are of both types, some being even more conventional than disciplined. In pre- and early-civilized times all knowledge was un-disciplined, and in primitive contemporary cultures, most may still be. In time, areas of knowledge which are not themselves the result of systematic inquiry are subjected to review in the light of verified knowledge and are expanded through the *application* of such knowledge. Virtually every craft, trade, profession, and other kind of human endeavour is today more an applied art, science, philosophy than merely a residual of ordinary experience, and many have a discernible, if not rigorous, substantive structure, if not a syntactic one. Though some theorists (Phenix,[12] Broudy, Smith and Burnett,[13]) hold that the curriculum of *general* education should be drawn exclusively, or at least preponderantly, from disciplined knowledge, it is clear that the cur-riculum for most *training*[14] and much *specialized* education is drawn from conventional wisdom or applied disciplinary knowledge.

Curriculum items

In an earlier paper[15] curriculum was stipulated to be 'a structured series of intended learning outcomes.' It is interesting that quite independently Goodlad and Richter[16] had arrived at a virtually identical definition, 'a set of intended learnings.' Gagne[17] holds to a similar view in defining curriculum as '. . . a sequence of content units . . .,' a content unit being '. . . a capability to be acquired . . .' His further stipulation that the content unit must be acquired 'under a single set of learning conditions' restricts the meaning of a curriculum *item,* but does not alter the basic agreement that curriculum deals with intended results, not the planned or actual experiences through which the results are achieved. The conventional definition of curriculum as 'planned learning experiences' is more appropriately associated with an *instructional plan.* Presumably many different instructional plans could be derived from a given curriculum.

It is useful to think of the curriculum development as occurring in two phases. The first entails a process of selection from the cultural reservoir, followed by an ordering or structuring of the selected elements, resulting in what might be called a *curriculum matrix* or master curriculum. The second phase involves a further selection from this matrix, without violating its structural imperatives, of a *curriculum* for a specific programme, institution, or group of institutions. Even after this second phase, the product still consists of *intended learning outcomes,* without reference to the instructional means of attaining them.[18]

The curriculum matrix consists of all the cultural content selected from the disciplines and practical enterprises, with indications of priorities, structural relationships, and type of outcome. A digital system for coding priority and ordering needs to be developed. A catalogue of curriculum items should provide instructional planners with all relevant information about each item in a concise, standardized form.

The best available scheme for classifying curriculum items is the widely known taxonomy encompassing three domains: cognitive, psychomotor, and affective. Alles and his colleagues[19] have suggested that the dichotomy between knowledge and intellectual skills within the cognitive domain[20] could be removed by re-defining cognitive domain category 1.00 as the cognitive operations of recognition and recall, ' . . . so as to make it more consistent with the concept of level.' The notion of level or intensity, so controlling in the affective domain analysis[21] is subordinated in the cognitive taxonomy to a typological or categorical scheme. The various classes essentially differ in kind, although their arrangement is allegedl loosely hierarchical on the basis of 'complexity.' However valid this notion of complexity may be with respect to the three major classes in the knowledge portion of the taxonomy, it is dubious with respect to the five intellectual skills. (Is analysis more complex than application, less complex than synthesis?) Moreover, there must certainly be a discontinuity between the two parts. Furthermore, the complexity criterion is clearly quite different from the criterion of internalization used in the affective domain.

The intellectual skills portions of the cognitive domain might more appropriately be construed as one end of the same continuum that is occupied by the psychomotor skills. It is not uncommon to view psychomotor skills as entailing physical and mental components (or motor and cognitive) varying from virtually entirely one, through all possible combinations of the two, to almost exlusively the other.[22] This continuum has been designated by Alles[23] as the *extensional* dimension as apposed to that of *intensity*. Indicating the motor component with a capital or lower-case S (skill) and the cognitive similarly with K (knowledge), he arrives at an asymmetric series: S, Sk, SK, sK. The logical next member of the series is K, which, as suggested above, might be considered to be the intellectual skills conventionally included in the cognitive domain.

As a basis for ordering the intensity dimension of the psychomotor domain, Alles[24] has proposed the principle of 'adaptive routinization.' *Routinization* entails ability to execute particular behavioural sequences ' . . . without continuous, deliberate, conscious attention and yet achieve functional adequacy, accuracy and speed,' and *adaptability* is the ability to do so in a variety of contexts. Using comparable literal symbols, with R representing Routinization and A, Adaptability, an intensity continuum might be visualized as: ra, Ra/rA, RA. Alles precedes even the pre-routine non-adaptive level with an 'initiatory level,' which one may recognize as corresponding to the first three levels (perception, set, guided response) in a taxonomy developed by Simpson[25]. Simpson's remaining two levels (mechanism and complex overt response) appear to reflect the routinization process without regard to versatility.

Most problematical of the three domains with respect to curriculum is the affective. It is by no means universally accepted that affective outcomes can be deliberately attained through instruction. Quite apart from the ethical consideration as to whether one person has the right to impose value systems on another, there is a popular notion that attitudes are 'caught rather than taught.' Carroll[26] excludes affective outcomes from his model for classroom learning, pointing out that whereas, in Skinnerian terms, '. . . learning tasks typically involve "operants," the attitudinal goals of education typically involve "respondents".' If affective outcomes are to be considered attainable through instruction, it is likely that they cannot be sought independently of cognitive or psychomotor learnings.

Indeed, it is not clear what distinction can be maintained between the affective domain and the 'Evaluation' category of the cognitive domain. Valuative behaviour appears to involve cognitive and affective components in varying combinations. Since Handbook II treats only of the intensity dimension of the affective domain, its extensional features are not clear. Perhaps they are best explicated in Broudy, Smith and Burnett's[27] discussion of evaluative maps and value exemplars, in which distinctions are made among attitudes, valuative concepts, and various kinds of norms.

Selection and structuring of curriculum items

With the well publicized acceleration in the expansion of the disciplined cultural content, the necessity for rational and continuous selection of curriculum items in increasingly evident. While the growth of scientific knowledge is most spectacular, much of it supersedes previous knowledge, whereas in humanities, such as history and the arts, the addition of new content, while possibly less precipitant, does not to as great an extent have the effect of supplanting or revising that which already exists. The problems of curriculum selection differ somewhat, therefore, from one realm to another.

Much work needs to be done to clarify the appropriate selection criteria and to devise efficient procedures for applying them. Whatever relevance the so-called needs and interests of learners may have to instructional techniques and timing, they do not, despite the prevailing professional mythology, seem to constitute curricular selection criteria. Similarly, although the traditional values and contemporary problems of a society are reflected in its culture, they provide little guidance for the selection of curriculum items. The analysis of adult activities[28] or the inventorying of 'persistent life situations'[29] seem appropriate to the development of a non-vocational training curriculum, but hardly compatible with educational curriculum development.

The rationale for curriculum selection is much clearer for training and specialized education than it is for general education. In the former the tasks to be performed and the conditions under which they are likely to be performed are known or at least available for task analysis. On the basis of such analysis, it is possible to select appropriate understandings, skills, and attitudes as curriculum content by applying the criterion of *utility* in performing the tasks. In general education, on the other hand, the circumstances in which learnings will be used and which ones will prove most useful cannot be predicted. Broudy, Smith and Burnett[30] have pointed out that whereas the outcomes of specialized education (or training) are used applicatively, those of general education serve primarily an interpretive function. For this purpose, structural (disciplined) cognitive and evaluative maps are necessary. This suggests that, in lieu of a task analysis, what is required is a disciplinary analysis using internal selection criteria of *significance* and *power* for further understanding of the discipline rather than the external criterion of specific utility. Bruner[31] makes essentially this point in his discussion of economy and power; Phenix's notion of 'representativeness' carries a similar import.

Obviously, some judgment as to the probable relevance of a discipline or aspect of a discipline to the contemporary world of affairs is appropriate, and effective instruction will doubtless include efforts to explicate, by way of illustration, specific relevances that are apparent. Nevertheless, if 'K' is highly relevant, and 'A' through 'J' are essential to the learning of 'K', then, though they may be notably irrelevant by external standards, the includion of 'A' through 'J' in the curriculum is entirely justified. Similarly, if 'L' is in itself of no practical value whatever, but extremely powerful in facilitating the learning of 'M' through 'Z', the selection of 'L' is warranted.

Only a specialist in a discipline can assess the internal significance of its substantive content. One is not free to extract at will isolated elements whose practical utility is most obvious, without regard to disciplinary structure. The integrity of clusters of concepts and skills must be respected and preserved.

The structural relationships within and among such clusteres serve as an important basis for the ordering of curriculum items. This is not to suggest exclusive reliance on logical structure as the ordering criterion. Quite apart from finished logical priorities, the substantive dimension of curriculum has, as Smith[32] has noted, '. . . elements related to one another asymmetrically,' that is, some learnings are prerequisite to the learning of others. It is quite possible, also, that careful experimentation will provide empirical evidence of a preferred ordering of given items, even where no rational reason for such order is apparent.

As a guide for instructional planning, the curriculum should on the one hand impose minimal restrictions in order to allow maximum flexibility in instructional sequencing. It is probable that for most curricular items, order is a matter of indifference. On the other hand, where there is some compelling basis for specifying order, the curriculum should provide this guidance for the instructional planners.

Much has been made in the past about the distinction between logical and psychological order. Even scientists have criticized the BSCS Blue version, which emphasizes molecular biology, for not observing the psychological requirement of proceeding from the familiar to the unfamiliar. One zoologist-psychologist, in a letter to the editor of *Science* (Vol. 155, Mar. 17, 1967, p. 1363) objected that while 'it may be the logical sequence to the graduate biologist . . .,' it '. . . comes very near to presenting the student with concepts and objects totally foreign to his experience and understanding.' It may be noted that Phenix[33] has argued that material drawn from the extraordinary rather than the familiar has a greater appeal to the imagination, and hence, enhances motivation. Obviously, however, a degree of novelty that introduces a discontinuity is dysfunctional. From Herbart's 'apperceptive mass' to Dewey's 'continuity of experience,'[34] the psychological characteristics of the learner have been dominant determinants of sequence. More recently, Miel has rejected logical ordering of curriculum.[35] Commenting that '. . . sequence in learning is useful only as it preserves continuity in education,' she recognizes as three possible threads of continuity in a curriculum, (1) abstract ideas or strategic concepts, (2) thought processes, and (3) feelings and human relations skills, but leaves the details of sequence to teachers or the learners themselves.

If, however, one holds to Piaget's notion of equilibration through assimilation or accommodation,[36] or to Ausubel's subsumption theory,[37] both psychological rather than logical in orientation, one cannot be as casual about leaving sequence decisions largely to the judgment of teachers or the impulses of learners. If the curriculum-instruction enterprise is viewed as essentially an effort to achieve isomorphism between an hypothesized individual cognitive structure or map and some valid external disciplinary structure, ordering decisions based on the latter must rest in part on reasonably accurate assumptions about the individual structure at any given time. The order of items 'B' and 'C' may, for example, be immaterial so long as one can assume the prior learning of 'A', but if not, then it may be essential that 'B' precede 'C'.

To some extent indications of priority in the selection of items have significance for ordering. Mager and Beach[38] include among six principles of sequencing vocational instructional units the notion of teaching first the skills that will permit low level functioning or, in effect, those most widely used. An analogous principle in educational curricula might be, insofar as possible, to teach the most powerful learnings before less powerful ones.

Whenever multiple criteria exist, compromises are necessary in their application, unless they are perfectly scalable. Similarly, compromises are necessary in procedures. Ideally, the procedure for selecting and ordering of curriculum items should entail a complete analysis of the various disciplines so that all of the potential curriculum items might be fed into a computer which, programmed with well-established ordering rules, would generate the optimum organization. A compromise is illustrated by the recent effort of the Committee on Undergraduate Instruction in the Biological Sciences to identify a content and structure for a basic college biology course by means of a detailed analysis of recently revised courses at four different institutions[39]. By recording all outcomes that were accorded as much as five minutes (0.1 instructional unit)[40] of attention and noting the sequential position of each, a composite curriculum for the course was developed. In general, selection and structuring criteria may be applied to items already in existing curriculums or implicit in existing instructional programmes and plans, with periodic review against the cultural source by experts familiar with the particular discipline or enterprise.

The instructional model

A definition or model of instruction must be comprehensive enough to encompass all possible instructional situations. It must serve for both training and instruction, for all domains of learning outcomes, for both academic and non-academic content, for divergent as well as convergent learning, for all ages, abilities, and backgrounds of 'instructees,' for large and small groups as well as single individuals, for situations with and without teachers, for teachers of varying competence and personality, for programmes, computers, simulation games, and responsive environments, and for all kinds of communities and every degree of availability of materials and equipment. It should not, however, include every instance in which learning occurs or studying takes place. There must be an *intent* on the part of some agent or agency to bring about learning, directly or indirectly. Moreover, it must be *learning*, and not mere behavioural change, that is sought. That is, as Carroll[41] indicates in his definition of 'learning task,' the individual must *become able* to do or understand something he was previously unable to do or understand, not simply *be induced* to do something he was already capable of doing. Learning does not always result in a change of behaviour, nor does a change of behaviour always result from learning.

The recent tendency to free instructional theory from learning theory, as well as from pre-conceived notions about what 'good' teaching is, has yielded a quantity of descriptive data on what teachers do in one kind of instructional situation, namely, the conventional classroom. This reversion to a previously bypassed 'natural history' stage in educational research has provided some insight into the logical operations occurring in instruction[42], to the amount and directness of teacher talk (Amidon and Flanders, 1963[43]; Amidon and Hough, 1967),[44] and to the pedagogical moves made by teachers and the meaning dimensions of classroom discourse[45]. In assessing which of the observed features define instruction, one must consider whether the physical presence of a teacher is assumed, whether some of the acts observed may be completely irrelevant or even counter-effectual, and whether certain provisions which might prove highly conducive to learning may have been missing in every situation studied.

It is difficult, apparently, to talk about instruction without using the two concepts of *influence* and *interaction*. Gage[46] has defined *teaching* as the 'process of influencing an organism to learn,' while Maccia[47] discussed instruction as 'influence toward rule-governed behaviour.' Strasser[48] defines instructional tactics as 'goal-linked influenced/ influencing behaviour of the teacher . . .' Whether teaching is a sub-set of instruction or vice versa depends on whether the frame of reference is the entire professional role of teachers or their role in a particular interaction. In the latter, there are complementary roles, and the influence, whatever may be meant by that term, is not uni-directional, as evidenced in Bellack's reflexive teaching cycles and by the effect of 'feedback' in branching programmes and the continual editing and revising done by CAI authors.[49] Nevertheless, the net effect of influence is predominantly in one direction, and the intention to influence is almost entirely so.[50]

The current popularity of 'interaction analysis' continues to focus attention on the interpersonal, social interaction, with its emotional overtones, that is inevitable in any instructional situation in which there is a group of 'instructees' or even a single one with an instructor. This pre-occupation with a situational factor that can be salutary, irrelevant, or detrimental serves to obscure the fact that the fundamental interaction in instruction is not among people, but between an individual and selected elements of his environment. In this transaction, to use a good Deweyan term, the instructor or programme author is not a participant, but a mediator, and often, a meddler. He is a stage manager and a director, but not an actor.

Most instructional models show a third element mediating between the teacher and the learner. Searles, viewing instruction as '. . . a process for the implanting of a structure in a mind,'[51] depicts a 'search image' (or idea) as mediating between the minds of the instructor and the learner. Actually, it would seem that the search image is the curriculum and that it is embodied in the instructional situation as an element of the instructor's 'mind' in the form of an intention. To the extent that this intention is reciprocated on the part of the instructee, Peirce's condition of 'thirdness,' which Gowin[52] has argued is necessary in instruction, is met.

Actions within the instructional situation may be classified as curricular, situational, and extraneous. That is to say, for certain features of the situation alternatives are possible but only within limits consistent with the intended outcomes; other features are responsive to situational variables without regard to curriculum; and finally, some observable features serve no curricular-instructional purpose whatever. The first category may be approximately equivalent to an *instructional curricular event*, as defined by Duncan and Frymier.[53]

Since the requirement curriculum makes of instruction is that learning experiences appropriates to intended outcomes occur, and since any learning experience must have an active and a substantive component, only two of the six functions which Jackson found teachers performing are *essential* to instruction, namely, *display* and *control*.[54] (See Figure 3.)

Language, broadly conceived, is the medium through which the transaction between the instructee and meanings is engineered. In instruction the message is the medium. It serves to (1) convey meaning with which the instructee can interact and (2) regulate the interaction. All instructional actions and language are either subsumable under one of these two functions or else they derive from special circumstances in the instructional situation rather than from the curriculum. In the classification system used by Bellack and his associates, the two functions

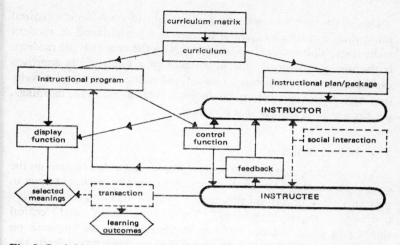

Fig. 3. Social interaction and intellectual transaction in the curriculum-instruction system

are represented by the substantive and the substantive-logical categories.[55] The enactive, iconic, and symbolic modes are applicable to both the display and control function as well as to the learner's responses.[56]

The display function

The curriculum restricts but does not prescribe the content and form of the message to be displayed in instruction. A cognitive knowledge outcome requires that data be displayed in some form, though the specific data selected for consideration are often optional. A skill-type outcome, whether cognitive or psychomotor, requires some sort of personal or depicted demonstration. In other words, the substance of the display may be either 'content' or 'process,' quite apart from the fact that the control function is concerned exclusively with process.

In computer-assisted instruction, the display function is carried out through such media as typewriter output, a cathode ray tube or tablet, supplementary reading material, film loops, audio or videotape, and materials kits. Most of these, as well as others, are available for conventional instruction, though the chief means of display continues to be 'teacher talk' or the lecture. As Brandwein has noted, '. . . the lecture, which, as generally practiced in the schools, plays a role in informing, is not to be considered a method of instruction; it is clearly one of the *materials* of instruction. . . .'[57]

One of the recent campaigns to improve instruction has emphasized the display function by seeking to introduce media based on modern technology. This emphasis is consistent with the view that the medium is the message. Recently the importance of a multi-media approach has been stressed. Whatever motivational value variety and novelty may have, from a curriculum standpoint, it is the message, the meanings, not the modes of display that is critical.

The control function

A second campaign for instructional improvement has centred on the control function and the kinds of actions instructees are called upon to perform. This concern for process has focused attention on 'discovery teaching,'[58] 'inquiry teaching,'[59] 'logical operations,' and 'critical thinking.'[60] There are two different justifications for the emphasis on these processes: (1) the processes themselves are important to learn, i.e., process is viewed as content[61] and (2) the substantive content of a discipline is best learned by the same methods of inquiry by which it was originally acquired.

The second of these propositions is highly debatable, except insofar as experience with the process is essential to an *understanding* of the methods of inquiry which gave rise to the content. Re-discovery, as a general method of instruction, was questioned more than a decade ago by Bellack[62] and more recently by Ausubel.[63]

The other proposition, that intellectual skills and methods of inquiry are important outcomes in their own right, is difficult to dispute. This is a curricular decision, not an instructional one, as in the previous case. It raises two questions. One concerns the degree of proficiency to be attained in the various processes. Except for maintenance purposes, there is no further justification for instructional attention to a process once the intended level of proficiency has been attained. The second question relates to the content toward which the process is to be directed. It is quite possible, when process is the intended outcome, that the substantive content is immaterial and is either left optional or arbitrarily designated, as in some elementary science programmes. It is also possible that significant substantive outcomes can be attained simultaneously with the process outcomes. Research is needed on the conditions giving rise to an 'information overload' when both types of outcome are sought concurrently. In any event, unless curriculum explicitly stipulates a process as an intended outcome, the only limitation on the instructional control function is that implicitly imposed by the *type* of substantive outcome to be attained.

Instructional planning

In some efforts to study instruction experimentally, e.g. Bellack,[64] Gage,[65] curriculum has been held constant without restricting instrumental content. In Gage's studies of 'explaining' as a micro-criterion, the activity portion was also, of course, controlled. However, in these, as in the other analyses of instructional discourse, the focus of attention has been the actual 'tactics' used, rather than the 'strategy' stipulated in the instructional plan. Thus, much of what is observed may not have been intended. Observational schemes for analysing instructional discourse and actions may reveal how the instructional acts were performed without reference to *what* acts were performed.

Many instructional acts are spontaneous; certainly most instructional language is extemporaneous. A change in curriculum may change the subject of the discourse, but cannot 'improve' its quality or change its pattern. A change in the instructional plan might change the quantity and perhaps the pattern, but cannot control the effectiveness of the discourse itself. Similarly, a change in curriculum or instructional plan might introduce different activities into the instructional situation, but not affect the skill with which they are carried out. Curriculum can exert an influence on instruction directly only as it is, consciously or unconsciously, an element in the conative system of the instructor (or, to some extent, the instructees), thereby controlling in a general way the extemporaneous responses to exigencies.

Primarily, however, curriculum influences instruction through the mediation of an instructional plan. Some of the observational research might well be directed to the question of what actions and language are used to implement a plan, and further analyses might be made of the process by which a plan is devised, given a curricular directive. The distinction between ineptness and inappropriateness is not trivial. It is undoubtedly easier to execute a plan than to devise one intelligently.

Some instructors are competent to read a properly formulated curriculum and from it to devise an appropriate instructional plan. If the curriculum reveals the type of outcome, including level of performance or sophistication, and provides structuring or ordering information, the instructional planner is faced with the task of selecting 'instrumental content' to be displayed, choosing or creating the media for displaying it, and deciding the general strategy by which the instructee's responses to it are to be controlled. These decisions require extensive knowledge of the subject under consideration, the materials that are available, the range of possible operations, and the probability of attaining a particular type of outcome associated with each of them.

Because of the substantive and pedagogical expertness required, such planning is increasingly being done *for* rather than *by* instructors themselves. These plans may take the form of instructional *packages,* in which display media are provided and control strategy is prescribed. Or they may be instructional *programmes* in which even the detailed control tacits are specified, and no implementation by an instructor is required. The instructor or institution deciding to employ a particular package or programme must accept the curriculum on which it was based.

In the total scheme, whether the curriculum and the instructional plan are developed by the institution or by an outside agency, the starting point is the curriculum matrix, which should serve all possible users. At this level, at least, a 'national curriculum' is highly desirable.

Neither the matrix nor a particular curriculum derived from it can, however, guide all aspects of instruction. Curriculum *assumes* individualization of instruction; any compromise through group instruction must be accounted for in the instructional plan and its implementation. Similarly, curriculum is silent on motivation and 'discipline' in the sense of behavioural control. These matters, though not essential aspects of instruction, must in most instances be dealt with to some extent. Likewise, curriculum does not specify the means of evaluation, though it furnishes the criteria for the evaluation of instructional outcomes.

Actually, there are seven points of evaluation in the full curriculum-instruction system. If the intended outcomes specified by the curriculum are satisfactorily achieved as actual instructional outcomes, it can be assumed that the entire system is functioning adequately. If the output is not satisfactory, however, one or more of six defects may be responsible. As suggested in Figure 4, the first step is to re-check the evaluation procedure itself—was it really appropriate for determining how well the intended outcomes were achieved? If not, a re-evaluation is called for. If, however, the evaluation procedure is vindicated, one might next ask whether the instructional plan was or was not carried out faithfully and skillfully. Closer monitoring of students' use of programmed instruction materials may be required. Or in the case of a live teacher, further experience with a new approach, or supervisory assistance, or in-service training may be necessary before the intended outcomes can be achieved satisfactorily.

If the execution of the plan seems not to be faulty, the appropriateness of the plan itself must be called into question, first in terms of the situation in which it was used and then in terms of the intended outcomes and their ordering, as stipulated by the curriculum. The content displayed, the mode and sequence of displaying it, the learning activities and 'contingencies of reinforcement' called for in the instructional plan, all require this dual evaluation.

When desired results are not obtained, even though presumably appropriate instructional plans have apparently been properly executed, doubt is cast on the curriculum itself. At the very least, the possible omission of essential prerequisites needs to be explored. But before further analysis it is not out of order to ask how important the curriculum items in question really were in the first place.

It is of course an oversimplification to suggest that unsatisfactory results are attributable to a major flaw in one component of the system. More likely they are due to minor deficiencies in a number of components, and their improvement depends on improved evaluation, improved instructional materials and techniques, improved instructional plans, and improved curricular ordering and selection. But it is well to distinguish among these components and not blame a curriculum for poor teaching performance or expect better teaching to compensate for an ill-conceived instructional plan.

Summary

In this paper an effort was made to sharpen the distinction between curriculum and instruction, and to clarify the relationship between them. When curriculum is viewed as a structured series of intended learning outcomes, instruction becomes the means by which intentions are translated into realities. The formulation of instructional plans or development of instructional 'programmes' or 'packages' is to be distinguished from the process of executing such plans. Each of these two aspects of instruction concerns two basic functions—display and control.

Similarly, the antecedent curriculum development system has two aspects, the design of a particular curriculum for a specific situation and the master curriculum or curriculum 'matrix' from which the specific one is derived. Again, both of these aspects involve two functions—the selection and structuring of the intended learning outcomes which are to be included.

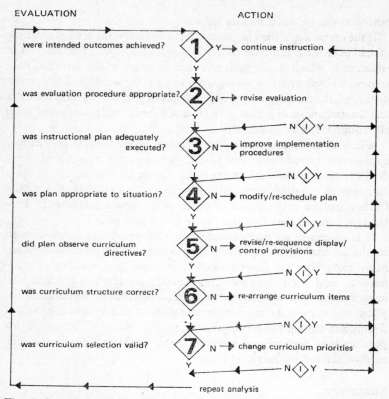

EVALUATION   ACTION

Fig. 4. Seven evaluation points in curriculum-instruction system (Y-yes; N-No)

Notes

1. Mauritz Johnson (1967), 'Definition and Models in Curriculum Theory.' *Educational Theory*, 17 (April), pp. 127–140.
2. B. F. Skinner (1968), *The Technology of Teaching*. Appleton-Century-Crofts.
3. Philip Phenix (1964), *Realms of Meaning*. McGraw-Hill.
4. Kenneth Henderson (1961), 'Uses of "Subject Matter".' In: B. O. Smith and R. H. Ennis (1961), *Language and Concepts in Education*. Rand McNally.
5. Jane Roland (1961), 'On the Reduction of "Knowing That" to "Knowing How".' In: B. O. Smith and Robert H. Ennis, (eds.), *op. cit.*, pp. 59–71.
6. John Goodlad and Maurice Richter (1966), *The Development of a Conceptual System for Dealing with Problems of Curriculum and Instruction*. University of California, Los Angeles.
7. Kenneth Burke (1945), *A Grammar of Motives*. Englewood Cliffs, N.J.: Prentice-Hall.
8. Philip Phenix (1964), *Realms of Meaning*. McGraw-Hill.

9. JOSEPH SCHWAB, 'Structure of the Disciplines: Meanings and Significances.' In: G. W. FORD and L. PUGNO (eds.), *The Structure of Knowledge and the Curriculum*. Rand McNally, 1964, pp. 6–19.

10. PHILIP PHENIX (1964), *Realms of Meaning*. McGraw-Hill.

11. PHENIX, *op. cit.*

12. PHENIX, *op. cit.*

13. HARRY BROUDY, B. O. SMITH and JOE BURNETT (1964), *Democracy and Excellence in American Secondary Education*. Chicago: Rand McNally.

14. Though many educationists refuse to distinguish between training and education the writer finds the distinction to be a useful one. Tyler, (see note 18) does also, defining training as '. . . that kind of learning where the total pattern is given . . .,' the efforts being directed at '. . . narrowing span of behaviour . . .,' whereas in education '. . . the emphasis is upon trying to open doors . . .'.

15. MAURITZ JOHNSON (1967), 'Definitions and Models in Curriculum Theory,' *Educational Theory*, 17 (April), pp. 127–140.

16. JOHN GOODLAD and MAURICE RICHTER (1966), *The Development of a Conceptual System for Dealing with Problems of Curriculum and Instruction*. University of California, Los Angeles.

17. ROBERT M. GAGNE (1966), 'Curriculum Research and the Promotion of Learning,' (paper presented to the American Educational Research Association, mimeo, 25p.).

18. RALPH TYLER (1963), 'Concepts, Skills and Values and Curriculum Development,' presented at Extension Curriculum Development Conference, Washington, DC, mimeo, 17p.

19. JINAPALA ALLES *et al.* (1967), 'An Attempt at Restructuring Some Conceptual Frameworks Used in Curriculum Development and Evaluation,' *Theoretical Constructs in Curriculum Development and Evaluation* (Ceylon Ministry of Education), pp. 1–17.

20. BENJAMIN BLOOM (ed.) (1956), *Taxonomy of Educational Objectives, Handbook I: The Cognitive Domain*. Longmans, Green.

21. DAVID KRATHWOHL *et al.* (1964), *Taxonomy of Educational Objectives Handbook II: The Affective Domain*. McKay.

22. HERBERT KLAUSMEIER (1961), *Learning and Human Abilities*. Harper and Row.

23. JINAPALA ALLES (1967), 'An Outline Analysis of Psycho-motor Aspects of Behaviour,' *Theoretical Constructs in Curriculum Development and Evaluation*. Ceylon Ministry of Education, pp. 18–23.

24. JINAPALA ALLES (1967), 'An Outline Analysis of Psycho-motor Aspects of Behaviour,' *Theoretical Constructs in Curriculum Development and Evaluation*. Ceylon Ministry of Education, pp. 18–23.

25. ELIZABETH SIMPSON (1965), *The Classification of Educational Objectives*. Urbana: University of Illinois.

26. JOHN CARROLL (1963), 'A Model of School Learning,' *Teachers College Record*, 64 (May), pp. 723–733.

27. HARRY BROUDY, B. O. SMITH and JOE BURNETT (1964), *Democracy and Excellence in American Secondary Education*. Chicago: Rand McNally.

28. FRANKLIN BOBBITT (1924), *How to Make a Curriculum*. Boston: Houghton Mifflin.

29. FLORENCE STRATEMAYER *et al.* (1947), *Developing a Curriculum for Modern Living*. New York: Teachers College, Columbia University.

30. HARRY BROUDY, B. O. SMITH and JOE BURNETT (1964), *Democracy and Excellence in American Secondary Education*. Chicago: Rand McNally.

31. JEROME BRUNER (1962), *The Process of Education*. Cambridge, Mass.: Harvard University Press.
32. B. O. SMITH and ROBERT ENNIS (1961), *Language and Concepts in Education*. Chicago: Rand McNally.
33. PHILIP PHENIX (1964), *Realms of Meaning*. McGraw-Hill.
34. JOHN DEWEY (1938), *Experience and Education*. Macmillan.
35. ALICE MIEL (1967), 'Sequence in Learning,' *Education Digest*, 32 (April), pp. 35–38.
36. JEAN PIAGET, 'Development and Learning.' In: R. E. RIPPLE and V. N. ROCKCASTLE (eds.) (1964), *Piaget Rediscovered*. Cornell University, pp. 7–19.
37. DAVID AUSUBEL (1963), *The Psychology of Meaningful Verbal Learning*. Grune and Stratton.
38. ROBERT F. MAGER and KENNETH M. BEACH, JR. (1967), *Developing Vocational Instruction*. Palo Alto: Fearon Publishers.
39. COMMISSION ON UNDERGRADUATE EDUCATION IN THE BIOLOGICAL SCIENCES (1967), *Content of Core Curricula in Biology*. Report of the Panel on Undergraduate Major Curricula (Publication No. 18, The Commission).
40. Those who consider a unit such as the conventional 50-minute lecture period hopelessly reactionary may prefer to view the unit as roughly equivalent to a micro-century.
41. JOHN CARROLL (1963), 'A Model of School Learning,' *Teachers College Record*, 64 (May), pp. 723–733.
42. B. O. SMITH and ROBERT ENNIS (1961), *Language and Concepts in Education*. Chicago: Rand McNally.
43. EDMUND AMIDON and NED FLANDERS (1963), *The Role of the Teacher in the Classroom*. Minneapolis: Paul S. Amidon and Association.
44. EDMUND J. AMIDON and JOHN B. HOUGH (eds.) (1967), *Interaction Analysis: Theory, Research and Application*. Boston: Addison-Wesley.
45. ARNO BELLACK *et al.* (1966), *The Language of the Classroom*. New York: Teachers College Press, Columbia University.
46. N. L. GAGE (1967), 'An Analytical Approach to Research on constructional Methods,' Research Memorandum 2, Stanford Centre for Research and Development in Teaching, mimeo, 16p.
47. ELIZABETH MACCIA (1964), *Instruction as Influence Toward Rule-governed Behaviour*. Occasional Paper, 64–155, Educational Theory Centre, Ohio State University, mimeo.
48. BEN STRASSER (1967), 'Conceptual Model of Instruction,' *Journal of Teacher Education*, (Spring), pp. 63–74.
49. ARNO BELLACK *et al.* (1966), *The Language of the Classroom*. New York: Teachers College Press, Columbia University.
50. B. O. SMITH (1963), 'A Conceptual Analysis of Instructional Behaviour,' *Journal of Teacher Education*, 14 (September), pp. 294–298.
51. JOHN E. SEARLES (1967), *A System for Instruction*. International Textbook Co.
52. D. B. GOWIN (1961), 'Teaching, Learning and Thirdness,' *Studies in Philosophy and Education*, 1 (August), pp. 87–113.
53. JAMES DUNCAN and JACK FRYMEIER (1967), 'Explorations in the Systematic Study of Curriculum,' *Theory into Practice*, 6 (October), pp. 180–199.
54. PHILIP JACKSON (1963), 'The Conceptualization of Teaching,' paper presented to American Psychological Association.
55. ARNO BELLACK *et al.* (1966), *The Language of the Classroom*. New York: Teachers College Press, Columbia University.

56. JEROME BRUNER (1966), *Toward a Theory of Instruction*. Belknap, Harvard University Press.
57. PAUL BRANDWEIN (1966), *Notes Toward a General Theory of Teaching*. Harcourt, Brace and World.
58. JEROME BRUNE (1966), *The Process of Education*. Cambridge, Mass.: Harvard University Press.
59. RICHARD J. SUCHMAN (1962), *The Elementary School Training Program in Scientific Inquiry*. Urbana: University of Illinois.
60. B. O. SMITH, 'A Concept of Teaching,' In: B. O. SMITH and ROBERT H. ENNIS (1961), *Language and Concepts in Education*. Chicago: Rand McNally, pp. 86–101.
61. J. CECIL PARKER and LOUIS RUBIN (1966), *Process as Content: Curriculum Design and the Application of Knowledge*. Chicago: Rand McNally.
62. ARNO BELLACK, 'Selection and Organization of Content.' Ch. 4 in *What Shall the High Schools Teach?* (ASCD Yearbook, 1956, pp. 97–126).
63. DAVID AUSUBEL, *op. cit.;* and 'Learning by Discovery,' *Educational Leadership*, 20 (November, 1962), pp. 113–17.
64. ARNO BELLACK *et al.* (1966), *The Language of the Classroom*. New York: Teachers College Press, Columbia University.
65. N. L. GAGE (1967), 'An Analytical Approach to Research on Instructional Methods,' *Research Memorandum* 2, Stanford Center for Research and Development in Teaching, mimeo, 16p.

Summary Appraisal

Both articles deal with the need for theoretical formulations in the field of curriculum. Schwab makes a compelling case for beginning with the practical (transactions) as a way to 'build back' to theory. This is an article which *must* be read and re-read by students of curriculum. Johnson's article is straightforward in its attempt to clarify relationships between intentions and transactions. In this sense, it serves as an excellent bridge between Part One and Part Two of this book. For the serious student of curriculum, these articles and the suggested readings which follow can provide a springboard for a career of inquiry. As comprehensive and thoughtful as the articles and readings are, they leave many questions unanswered which merit investigation in the years to come. Some of these are:

What sources should be used to determine educational goals and objectives? How are values made explicit in the selection of these objectives? What are the relationships between goals and objectives? What is the usefulness of a statement of educational objectives in making other curriculum decisions?

What components must be considered in organizing the curriculum for effective instruction? Who selects curriculum content and/or organizing elements (concepts, generalizations, topics)? What are the criteria for their selection? What are the criteria for the selection of organizing centres (learning opportunities)? What are the relationships between goals and objectives on the one hand and organizing elements and organizing centres on the other?

What forms of evaluation are appropriate to curriculum decision makers? What is the relationship between evaluation and goals and objectives? How is evaluation data to be used?

Suggested Readings

BEAUCHAMP, GEORGE A. (1975). *Curriculum Theory*. 3rd Edition. Wilmette, Illinois: The Kagg Press.
The author sets forth the need for us to become more 'scientific' in our approach to the problems of curriculum. He explores theory in related areas and develops the concept of curriculum theory. Finally, he develops one curriculum-theory model which contains: (1) a group of assumptions and postulates, (2) a list of technical definitions, (3) provision for curriculum planning, and (4) a description of a curriculum design. The author recognizes the limitation of his model, but in its construction he demonstrates one avenue which may lead to more adequate theory building and research in the field.

GOODLAD, JOHN I. with MAURICE N. RICHTER, JR. (1966). *The Development of a Conceptual System for Dealing with Problems of Curriculum and Instruction*. Cooperative Research Program. Washington DC: US Office of Education, Project No. 454.
This monograph sets forth a conceptual system valuable to those who are interested in empirical work. It builds on the work of the classicists (Bobbitt, Herrick, Tyler) and also sets forth concepts valuable to those who wish to observe what curriculum workers do. The conceptual system suggests answers to the problem of who makes what decisions as well as to the problem of the interplay between funded knowledge and conventional wisdom. This is a very important reading for those interested in curriculum as intentions and curriculum as transactions.

SCHAEFER, ROBERT J. (1971). 'Retrospect and Prospect' and TYLER, RALPH W., 'Curriculum Development in the Twenties and Thirties.' Both appear in *The Curriculum: Retrospect and Prospect*, The Seventieth Yearbook of the National Society for the Study of Education, Part I, University of Chicago Press, Illinois. These two chapters, together, give their readers a brief but good overview of the works of the early curriculum theorists in the United States, including the work of the Committee on Curriculum-Making of the National Society for the Study of Education which resulted in the now famous Twenty-Sixth Year Book. Other chapters in *The Curriculum: Retrospect and Prospect*, notably those of McClure and Macdonald are worthwhile reading for those interested in theory and empirical work.

General Bibliography for Part One

Books

ASHTON, P. M. E. *et al.* (1975). *Aims in Primary Education.* London: Macmillan Educational.

EISNER, ELLIOT W. (ed.) (1971). *Confronting Curriculum Reform.* Boston: Little, Brown.

GOODLAD, JOHN I. *et al.* (1974). *Toward a Mankind School: An Adventure in Humanistic Education.* New York: McGraw-Hill.

GROBMAN, H. (1968). *Evaluation Activities of Curriculum Development Projects.* AERA Monographs in Curriculum Evaluation. Chicago: Rand McNally.

HARLEN, WYNNE (1975). *Science 5–13: A Formative Evaluation.* London: Macmillan Educational.

HIRST, P. (1974). *Knowledge and the Curriculum.* London: Routledge and Kegan Paul.

HOLLEY, B. J. (1974). *A-Level Syllabuses: History and Physics.* London: Macmillan.

KLIEBARD, H. M. (1972). 'Exemplars of Curriculum Theory,' in LAVATELLI, C. S. *et al.* (eds.) *Elementary School Curriculum.* New York: Holt, Rinehart and Winston.

LAWTON, D. (1973). *Social Change, Educational Theory and Curriculum Planning.* London: University of London Press.

PARLETT, M. and HAMILTON, D. (1972). *Evaluation as Illumination.* Occasional paper 9. Edinburgh: Centre for Research in Education.

REID, W. A. and WALKER, DECKER (eds.) (1975). *Case Studies in Curriculum Change: Great Britain and the United States.* London: Routledge and Kegan Paul.

SEGUEL, M. L. (1966). *The Curriculum Field: Its Formative Years.* New York: Teachers' College Press.

STUFFLEBEAM, D. L. (1971). *Educational Evaluation and Decision Making.* Itasca, Illinois: F. E. Peacock.

TANNER, D. and TANNER, L. (1975). *Curriculum Development: Theory into Practice.* London: Collier, Macmillan.

WHITE, J. P. (1973). *Towards a Compulsory Curriculum.* London: Routledge and Kegan Paul.

WITTROCK, M. C. and WILEY, D. E. (eds.) (1970). *The Evaluation of Instruction.* New York: Holt, Rinehart and Winston.

Articles

GREENE, M. (1971). 'Curriculum and Consciousness,' *T. Coll. Rec.*, 73, 253–269.

HOGBEN, D. (1972). 'The Behavioural Objectives Approach: some problems and dangers,' *J. Curr. St.*, 4, 1, 42–50.

INGLIS, F. (1974). 'Ideology and the Curriculum: the value of assumptions of system builders,' *J. Curr. St.*, **6**, 1, 3–14.

JOHNSON, M. (1967). 'Definitions and models in curriculum theory,' *Ed. Theory*, **17**, 127–140.

JOHNSON, M. (1969). 'The translation of curriculum into instruction,' *J. Curr. St.*, **1**, 2, 115–131.

KLIEBARD, H. M. (1970). 'Reappraisal: the Tyler Rationale,' *Sch. Rev.*, 259–272.

STAKE, R. E. (1968). 'Testing in the evaluation of a curriculum development,' *Rev. Ed. Res.*, 38, 77–84.

STAKE, R. E. (1970). 'Objectives, priorities and other judgement data,' *Rev. Ed. Res.*, 40, 181–212.

STENHOUSE, L. (1971). 'Some limitations on the use of objectives in curriculum research and planning,' *Paedagogica Europaea*, 78–83.

WALKER, D. F. and SCHAFFARZICK, P. (1973). 'Comparing curricula,' *Rev. Ed. Res.*, **44**, 1, 83–111.

WESTBURY, I. (1970). 'Curriculum evaluation,' *Rev. Ed. Res.*, 40, 239–260.

WESTBURY, I. and STEINER, W. (1971). 'Curriculum: a discipline in search of its problems,' *Sch. Rev.*, 243–267.

WILLIS, G. H. (1975). 'Curriculum criticism and literary criticism,' *J. Curr. St.*, **7**, 1, 3–17.

PART TWO

The Curriculum in Transaction

Introduction

PART TWO

The Curriculum in Transaction

In Part One we have illustrated various ways of studying the issues raised by the question: *What should be taught and studied in our educational institutions?* In Part Two we shall look at what happens as this question is translated into what *is* taught and studied in schools and colleges and how what is taught and learned may be studied as the curriculum in transaction, as the ongoing reality of educational practices.

At the outset it is important to recognize that it is the content of education on which we need to focus attention, on how this is developed, changed and transacted. It is, of course, not always possible to draw hard and fast distinctions between the substance of learning experiences and the methods used in creating them: medium and message are not easy to disentangle. It is, nevertheless, important for students to maintain an awareness not only of where curriculum issues end and teaching and instructional ones begin but also of how in fact content and method interact.

Just as problematic is the study of what happens to the intended curriculum in the classroom in the hands of the teachers and the minds of the taught. The papers of Chapter 7 each throw light on the nature of this problem showing not only how the *de facto* curriculum, what is actually taught, may be shaped by assumptions which are not always made explicit but by a language which may seem all too explicit at times.

As complex, and about which more needs to be known, are the processes of curriculum change and innovation. These processes together with those of curriculum development and the translation of curriculum into teaching and learning have been the object of research in ways illustrated in Walker's paper on curriculum development and those of Westbury and Barnes on the curriculum in operation. How and in what form more of the field of curriculum studies can be brought under the rationality of research is dealt with in the last chapter.

In the first paper of this last chapter: *What Curriculum Research?* Walker attempts a reconstruction of the grounds on which research into the curriculum can stand. He does this with cogency and force echoing in some ways the criticisms which Schwab raised in his *The Practical: A Language for Curriculum* in Part One but also showing what 'the practical' means in research terms and it is this emphasis on the possible and the examples given in the two papers following which provide the hope that as with other areas of study, research can be of help to the student of the curriculum.

Chapter 5

Curriculum Development

Introduction

There is a sense in which it may be said that there is nothing new about the process of curriculum development and yet there is all to learn. This apparent contradiction arises because since the time that Plato proposed a curriculum for the Guardians of his Ideal State until relatively recently we have taken the process of curriculum development for granted, reflected hardly at all on its nature and attempted little or no analysis of its characteristics. With Franklin Bobbitt began a more systematic approach which was followed by the work of Ralph Tyler, Benjamin Bloom, Hilda Taba, John Goodlad and their associates. However, though this more systematic approach led to a rationale for curriculum development based on the selection of educational objectives, the creation of learning experiences through which to achieve them and the evaluation of the extent to which the objectives were achieved, it did not account fully for the interplay of the different aspects of the process of curriculum development. It is to this interplay that the papers of this Chapter, each in its own terms, is addressed.

The data-source for each paper differs. Walker depends on reports of curriculum projects, and Lamm on theories of instruction. Each author develops a somewhat different but self-consistent view of curriculum development (or planning). Lamm's approach is the more eclectic drawing on philosophy, on cultural and social expectations and on what he terms 'a metatheory of instruction', that is, on a theory about theories of instruction, on what each implies for the behaviour of the teacher and the student. The result of Lamm's analysis is to raise important questions about how far the process of curriculum planning as a guide to teachers should include an indication of the methods of teaching to be employed.

Walker uses a rather different approach. His concern is to reveal the principles employed by educationists when they are involved in the process of curriculum development. His method is first to describe what they do in general terms and secondly, attempt to explain why they do it. His approach is an empirical one concerned to account for the way curricula are developed. Lamm is more concerned to develop a general model for curriculum development rooted in broad conceptions of instruction and education. It is on the contrast and compatibility of the two ways of conceiving and characterizing curriculum development that one should focus in this Chapter as well as on the kind of data each author draws upon for his argument.

Readings

*A Naturalistic Model for Curriculum Development**

Decker F. Walker *Stanford University*

This paper presents a model of curriculum development as it is practiced in modern curriculum projects. It is a naturalistic model in the sense that it was constructed to represent phenomena and relations observed in actual curriculum projects as faithfully as possible with a few terms and principles.[1]

The field of curriculum already can boast an outstandingly successful model of curriculum development based on the work of a generation of curriculum theorists from Franklin Bobbitt to Ralph W. Tyler. The formal elements of that model—the classical model—are the objective and the learning experience. Its logical operations are determining objectives, stating them in proper form, devising learning experiences, selecting and organizing learning experiences to attain

---

* This article has been reproduced from *School Review* (November, 1971) by permission from the author and The University of Chicago Press.

given outcomes, and evaluating the outcomes of those experiences. This model has undergone 50 years of continuous development and use. It has facilitated the systematic study of education, and it has served as the basis for a respectable and growing educational technology.

For all its successes, however, this classical model seems not to have represented very well the most characteristic features of traditional educational practice.[2] In most cases when teachers or subject matter specialists work at curriculum development, the objectives they formulate are either a diversion from their work or an appendix to it, not an integral part of it. It may be that curriculum developers, to the extent that they deviate from the classical model, are wasting effort or, worse, misdirecting children's education. But it is also possible that the classical model neglects or distorts important aspects of contemporary practice in curriculum development. If so, a model of curriculum development frankly based on practice should illuminate novel facets of the curriculum development process, correct misconceptions about that process, and enable us to understand both the failures and the successes of the classical model.

The naturalistic model

The model of the process of curriculum development to be presented here consists of three elements: the curriculum's *platform*, its *design*, and the *deliberation* associated with it.

The curriculum developer does not begin with a blank slate. He could not begin without some notion of what is possible and desirable educationally. The system of beliefs and values that the curriculum developer brings to his task and that guides the development of the curriculum is what I call the curriculum's *platform*. The word 'platform' is meant to suggest both a political platform and something to stand on. The platform includes an idea of what is and a vision of what ought to be, and these guide the curriculum developer in determining what he should do to realize his vision.

The second formal element in the model, *deliberation*, is aptly characterized by Schwab as follows:

[Deliberation] . . . treats both ends and means and must treat them as mutually determining one another. It must try to identify, with respect to both, what facts may be relevant. It must try to ascertain the relevant facts in the concrete case. It must try to identify the desiderata in the case. It must generate alternative solutions. It must take every effort to trace the branching pathways of consequences which may flow from each alternative and affect desiderata. It must then weigh alternatives and their costs and consequences against one another, and choose, not the right alternative, for there *is* no such thing but the best one.[3]

A curriculum's *design*,[4] like an automobile's design, is the set of abstract relationships embodied in the designed object. The design is the theoretically significant output of the curriculum development process. When it is embodied in a material form, a curriculum's design, like an automobile's design, presents itself to us as a single material entity, a Gestalt, which must then be represented in some schematic way if we are to deal with it analytically.

We are accustomed to speaking of curricula as if they were objects produced by curriculum projects. The trouble with this view is that the curriculum's effects must be ascribed to events, not materials. The materials are important because their features condition the events that affect those using the materials. The *curriculum's design*—the set of relationships embodied in the materials-in-use which are capable of affecting students—rather than the materials themselves are the important concerns of the curriculum specialist.

The trouble with the concept of design is that the curriculum's design is difficult to specify explicitly and precisely. A method is needed for representing the potentially effective features of a set of curriculum materials schematically so that design elements can be identified and treated analytically. One way to specify a curriculum's design is by the series of *decisions* that produce it. A curriculum's design would then be represented by the choices that enter into its creation. Just as an experienced architect could construct a model of a building from a complete record of the decisions made by the building's designer as well as from a set of blueprints, so a curriculum developer could substantially reconstruct a project's curriculum plan and materials from a record of the choices they made. It may seem awkward to represent a design as a series of decisions, but I hope to show that such a representation has many features that will appeal to both theorists and researchers.

In the development of any curriculum some design decisions will be made with forethought and after a consideration of alternatives. These decisions make up the curriculum's *explicit* design. But the curriculum developer adopts some courses of action automatically, without considering alternatives. In these cases it is awkward to speak of a decision, even though the result is the same as if a decision has been overtly made. These unconsidered choices make up the curriculum's *implicit* design.

A curriculum's implicit design can never be completely specified in this mode of representation because the number of decisions, implicit and explicit, that underlie a project's materials is impossibly large. This limitation is not serious, however, for with accurate records any question that can be asked about the implicit design can be answered. In framing the question the questioner must ask how a particular issue was decided, and this characterization of the issue defines the decision of interest. Theoretically, at least, records of the curriculum maker's behaviour should reveal the course of action he chose at that point, even though he did not formulate the decision himself.

In this naturalistic model, then, the theoretically interesting output of the curriculum development process is not a collection of objects, not a list of objectives, not a set of learning experiences, but a set of design decisions. The process by which beliefs and information are used to make these decisions is *deliberation*. The main operations in curriculum deliberation are *formulating decision points, devising alternative choices* at these decision points, *considering arguments* for and against suggested decision points and decision alternatives, and, finally, *choosing* the most defensible alternative subject to acknowledged constraints.

The dynamics of the naturalistic model

The animating principle in curriculum deliberation is the desire for defensibility, for justifiability of decisions.[5] The curriculum designer wants to be able to say he was constrained either by circumstances or by his principles to decide as he did. To be constrained by circumstances is the curriculum designer's strongest possible justification, for then he has no genuine choice. If every decision were dictated by circumstances beyond his control, however, he would have no freedom to remake the world as he wished it to be. But when all circumstantial constraints are considered the curriculum designer finds he still has options left. It is his commitment to making these remaining choices in a defensible way that leads him to search for additional principles which are not natural, but man-made. The curriculum developer expects that these *conventional* principles will be accepted not as facts of life but as expressions of a shared view of the way life can and should be. Taken together, these natural and conventional principles provide enough constraints to enable the decision maker to resolve consistently issues that arise and to justify his decisions on the ground that anyone who acknowledged his principles would choose as he chose.

Needless to say, the derivation of curriculum-making constraints from natural and conventional principles and the application of these constraints to decision making is a horribly complicated job. We should not be surprised, therefore, to find that curriculum deliberations are chaotic and confused. Alternatives are often formulated and defended before the issue has been clearly stated. Feelings run high. Personal preferences are expressed in the same breath with reasoned arguments. But we must not be misled into believing either that such confusion is worthless or that it is the inevitable consequence of deliberation. Deliberation is defined by logical, not social psychological criteria, and it may take many forms. The most common form in current practice is argumentation and debate by a group of people. But it could be done by one person, and no logical barrier stands in the way of its being performed by a computer.

The heart of the deliberative process is the justification of choices. This justification takes the form: 'If you accept *this,* then you must choose *that.*' In justifying a choice we appeal to that which is already accepted in order to secure approval for our less-well-accepted choice. Those assumptions which the curriculum designer accepts and which serve as the basis for the justification of his choices constitute the curriculum's platform. Almost anything that is accepted as good, true, or beautiful can be part of a platform. Certainly beliefs about what exists and about what is possible are necessary parts of any platform. I call such beliefs *conceptions.* 'We believe there is a learnable strategy for discovering one's unspoken notions, one's unstated ways of approaching things,' states a conception of what is learnable.[6]

Beliefs about what relations hold between existing entities, that is, beliefs about what is true, I call *theories.* 'The teacher imparts attitudes toward a subject and, indeed, attitudes toward learning itself,' states a theory of the development of attitudes toward learning.[7]

Beliefs about what is educationally desirable, that is, beliefs about the good and the beautiful in education, I call aims. 'We teach a subject not to produce little living libraries on that subject, but rather to get a student to think mathematically for himself, to consider matters as a historian does, to take part in the process of knowledge-getting,' states an aim in general terms.[8] Educational objectives are one form in which aims can be stated.

These three platform components—conceptions, theories, and aims—

are sophisticated products of reflections on life and on education. However, a curriculum maker's actions are frequently based on less carefully conceptualized notions. Two kinds of less explicit but nevertheless powerful platform components are worth our attention: *images* and *procedures*. Images specify the desirable simply by indicating an entity or class of entities that is desirable without specifying why or in what way it is desirable.[9] Heroes are cultural images. So are outstanding works of art of admired scientific theories. Procedures specify courses of action or decision that are desirable without specifying why or in what way they are desirable. 'Be honest' and 'Minimize the time necessary to learn' are procedures since they specify a method of operation without specifying why or in what way that method is a good one.

Frequently the curriculum developer cannot decide among a set of alternatives either because all the alternatives are consistent with his platform or because none are, or because he does not have enough informationa to determine whether they are consistent with his platform. In these cases the curriculum designer must seek additional information in order to make a justifiable decision. Even when his platform principles make him confident that his choice is a good one, the responsible curriculum maker will often seek empirical confirmation of his beliefs. Data, while not part of the platform, can be a most persuasive basis for justification.

The curriculum designer may feel justified in a particular decision whenever he regards it as consistent with his platform and the information available to him. But judging the consistency of a decision alternative witha system of platform principles and a body of data is a complicated affair. Any decision is likely to fall under the purview of several platform principles and be judged more or less desirable in their separate lights. Also, the platform itself is likely to contain conflicting tendencies, if not outright contradictions, which only appear when the consequences of various principles are thoroughly worked out. For both these reasons and more a curriculum designer may change his platform as his work progresses.

In current practice, however, such changes seem to be relatively minor. For the most part they consist of elaborations of existing principles and adjudications of unanticipated conflicts. These minor alterations are preserved and kept consistent through the action of *precedent*. When a situation arises that is substantially the same as one already encountered, the curriculum designer need not laboriously justify the new situation in terms of platform principles; he can simply cite precedent. The application of precedent is such an important component of curriculum planning that I find it convenient to speak of

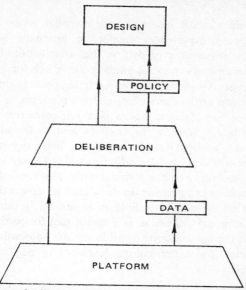

Fig. 1. A schematic diagram of the main components of the naturalistic model

the body of precedents evolved from the platform as *policy* and reserve the word platform for principles accepted from the start.

This completes the naturalistic model. The diagram in figure 1 shows the major components of the model and their relationships. The platform is shown as the base on which further work rests. Platform principles together with whatever data, the project collects are the raw materials used in deliberation, in the course of which curriculum materials are designed. The design stands at the apex of the structure to indicate both its status as the ultimate end of the process and its dependence upon the other components.

This model is primarily descriptive, whereas the classical model is prescriptive. This model is basically a temporal one: it postulates a beginning (the platform), an end (the design), and a process (deliberation) by means of which the beginning progresses to the end. In contrast, the classical model is a means-end model: it postulates a desired end (the objective), a means for attaining this end (the learning experience), and a process (evaluation) for determining whether the means does indeed bring about the end. The two models differ radically in the roles they assign to objectives and to evaluation in the process of curriculum development.

In the classical model objectives are essential, since, without an objective, learning experiences cannot be rationally selected and assessed. In the naturalistic model, on the other hand, objectives are only one means among others for guiding our search for better educational programmes. Objectives are not a starting point in this model but a late development of the curriculum maker's platform.

Evaluation in the classical model is a self-corrective process for determining whether learning experiences lead to the attainment of given objectives.[10] Without it, all is speculation. In the naturalistic model this kind of evaluation is not *logically* necessary. Design decisions *can* be justified by reference to the platform only. However, the empirical data that evaluation can provide on the effects of design decisions can be compelling evidence in a justificatory argument. In other words, in the naturalistic model evaluation is a useful tool for justifying design decisions, even though it is quite possible and not nonsensical (although probably unwise) for a curriculum developer to neglect systematic formal evaluation.[11]

The naturalistic model and curriculum research

If the naturalistic model represents the process of curriculum development faithfully, then we must revise many of our ideas about the conduct and evaluation of curriculum projects. For example, the USOE's requirement that persons seeking funds for curriculum development state their objectives behaviourally when they submit their application makes no sense if, as I believe, a defensible set of objectives is the output of deliberation based on a platform. If detailed information about the applicant's plans is needed before a grant can be awarded, that information is more fully and easily communicated by a platform which includes conceptions, explanations, images, and procedures as well as general aims.

Some curriculum practices predicated on the naturalistic model differ substantially from current practices. I wish to focus attention here on the implications of this model for research in the field of curriculum.

This model must be more fully developed before it can dependably guide research. But this elaboration and development itself requires research. In particular, a large investment of intellectual labour is necessary to create research techniques that will permit the study of curriculum designs and their platforms and deliberations. Assuming that such techniques can be developed, the model could contribute to curriculum research in several distinct ways.

1. *The model itself contains propositions that need to be tested.* According to the model, curriculum designers have platforms which strongly influence their deliberation and their final design. Do curriculum development groups in fact share a greater body of common beliefs than on would expect of groups of similar composition? Do the curriculum developer's justifications appeal to this body of shared beliefs? Do curriculum-making groups with similar platforms conduct similar deliberations and produce similar curriculum designs?

2. *The model provides a conceptual basis for descriptive studies of curriculum development.* Despite a decade and a half of unprecedented activity in curriculum development we know very little about the methods of operation of curriculum development groups. In what ways have the platforms of the different groups operating within a subject matter area differed? How have the platforms of groups in one subject field differed from those in the other fields? What platform elements are common to most contemporary curriculum projects? What kinds of issues arise in curriculum deliberations? How many alternatives does a curriculum development group typically examine in deciding a question? On what sources do they draw in formulating and justifying decision points and decision alternatives? It is too late for us to ask these questions of the projects which are now having such a great influence over what children learn, but we can resolve to do better. Until we can answer such basic descriptive questions we cannot hope to make much headway on deeper questions in curriculum theory.

3. *The model provides a conceptual basis for studies of the effectiveness of various design elements.* Studies of the effectiveness of contrasting educational 'treatments' have been notoriously sterile. Yet, if different curriculum designs do not produce different results, curriculum development is a futile enterprise. One of the most pressing empirical tasks in the field of curriculum is the rigorous establishment of connections between curricular variables (i.e. design elements) and learning outcomes. At present we are in a position to say with some confidence that a physics course produces learning that would not have occurred had the student not taken a course in physics. Evaluation studies of the new curricula have given us evidence which shows that students who take physics courses which have somewhat different aims will have

greater success achieving those aims emphasized in their course and less success with the aims emphasized in another course. But we need evidence that some of the subtler design features to which curriculum makers give so much thought have observable effects on students.

Many of the new courses in mathematics and science have students manipulate physical materials as a means of teaching abstract concepts and relations. Since these materials are relatively expensive, a systematic determination of the additional learning ascribable to this design feature would help to justify the costs of the materials. Furthermore, an understanding of the role of manipulation in facilitating learning would be of great scientific importance. An evaluation study would normally consider the curriculum as an undifferentiated 'treatment.' What is needed, however, is a determination of the effects of a single design element.

One possible approach to the difficult research problem of isolating the effect of a single design element might be to excise the element (in this case manipulation) from the curriculum's platform and deliberation in all cases where it can possibly be removed. When necessary, the omitted design element could be replaced by a resonable but much less costly alternative.[12] (Thought experiments or imaginative visualization might serve as alternatives to manipulation of materials.) If small-scale intensive studies show no important differences in the learning of groups exposed to the design element and groups given a comparable curriculum without the design element, then the value of this element would be called into question. If differences are found, the nature and extent of these differences should be valuable clues to the learning process by means of which the design element produces its effects.

4. The model could facilitate curriculum research *by making it possible to formulate succinctly questions that have not received enough attention from curriculum specialists*. A model suggests certain questions for research simply because they are so easily framed in the model's terms. The classical model has encouraged studies of the best form for objectives and of the results of various ways of formulating objectives. The naturalistic model, because it employs different terms, suggests other questions. Justification is an important component of the naturalistic model. But the same choice can be attacked and defended on many different grounds. Which grounds are appropriate? Which kinds of grounds should be accorded greater weight? Which in fact receive greater weight in curriculum developers' deliberations? The study of the logical and empirical foundations of the process of justifying

curriculum decisions is an important and neglected problem in the field.

Another neglected problem in curriculum concerns the ordering of decisions. Considering some questions before others can make a tremendous difference in the final design. A curriculum developer in his early work can so restrict the scope of his remaining decisions as to inadvertently close off whole fields of options. Should the curriculum developer make the choice he regards as crucial at an early stage in his work? What are the consequences of bringing different kinds of questions into the deliberations at different points? What areas of decision are interrelated in such a manner that making decisions of one kind reduces options in related areas in ways other than through reduction of resources?

5. *The model should help to identify problems from other fields whose solution would facilitate curriculum development.* Curriculum designers rely explicitly and implicitly on natural and conventional principles in their platforms and their deliberations. Frequently these principles are not tested propositions. They are condensations of practical experience, conventional wisdom, speculative hypotheses, or simply hunches. Perhaps curriculum developers should avoid such 'principles,' but they do not. We have insufficient experience with curriculum development to assess the extent to which these unverified principles prove to be true, so we cannot say whether curriculum makers are wise to rely on such principles. But it seems that the recent wave of curriculum projects, by operating on hypothetical psychological principles about such phenomena as discovery learning, has stimulated psychologists to investigate some questions they had not raised before. A more systematic study of the platforms and deliberations of curriculum development groups should uncover more such principles in need of investigation by our colleagues in other fields.

An example of a principle that curriculum projects seem to employ implicitly, but which has received little disciplined attention, is the role of consistency of experience in attaining certain kinds of long term learning. A curriculum developer interested in fostering inquiry will avoid any suggestion of dogmatism or arbitrary closure in his curriculum plans and materials because he believes it will detract from the course's effectiveness in developing an inquiring approach to learning. He fears that one or two experiences inconsistent with this attitude would destroy weeks of effort spent demonstrating the value and usefulness of the inquiring mode. To my knowledge this problem has been neither formulated nor investigated by educational psychologists.

Notes

This paper is based on an earlier paper entitled 'An Empirical Model of the Process of Curriculum Development' presented at the 1970 Annual Meeting of the American Educational Research Association in Minneapolis.

1. The model is based on reports of projects such as WILLIAM WOOTON'S (1965), *SMSG: The Making of a Curriculum*. New Haven, Conn.: Yale University Press; RICHARD J. MERRILL and DAVID RIDGWAY'S (1969), *CHEM Study: The Story of a Successful Curriculum Project*. San Francisco: W. H. Freeman & Sons; and ARNOLD GROBMAN'S (1969), *The Changing Classroom*, BSCS, Bulletin no. 4. Garden City, N.Y.: Doubleday & Co; and on the author's first-hand observation and study of one project as reported in 'Toward More Effective Curriculum Development Projects in Art', *Studies in Art Education* Winter 1970, and in 'A Case Study of the Process of Curriculum Development,' mimeographed. Stanford University, July 1969.

2. The classical model is, of course, intended to be prescriptive rather than descriptive, but those who recommend it as a norm imply thereby that practice guided by the model does what ordinary practice does, only better. The following articles are only a small sample of the rather sizable literature on the shortcomings of the classical model when it is applied to the classroom teaching or traditional curriculum development efforts: J. MYRON ATKIN (1963), 'Some Evaluation Problems in a Course Content Improvement Project,' *Journal of Research in Science Teaching*, 1, 1, 129–32; ELLIOT W. EISNER (1967), 'Educational Objectives: Help or Hinderance?' *School Review*, 75, 3, 250–60; PHILIP W. JACKSON and ELIZABETH BELFORD (1965), 'Educational Objectives and the Joys of Teaching,' *School Review*, 73, 3 (Autumn), 267–91; JAMES B. MACDONALD (1966), 'The Person in the Curriculum.' In: HELEN F. ROBISON (ed.) *Precedents and Promise in the Curriculum Field*. New York: Teachers College Press.

3. JOSEPH J. SCHWAB (1969), 'The Practical: A Language for Curriculum,' *School Review*, 78, 1 (November), 1–23. Also see DAVID P. GAUTHIER (1963), *Practical Reasoning*. New York: Oxford University Press, for an excellent philosophical treatment of deliberation.

4. The term 'curriculum design' first explicated by Herrick (see 'The Concept of Curriculum Design.' In: VIRGIL E. HERRICK and RALPH W. TYLER (1950), *Toward Improved Curriculum Theory*. Chicago: University of Chicago Press), and used to mean the major distinctive features of a curriculum is closely related to, but distinct from, the phrase 'a curriculum's design' used here. My usage applies the latter term to the *complete set* of abstract relationships embodied in the curriculum materials, whereas Herrick's usage confines the former term to the *prominent* and *distinctive features* of what I have called the curriculum's design. The same ambiguity attends the use of the word design in other contexts. When we speak of the 1967 Valient's design, for example, we can mean the entire design including all details, although we ordinarily mean only the distinctive and prominent features of the design.

5. ISRAEL SCHEFFLER (1958), 'Justifying Curriculum Decisions,' *School Review*, 66, 4 (Winter), 461–72.

6. JEROME BRUNER (1966), *Toward a Theory of Instruction*. Cambridge: Mass.: Belknap Press, p. 93.

7. *Ibid.*, p. 123.

8. *Ibid.*, p. 72.

9. The idea that vague notions can nevertheless be effective by virtue of being represented in a concrete model I got from Thomas Kuhn's notion of paradigm (*The Structure of Scientific Revolutions*. Chicago: University of Chicago Press, 1962). The idea that the force of such vague ideas arises from our admiring them but not knowing why comes from MORRIS WEITZ'S essay, 'The Nature of Art'. In: ELLIOTT W. EISNER and D. W. ECKER (ed.) (1966), *Readings in Art Education*. Waltham, Mass.: Blaisdell Publishing Co.

10. The concept of evaluation involved in the classical model and the only type of evaluation directly relevant to the process of curriculum development is what MICHAEL SCRIVEN has called *formative* evaluation 'The Methodology of Evaluation.' In: R. W. TYLER (ed.) (1967), *Perspectives of Curriculum Evaluation*. Chicago: Rand McNally & Co.

11. Evaluation as the assessment of educational decisions is not a new idea. This conception gets its earliest clear treatment in LEE CRONBACH'S (1963) article, 'Course Improvement through Evaluation', *Teachers College Record*, May, 672–86.

12. Scriven (n. 10 above, pp. 68–69) has suggested a similar procedure for obtaining a valid control 'treatment' for comparison with exposure to a curriculum produced by a project. He suggests that cut-rate 'new curricula' be created, whereas I suggest here that one design element be improvised in this way.

Teaching and Curriculum Planning*

Z. Lamm *School of Education, Hebrew University of Jerusalem*

The Objective

The objective of this article is to make explicit the relationships between theories of instruction and curriculum planning through analysis of the various theories of instruction. This analysis proposes a classification of the theories of instruction and examines the criteria which characterize each of them.

The problem

The impression one gets when reading so-called principles of curriculum planning is that these are designed as if they are to take the place of theories of instruction. It may be that this tendency arises from

* This article has been reproduced from the *Journal of Curriculum Studies* (1, 2, 1969) by permission of the author and Wm. Collins Sons and Company Ltd.

the weakness of many current theories of instruction.[1] This weakness is also apparent in the deductive speculations made in order to adapt learning theories to teaching situations as if the process of teaching were merely the learning process in reverse. In this state of affairs curriculum planning by manipulating various principles of learning theories tends to become a substitute for a theory of instruction.

A theory of instruction aims apart from its descriptive functions, to serve as a set of controls on teachers' behaviour and is intended to create conditions considered indispensible for the occurrence of learning. Even the most comprehensive knowledge of the nature of learning is not identical with a knowledge of those rules which should govern teachers' behaviour.

To plan curricula means to anticipate actions to be made according to a given state of a certain group of pupils and actions which are directed toward desired goals. In order to decide what actions lead to these goals the findings of the psychology of learning are necessary but these alone are not sufficient. A curriculum is a product of deliberations concerning the pupil and his ways of learning which take into consideration the behaviour of the teacher, the nature of content or subject matter and the aims of teaching. Thus, the psychology of learning alone is an insufficient source for curriculum planning. Moreover, the use of the psychology of learning as its only theoretical source will unavoidably cause planning to be biased as if teaching were taking place under laboratory conditions.

The teaching situation is from one point of view narrower than the situations explored by theories of learning, for not all learning is carried out by means of teaching. On the other hand the teaching situation is more complex than the situation explored by learning theories, more factors being involved. This situation can only be explained with the aid of a more comprehensive theory than the theories of learning actually are or are intended to be. For the time being such a theory has not been formulated, let alone proven. This explains why some models of curriculum planning tend to become substitutes for such a theory.

A model of curriculum planning is by definition neutral in relation to the aims of teaching. Since there is also always a certain relationship between aims and means, principles of planning can only be valid so long as they are really formal and neutral logical structure. In the case of theories of instruction and teaching which are structures built upon preference for certain ends over others this condition does not hold. Curriculum planning cannot be carried out without a theory of instruction to direct it, since not every kind of curriculum will fit any kind of instruction. Models of curriculum planning can generate workable curricula only when based upon a theory of instruction, otherwise they are liable to remain sterile logical structures.

A metatheory of instruction

Many and varied criteria have been advanced by different philosophers for judging whether a statement should qualify for the term 'theory'. If three commonly advanced criteria are accepted—that statements must be couched in general not specific terms, that statements must in themselves be logical and be related to one another logically so as to form a coherent whole and that statements must be verifiable by an acknowledged method of verification—if these criteria are accepted, the majority of statements made about instruction would not be classed as theory. A metatheory of instruction is therefore proposed to serve curriculum theory as a map of the field in which curriculum planning is to be carried out.

A semantic analysis of a large sample of statements was carried out by the author. The sample was derived from six sources: (1) written evidence given by teachers about their work; (2) attempts, made by teachers, at systematization of their personal experience; (3) speculative conceptions of teaching; (4) implications or deductions from philosophical, psychological and other theories; (5) applications from relevant finding of non-educational research; (6) findings of research studies on teaching. A two stage analysis was carried out on the source data aimed at (a) fixing the boundaries, topics, kinds of discussion of the field, (b) discovering criteria for classification of the various and often controversial views about the topics exposed in the former stage. Seven dimensions along which the various theories of instruction can be classified into three patterns were found. Each of these patterns represents, on the one hand, the controversial views about instruction and on the other, three different sets of activities which nevertheless are named by the common term: instruction. These seven dimensions are:

(I)   The nature and the source of aims
(II)   The nature of desired achievements
(III)   The status of the learner
(IV)   The status of the contents of teaching
(V)   The status of the teachers
(VI)   The conception of the social functions of teaching
(VII)   The psychological interpretation of learning

The analysis of the various theories and their derivations within these dimensions shows the extent of logical dispersion of approaches in each of them. Moreover, it shows that this dispersion, though specific in content in any of these dimensions, shares a similar structure in all of the theories.

Using the products of analysis of the investigated theories it was possible to reconstruct models of theories of teaching along the lines of the above-mentioned dimensions. Such a reconstruction yields three models of 'pure' theories of instruction. These are:

1. A pattern of teaching which is considered primarily as a process of instruction by imitation.
2. A pattern of teaching which is considered primarily as a process of moulding.
3. A pattern of teaching which is considered primarily as a process which promotes the educability of the pupil.

These reconstructed theories are, of course, artificial structures. Only a few deliberations about teaching correspond to these reconstructions. Most theories of instruction are fusions of views which logically belong to two or to all of these patterns. For the time being we shall leave open the question whether the lack of a logical unity in most of the theories of instruction is a result of ignorance or whether this can be explained by the fundamental characteristics of the instructional process. In any case these reconstructed patterns seem to be useful as theoretical frameworks for the investigation of the process of teaching. By identifying the characteristics of teaching they can be used as criteria for analysing theories of instruction. Following this procedure we shall describe the three patterns of instruction briefly along each of the seven proposed dimensions of analysis.

A. The imitation pattern

(I) The ends guiding this pattern can be defined as extrinsic. Extrinsic aims in instruction (as well as in education) are those whose validity is supported by values other than the needs of a developing human being. These values are created by prevailing social demands. It would be a hard task to prove that the ends justified by social demands stem in fact from an individual's inner needs, despite the fact that they are often represented as such. These claims, which are merely rationalizations, are from the logical point of view evidently *a posteriori* structures. First there were the aims forced on teaching by social pressure, and only later, may be as lip service to educational ideologies of our time, came the interpretation of these aims as if they fitted the needs of a growing personality.

In this pattern of instruction teaching aims to adapt pupils' behaviour to uniform social conventions by evoking behaviour congruent with social demands, even in cases in which these demands negate the needs of an individual and his development.

(II) The desired achievement in this pattern of teaching is the ability to reproduce accurately, as far as possible, the behaviour taught. Any dissimilarity to an accepted model, in spelling for example, is considered as failure. Success, in cases like this, is measured by the degree of similarity of performance to the given example. These examples to be imitated are to be found in all spheres of life. Among them will be found basic intellectual skills (reading, writing), some social habits (manners), stereotyped ways for the manifestations of emotions, modes of using tools and instruments, etc. The less these achievements are influenced by the performers' individuality, taste, style and so on the higher they are evaluated.

(III) The assumption that all the learners are alike must to some degree be accepted, by those who are concerned with teaching according to the pattern of imitation. One cannot expect an accurately reproduced behaviour if one does not take for granted that all learners have some identical traits in common. This is true even where some effort is made to adjust methods of instruction to the individual pupil. It follows that one set of aims is considered valid for all pupils, who are presumed to be able to perform alike even if their mode of learning is not exactly the same. This assumption brings about a recognition of individual differences.

(IV) Whatever its content teaching in this pattern is guided by a ritual approach. Sometimes the ritualized content is but a small part of the total content taught, and sometimes almost everything taught is so perceived.

Justification of imitation as a teaching method derives from the consideration of some selected content as being value *per se*. Such considerations stem from various sources. One is a sacred approach to specific items of knowledge which are regarded by communities, societies or cultures as indispensible. The other is a utilitarian approach to items of knowledge which are regarded as being so useful as to warrant their transmission to the growing generation in their original form.

(V) In a society which defines a teacher as the trainer of the next generation in specific modes of behaviour, his status is merely that of a craftsman. Such an artisan—teacher has to fulfil 'orders' without asking about the aims of his actions and is limited even in his choice of means. This type of instruction is strictly controlled by the community whose members feel able to exercise control since they have been taught in the same way when young.

(VI) The philosophy which guides this pattern of instruction can be epitomized as a philosophy of socialization in its narrowest sense. According to this interpretation teaching is a device for the preparation of the growing generation to take their part in normative social activities, change being undesirable. The presumed role of instruction, which is the explicit or implicit justification of the imitation pattern, may be outlined as follows: the actual behaviour of adults serves as a teaching model. This model is to be transferred unaltered. It follows that teaching has a social role in ensuring stability rather than facilitating change.

(VII) The preferred mode of the imitation pattern of teaching is conditioning. To teach means to arrange the conditions of learning so that a particular response will be stabilized and the required response will be manifested whenever the appropriate stimulus appears.

B. The pattern of moulding

(I) The ends guiding the moulding pattern of instruction are of two kinds: intrinsic and extrinsic. The intrinsic aims derive from regarding such human features as character, intellect and emotion, as objects for educational treatment. The extrinsic aims find expression in terms of functions which an individual fulfils in the state, society and community. The moulding pattern is guided by both of these kinds of aims. To mould means to develop the individual's traits (character, intellect, emotions, etc.) according to a given model such as good citizen, religious person, patriot, etc. Here arises an indispensable tension between the two kinds of ends which is relieved in this pattern of teaching by the subsumption of the intrinsic aims to the extrinsic ones. To mould according to a given model means to develop the human powers as long as this development does not contradict the essentials of the model.

(II) The nature of the desired achievement in this pattern of instruction is the ability to behave according tolearned principles of behaviour. The pupil should be able to think about problems which have not been met before, in the same way as he has been thinking while solving problems in the course of learning to evaluate, for example, new works of literature, using the criteria exercised in the evaluation of previously studied works, to behave in unfamiliar situations according to the rules of behaviour already learned. This approach implies that the criterion for evaluation of teaching is the exact transferability of the pupil's learning activities in school to new situations.

(III) A student exposed to the moulding pattern of teaching is regarded as somehow being different from his peers who have not. However, as in the imitation pattern, the group concept still governs the definition of the individual pupil. Despite this approach it is recognized that each pupil will possess individual traits. Moulding according to a given model must imply that all students can be changed in some desired direction. This changeability is a supposed common trait of all students. Their individuality is recognized, and the recognition manifests itself in demands for specific techniques by means of which the individual pupil will be shaped according to the common end. This pattern of instruction in principle permits the individualization of methods, providing that the different methods will bring about the same goals. The methods, i.e. modes of motivating pupils' learning, kinds of operations performed by the learners and the ways of evaluation of progress, can be different in case of different pupils as long as their product is the pupil's ability to behave (intellectually, emotionally, etc.) according to given principles.

(IV) Content is taught in order to bring about the internalization of principles then implied. Shaping a taste for literature can be done only by reading literary classics. Yet this reading does not aim solely at knowing these works but is in addition intended to mould the pupil's discriminatory ability. The same can be said about science or history teaching. Their end is not only knowledge of the actual content which was taught but also the use of the structural principles involved. These structural principles are considered to be the original meaning of the contents. The teaching of the original meaning, as opposed to original appearance, allows for manipulation of content. This can be rewritten, re-represented and re-interpreted according to the learner's abilities, motivations and interests, but only as long as its original meaning remains untouched.

(V) The teacher suitable for the pattern of moulding is one whose personality traits fit a model of personality appreciated and acceptable to existing cultural groups. He is expected to be a representative or an example of this culture because, in distinction from a society where the imitation pattern is used, not all members of society are considered capable of evaluating everything the teacher does. The teacher in the framework of the moulding pattern is much more independent. Only other members of the community who are regarded as 'men of culture' are considered to be entitled to interfere with and judge his teaching. The teacher is no longer regarded as a craftsman but rather as an agent of a culture the principles of which serve as criteria for the evaluation both of the various aspects of the community and of the personalities of its members. Because such a teacher is expected to interpret the contents of a culture and to adapt the methods in his teaching, his status is higher than the status of a craftsman whose methods are merely traditional. His status is not yet however that of a member of a profession, since members of the community who are not teachers but just educated people are entitled to judge his actions and behaviour.

(VI) Changing a pupil's personality in order to ensure his participation in a certain culture implies that as yet he does not share this culture. The process which brings about the internalization of cultural patterns is acculturation. This term may serve to define the social meaning of teaching according to the moulding pattern. Moulding is nothing less than bringing about the internalization of given cultural patterns by the growing generation until their autonomous functioning within that culture is ensured. To function within a culture means to be able to behave and to evaluate one's own and other's behaviour according to the norms and the values of that culture. Such achievements can be attained only when the growing person has internalized these norms and values rather than learnt them. Thus in this pattern the social function of teaching is to bring about personality changes, i.e. changes in modes of thinking, attitudes and in overt behaviour approaching patterns derived from a given culture.

(VII) Ideas may be interpreted both as concepts and principles. Moulding a personality according to a given pattern of culture means to cause a human being to learn to respond to concepts and principles in ways accepted by that culture. The preferred mode of learning in this pattern of teaching is therefore the learning of concepts and principles and to some degree, of problem solving with the use of the same concepts and principles.

C. The pattern of promoting educability

(I) In this approach to teaching intrinsic aims control the extrinsic ones. Developing human powers necessarily involves the use of a variety of content which is structured according to some rules, principles or systems. Thus teaching any content results in the last analysis, in determining the pupil's thoughts, shaping his emotions and moulding his character. Since there is no way of developing human powers, such as intellect, emotions and character without content and since most content is ruled by some discipline, system of principle, it is charged with moulding capacity.

In the pattern of promoting educability by teaching it is assumed that the individual's development should not be curtailed by the structure of content, by the spirit of existing values or habits or by any other conventions. All these may be used as means in education as long as they support the development of the individual's powers. But when the content endangers the development of the individual by stunting his capacity to grow it stops serving as a useful means of achieving educational aims as understood in this pattern.

(II) The desired achievement in this pattern can be described as creative behaviour anchored in an autonomous personality. By autonomous personality is meant a person who is capable of using freely his various powers in appropriate situations, and the ability to judge and evaluate his actions as if they were not his own, and thus be able to act according to his own decisions. Autonomy is, therefore, the desired final product of the development pattern of teaching.

(III) In this kind of teaching the pupil is considered a unique person, whose characteristics have to be taken into account. The fact that he learns together with other pupils has only technical significance and should not prescribe the methods of dealing with the individual pupil. Here individualization is not restricted to the adaptation of suitable methods of teaching to individual learners as it is in the moulding pattern, but in the first place demands adaptation of suitable aims to the individual. All aims, or the same aims cannot be considered suitable for all pupils. Aims of education in this pattern derive from consideration of the individual pupil and not from external demands. The pupil's basic traits are one of the departure points for defining aims, which therefore cannot be anything but individual aims.

(IV) Content is an inevitable ingredient of teaching. One cannot teach without teaching something. This is the reason for the use of content even in this pattern. But as we have seen content in teaching can be regarded either as aims or as means. In this pattern of instruction, however, it is considered exclusively as means. It is to serve as tools for training the powers of the pupil, and, because the desired achievement is creativity, there is no doubt that any manipulation of it is legitimate. The aim here is not to establish the rules of the content as authorities in the pupil's life but rather to ensure the emergence of the pupil's powers of judgment over the content within his experience.

(V) The definition of the teacher's role, in this pattern of teaching includes diagnostic functions with regard to two different objects. The first is the learner, whose aptitude and traits are to be diagnosed. The second is the content, which has to be diagnosed as tools serving particular ends in the development of the pupil. This two-fold function included in the definition of the teacher's role brings it near to, if not into, the ambit of professional roles. Teaching is here considered as a professional occupation, the practice of which, as that of other professions, cannot be judged by those who are not members of this profession. Teaching is a kind of specialization, akin to medicine or law, in which the process of decision-making about means and methods is independent of any external authority.

(VI) The social meaning of teaching presumed in the framework of this pattern is one of individuation. Individuation has a social meaning because society is, in the last analysis, the sum total of what its members are. This statement does not contradict the assumption that society is, in some ways, an independent phenomenon. Even when defined as an independent phenomenon society is dependent upon the levels and kinds of persons within it. Individuation means cultivating the best of the human being's abilities on the assumption that the potential best is inherent in human nature and must be developed, but not moulded, educated but not shaped. It follows that an autonomous personality is a decisive factor in the functioning of a society, and the task of instruction is to ensure the development of such a personality. But individuation means more than this. It is considered the main path for ensuring the self-realization of a human being as such. According to this conception the full development of a human being is not in conflict with the interest of a sane society. On the contrary they mutually support each other as long as the nature of both is observed.

(VII) The psychological meaning of the means preferred in this pattern of teaching is brought out in such terms as insight, inventiveness, originality, self-expression and innovation which are characteristic of creativity in its various appearances and levels. Techniques which endanger the emergence of creativity are rejected in this style of teaching. The creative approach to teaching is supposed to stimulate a creative approach to learning. This approach is not restricted only to the teaching of the arts (where it is accepted to some degree within the moulding pattern) but even in science teaching, in physical education and in many other school activities.

These criteria derived from an analysis of the content of theories of instruction can be summarized in Table 1.

The metatheory of instruction and curriculum planning

Most curricula, like most of the prevailing theories of instruction cannot be identified with one single pattern of the above classified patterns. There are areas of teaching planned according to the principles of imitation, others according to those of moulding and some according to the principles of promoting educability.

Areas of teaching can be roughly classified into six categories: (1) Humanities (literature, history, philosophy, etc.), (2) Arts (music, drawing, dance, etc.), (3) Sciences, (4) Social sciences, (5) Arts and crafts, and (6) Physical education. This is of course a simplification even for our purpose, because in each of these categories different kinds of teaching are practised, but it will suffice as an example. All decision in these six areas may be guided by any one of the three possible patterns of teaching. But then there is a possibility that teaching in one of the areas, let us say in the humanities, is directed by the pattern of imitation; teaching in another, let's say in science, is directed by the pattern of moulding, and teaching in a third area, let's say in crafts, is directed by the pattern of promoting educability. Decisions in any of the six areas of teaching (and there are actually more than six) may be guided by any of the three patterns of instruction. Thus as a result of a *formal* analysis we may find a large number of possible theories of instruction

Table 1: Criteria for defining patterns of instruction

Dimensions for analysing theories of instructions	A. IMITATION	B. MOULDING	C. EDUCABILITY
(I) NATURE OF AIMS	extrinsic aims only	extrinsic aims control intrinsic ones	intrinsic aims control extrinsic ones
(II) NATURE OF DESIRED ACHIEVEMENT	ability to perform according to given models	ability to act according to given principles	ability to discover new principles and test them
(III) STATUS OF THE LEARNER	solely as a member of a social group	as a member of a heterogeneous group	as a unique individual
(IV) STATUS OF THE CONTENTS	ritualistic—to be transferred in original form	manipulative—to be transferred in original meaning	instrumentalistic—as a means to develop pupil's powers
(V) STATUS OF THE TEACHERS	as a communal employee	as a cultural agent	as a professional
(VI) SOCIAL FUNCTIONS OF TEACHING	a means of socialization	a means of acculturation	a means of individuation
(VII) PSYCHOLOGICAL INTERPRETATION OF LEARNING	conditioning	concept and principle learning	problem solving and creative thought

in which different combinations of patterns are suggested for teaching in the various areas. Similarly it may be found that various combinations can be discovered within a single teaching area, (e.g. in the Humanities area we might find imitation guiding the teaching of sonnet writing, moulding in further literary taste and creativity in the writing of compositions).

When a certain curriculum consists of an intermingling of two or three patterns the problem arises which of these patterns will dominate the results. We must point out here that although it may be true that some personalities are so structured that the results of the three teaching patterns may exist independently in most cases it is to be expected that one of the patterns will govern the overall behaviour of any one personality.

Teaching of reading and writing (considered as technical skills) is teaching by imitation. In order to pass from the stage of reading and writing to the stage of creativity in reading and writing (such as dramatic recitation or creative writing) one has to read and write according to some accepted rules and conventions, i.e. to be moulded. Thus, in order to reach the aims of the development pattern teaching has to avoid premature automatization, such as may occur when skills are taught under imitation controls or principles are taught under moulding controls.

It may seem to follow that teaching can be defined as a hierarchy of patterns. The lowest of these is the pattern of imitation, the aims of which have to be attained in order to attain the aims of the higher pattern—moulding, and the aims of moulding having to be reached in order to make pupil development possible but usually the aims of the lower patterns may be attained in a way which prevents any serious achievement in the higher patterns. Imitation can bring about automatization of responses so that the individual loses the plasticity to change according to the moulder's intentions, and moulding can become final and thus prevent further development. The aim of analysing the interrelations among the different patterns of teaching in the various areas is to elucidate the possibilities of passing from the lower patterns to the higher ones; i.e. from imitation to moulding and from moulding to development.

Notes

1. Cf. N. L. GAGE (1963), *Paradigms for Research on Teaching: Handbook of Research on Teaching*. Chicago: Rand McNally, pp. 94–142.

Summary Appraisal

Apart from the differences in method and ways of conceptualizing the process of curriculum development presented in the preceding papers, one should note also the justification which each author accords his work. Walker suggests several ways in which his 'naturalistic' model will contribute to curriculum research including a reappraisal of the process of curriculum evaluation. Lamm with marking a clear path through the complex relationships between curriculum planning and the conduct of teaching. In the light of these concerns one should speculate on the extent to which the particular concern may have shaped the method employed and concepts or principles developed by each author.

Suggested Readings

MacDonald, J. B. *et al.* (Eds.) (1965). *Strategies of Curriculum Development: Writings of the Late Virgil E. Herrick*. Columbus, Ohio: Charles Merrill.
Herrick was a pioneer in the study of curriculum development and was much concerned to develop principles to guide curriculum design. He was sensitive to both the larger issues of educational value and to the practicalities of school and classroom. This collection of writings shows how very close the man was to the real issues of learning and teaching while at the same time being conscious of the need to see the meaningfulness of these activities as purposeful and planned.

Tyler, R. W. (1950). *Basic Principles of Curriculum and Instruction*. Chicago: University of Chicago Press.
A classic in the field introducing one to the paradigm of Educational Objectives—Learning Experiences—and Evaluation which has informed much thinking about curriculum development over the last two decades.

Taylor, P. H. (1970). *How Teachers Plan their Courses*. Slough: NFER.
This is an empirical study using data arising from discussions with teachers, analyses of their schemes of work and replies to questionnaires to construct a model of their perceptions of the process of curriculum development. It may usefully be compared and contrasted with Walker's approach recounted in *A Naturalistic Model of Curriculum Development*.

Taylor, P. H. and Johnston, M. (1974). *Curriculum Development: A Comparative Study*. Slough: NFER.
Ten essays introduce the reader to styles of curriculum development in different national contexts and show the relationship of curriculum to general educational concerns. Both centralized and decentralized systems are illustrated. An introductory and a concluding essay raise issues common to curriculum development wherever it is found and attempts to clarify them.

Chapter 6

Curriculum Change and Innovation

Introduction

Countless curriculum changes and innovations have been introduced
to schools during the twentieth century, particularly during the last
two decades. One hears of new maths, new science, new social studies,
inquiry training, computer assisted instruction and the like. And yet,
when one looks at the schools of today it becomes easy to conclude, as
do Goodlad and Klein (1970), that promising innovations are 'blunted
on the classroom doors.' One problem, of course, is our tendency as
curriculum workers to forget that neither curriculum as intentions nor
curriculum in transaction occurs in a vacuum. Curriculum change is
more than adding, deleting or altering content or a given sequence of
instruction. It is more than testing a new programme and disseminating
it with the hope that it will be adopted. We need to back off and look
at schools as total cultural systems. From there we can begin to construct
and implement curricula which interact with societal needs, internal
school norms, human resources, student expectations and needs,
organizational characteristics, and the like. Each of the papers in this
chapter deals with curriculum change as it is related to such cultural
variables.

Goodlad begins his thoughtful article by suggesting that curriculum,
in theory and practice, is now ready for the tenets of Progressive
Education. Then, after reviewing curriculum changes from the 30s
through the 70s in the United States, he sets forth a series of proposals
for curriculum change which should be considered as we move through
the 70s into the 80s and beyond.

First, the curriculum planning process, as carried on in curriculum study centres, must involve a continual dialogue among persons at all levels of decision making. Such dialogue must address itself to the commonplaces of curriculum. In short, curriculum must become a field of study. The proposal leads naturally to a second one: dialogue most be carried beyond verbal abstraction to a level of model building and simulation. Third, a network of experimental schools should be established to test such models and simulations, while at the same time reversing the process to build theory from practice as Schwab suggests in Chapter 4 of this book. Fourth, we need experimentation with alternative modes of instruction derived from curricular structure. Fifth, classroom curricula are not enough. In addition to school curricula are curricula of television, of work, of leisure. We must consider schooling as only a part of education.

The relation between the organization of schools and the persistence of curriculum innovation is the subject of the research report by Shipman. The report was extracted from a follow-through study of 38 secondary schools involved in the Schools Council Integrated Studies Project based at Keele. The object of the research was to find how different aspects of school organization influence the success or failure of the trial of curricular materials and new teaching methods. The findings of the study seem to suggest that involvement of teachers at the local level is critical to the success of the innovation. The author concludes that the school which is likely to introduce and implement a planned innovation successfully would:

—have teachers who feed back information to the project

—have teachers who accumulate supplementary materials

—have teachers who had volunteered knowing that they would be involved in innovation

—reorganize its timetable to provide planning time for teachers involved in innovation

—have a head teacher who supported the innovation but did not insist on being personally involved

—have a low staff turnover among key personnel

—be free of any immediate need to reorganize as part of a changing local school structure

Reference

GOODLAD, J. I. and KLEIN, F. *et al.* (1970). *Behind the Classroom Door.* Worthington, Ohio: C. A. Jones Publishing Co.

Readings

Curriculum : A Janus Look[1]*

John I. Goodlad *Institute for Development of Education Activities and University of California, Los Angeles*

On three counts the Roman god, Janus, is relevant to what I am about to say. First, Janus has been represented as having two faces, one looking forward and the other backward. I look from the present into the recent past and from the present into the imminent future. Second, Janus was the animistic spirit of doorways and archways. I speak to the problems of cutting doorways between and building archways over different levels of curriculum decision-making. Third, Janus in Roman mythology, was guardian of the gate of heaven (the 'opener' and the 'shutter') and god of all beginnings. Those of us who work in curriculum might be expected, then, to invoke Janus in making our beginnings and to reckon with Janus at the ending believed by some to be still another beginning.

Recent curriculum emphasis

Curriculum in theory and practice, is now ready for the tenets of progressive education. In fact, a large part of progressive education that once was embodied in the conventional wisdom—if not the professional practice—of educators is now embodied in the conventional wisdom of a new generation of educators. But they didn't learn it from their history books. They acquired it, in part, from the discipline-centred curriculum reform movement and its accompanying psychological baggage that moved in behind the dying, propaganda thrusts of life-adjustment education.

* This article has been reproduced from the *Journal of Curriculum Studies* (1, 1, 1968) by permission of the author and Wm. Collins Sons and Company Ltd.

The first (1951) and last (1954) reports of the two Commissions on Life Adjustment Education for Youth almost coincide with the creation of the National Science Foundation (1950), which came to finance many curriculum reform projects in subsequent years, and the appearance of products from the University of Illinois Committee on School Mathematics (1951), perhaps the earliest of the organized, inter-disciplinary groups.[2] And the death of the Progressive Education Association (1955) and of its journal (1957) coincide in time with the early efforts of Jerrold Zacharias to organize his fellow scientists for school curriculum reform[3], and with Sputnik (1957). The decade of the '50s marks the ending of one era and the beginning of another.

My statement that a new generation of educators is learning the conventional wisdom of one era from the conventional wisdom of another appears, at first glance, to be enigmatic if not in error. The beginning of the new era certainly did not take its rhetoric from the dying gasps of life adjustment education. Progressive education already had lost its intellectual vigour before the life adjustment movement fell victim to the fusillade of attacks ultimately intended for the larger, longer parent movement.[4] What is now currently referred to as the current curriculum reform movement[5] had no orthodoxy throughout most of the decade of the '50s. It simply was *against* what appeared to be excesses as expressed in earlier pedagogical cant—'the whole child,' 'persistent life situations,' 'intrinsic motivation,' and particularly 'teaching children, not subjects'—and *for* what appeared to be neglected —subject matter as perceived by specialists in the disciplines. In 1938, Boyd Bode had predicted, '. . . if it (progressive education) persists in a one-sided absorption in the individual pupil, it will be circumvented and left behind.'[6]

Change, by definition is away from what exists or appears to exist. And change is likely to be excessive or give the appearance of excess when what it seeks to replace is or appears to be excessive. Perhaps this is why the new, discipline-centred curriculum reform movement acquired an orthodoxy so soon. In the decade of the '60s, its own central tenets became a cant: 'discovery method,' 'intuition,' 'structure of the disciplines,' and even 'learning by doing.' Shades of John Dewey and William Heard Kilpatrick!

It is no small irony that, as the current movement grows from its suburban middle-class beginnings to encompass concern for students in harsh, urban environments, it sounds some notes that echo reports of the Commission on Life Adjustment Education for Youth. It is an even greater irony that it was Jerrold Zacharias, a key figure in vitalizing curriculum content, who spoke passionately from the floor of the 1965 White House Conference on Education urging greater consideration for children, for boys and girls, in the deliberations and recommendations.

Will we have come full cycle by 1970? If so, and more important, what will we have learned from the preceding two decades that will be put to good use in curriculum reform of the succeeding two? Clearly, we did not apply in the '50s and '60s what we might have learned from the '30s and '40s.

Jerome Bruner, who shares credit for concepts (particularly 'intuition' and 'structure') underlying current curriculum reform, likewise shares blame for our failure to draw concepts from the past to balance excesses in the present. By not referring to two generations of curriculum inquirers and inquiries, some of which included thinking very much like his own (although rarely so well stated), in his highly personalized report of the 1959 Woods Hole Conference,[7] Bruner's contribution was not cumulative. Indeed, neither the links to nor the differences from John Dewey, Charles H. Judd, and Franklin Bobbitt, to name only a few, were stated. And since most of Bruner's readers were not readers of these earlier men it is not surprising that, for example, the concept of inquiry was born anew.

But linkages to the past might not have changed anything anyway. A new generation of curriculum makers was ready for the proposition '. . . that any subject can be taught effectively in some intellectually honest form to any child at any stage of development' (p. 33). Others among Bruner's observations fell on deaf ears: 'Is it worth while to train the young inductively so that they may discover the basic order of knowledge before they can appreciate its formalism?' (p. 47). 'But the danger of such early training may be that it has the effect of training out original but deviant ideas' (p. 48). 'There is a surprising lack of research on how one most wisely devises adequate learning episodes for children at different ages and in different subject matters' (p. 49). '. . . it may well be that *intrinsic* (italics mine) rewards in the form of quickened awareness and understanding will have to be emphasized far more in the detailed design of curriculum' (p. 50).

Two sentences in particular take us back to the '30s: 'We might ask, as a criterion for any subject taught in primary school, whether, when fully developed, it is worth an adult's knowing, and whether having known it as a child makes a person a better adult' (p. 52). '. . . a curriculum ought to be built around the great issues, principles and values that a society deems worthy of the continued concern of its members' (p. 52). Could we be reading George S. Counts? If we add to this last quotation what Bruner does not quite say—that the students themselves should choose from among these great issues in determining their curriculum, we could be reading Harold Alberty. And Bruner comes close: 'Perhaps anything that holds the child's attention is justified on the ground that eventually the child will develop a taste for more self-controlled attention . . .' (p. 72). Imagine a Bruner, 20 years younger, fashioning with Alberty the core curriculum!

No, the 1960 breed of curriculum makers no more heard this side of Bruner than they heard the disclaimer in the 1951 report of the Commission on Life Adjustment Education for Youth: life adjustment education '. . . emphasizes active and creative achievements as well as an adjustment to existing conditions; it places a high premium upon learning to make wise choices . . .'[8] Had the several statements I have lifted from Bruner and more like them constituted the essence of his book, Bruner would have been a less significant figure in the current curriculum reform movement and certainly would not have contributed to its orthodoxy. His several bold hypotheses, clearly counter-cyclical to the perceived excesses and deficiences of the progressive education era, made the difference and contributed significantly to the innovative thrust of the '60s.

It is quite possible, however, that a much older Bruner, witnessing but perhaps not contributing to a new curriculum reform, will prefer to remind us of his secondary rather than his primary propositions. Because in these lies something of the shape of what might be expected of curriculum innovation in the '70s and '80s. An older Dewey, too, viewing in dismay what he was charged with having wrought, sought to remind us of the full breadth of his argument. In that part of Dewey we chose to forget lay the seeds of at least part of what has happened in the '50s and '60s.

There is tragedy in the distorted emphases of an era, no doubt of that. Personal tragedy and societal tragedy. Curriculum planning, like other human phenomena, suffers at any given time because of preoccupations that obscure other relevant emphases. But it is these over-emphases, too, that give societies their innovation spurts and the individuals who spawn them their *raison d'etre*. Perhaps the poet Yeats was thinking of tragedy in this dual sense when he said: 'We begin to live when we have conceived of life as tragedy.'

But excesses can become neuroses and neuroses, in turn, interfere with rational functioning, inhibiting the power of individuals and the power of societies to right themselves. Lawrence Kubie reminds us that neuroses, rather than being inevitably correlated with the creative process, distort and corrupt it.[9] A society must seek to right itself, then, before the creative thrust of innovative excess becomes neurotic, inhibiting the creative energy needed for the counter-cyclical thrust. The time is come, I think, to right the emphases of a creative curriculum thrust that has spanned two exciting decades.

Undoubtedly, an innovative period in curriculum innovation lies ahead for the '70s and '80s. It will be more counter-cyclical, I believe, to the '50s and '60s than to the '30s and '40s. These decades, too, will have their excesses, probably in the form of their most creative thrusts. The challenge—conspicuously ignored in the past as no doubt it will be ignored in the future—is to capitalize on the excesses of the past while sustaining new excesses into the future.

Perspective on curriculum analysis

Curriculum planning involves at least two very different kinds of processes. First, there are political and legal considerations. Controlling agencies set forth guidelines which sometimes take on the character of law. He who would understand curriculum planning or any curriculum in all its ramifications perforce must understand the political-legal structure within which it exists.

Second, curriculum planning is a substantive enterprise in that it has certain perennial foci of intellectual attention, commonly identified as considerations of ends and means. Thus, there are commonplaces which can be treated from differing perspectives in the same way that commonplaces of philosophical thought—the nature of knowledge, man, and the good life, for example—can be treated from differing perspectives. To the extent that such commonplaces are, indeed, common in curriculum discourse and to the extent that this discourse is made rigorous by relevant logical-deductive inquiry and empirical research, a field of study emerges.

Viewed against these criteria, curriculum as a field of study is, at best, embryonic. There is and has been vigorous discourse about ends and means: objectives and how to derive them, objectives and whether to have them, objectives and how to define them; content and its validation, content and its organization, content and its ossification; and so on. There has been effort, too, to arrange these commonplaces so as to give some rational guidance to curriculum building. There has been little model- or theory-building; both have suffered from a paucity of descriptive and experimental data. And the dialogue has suffered from general omission of inclusion/exclusion criteria. As a consequence, participants rarely appear to be addressing themselves simultaneously to the same commonplaces and so talk right past each other. The dialogue might be described better as a series of monologues.

My colleagues and I, not to be outdone, have formulated a kind of team monologue, on the assumption presumably that several persons talking as one past everyone else are better than one person talking all by himself past everyone else. Building on the work of Ralph Tyler,[10] we have formulated a tentative conceptualization of some ends-means commonplaces in curriculum and have superimposed a tentative conceptualization of the political structure within which curriculum planning might be conducted in a complex society.[11] We have come up with a model—still in revision—which is brazenly intended for enriching curriculum discourse (even if systematically rejected) and increasing rationality in curriculum making (which, of course, it will not do if rejected, whether systematically or unsystematically!).

The details of this model serve little purpose here. But its broad outline provides a framework which, even if only glimpsed, may reduce somewhat the extent to which I talk past you. By developing a model of the substantive commonplaces of curriculum and of the political considerations in curriculum planning, we have a backdrop for appraising ideological formulations of what curricula or a curriculum should consist of. Thus, we can systematically appraise the recommendations of James B. Conant for the American high school[12] and compare these with other recommendations, keeping the same commonplaces in view throughout. Similarly, we can place the proposals of Jerome Bruner[13] in historical perspective, predict the inclusions and exclusions likely to result in practice from applying his emphases and perhaps even formulate the proposals necessary to balance these emphases. Assuming some soundness in the model (and I further assume its improvement and the formulation of alternative models through continuing inquiry) and some use of it, we might anticipate parallel growth in the viability of ideological curriculum proposals, less blind faith in the ill-formed curricular pronouncements of political or military heroes, and less skittering about from emphasis to emphasis, fad to fad.

Such a model provides, also, a backdrop for analyzing how the political structure functions with respect to curricular decisions and even for planning how to go through it or around it in seeking to influence the curricula of schools, classrooms, and students. Because ideological curricula, to affect those for whom they are intended, must penetrate or circumvent the political structure.

Our model poses three levels of decision-making: societal, institutional, and instructional.[14] We do not say that all three should exist. There are no 'shoulds' in our model other than the overriding implication that its categories and suggested processes are appropriate to a conceptual model of curriculum. But we do imply that curriculum decisions are likely to be made at all three levels in a complex society. (In a simple society, these levels are likely to be collapsed into two or even into one.) In the United States, local, state, and even federal authorities make curricular decisions that affect what is studied by the nations' children and youth. These are societal decisions. Teachers, acting in concert, develop curriculum guides for their schools and school systems, paying varying degrees of attention to societal decisions. These are institutional decisions. And teachers, acting alone, formulate plans for specific groups of students entrusted to them, again ignoring or paying their respects to societal and institutional decisions. These are instructional decisions.

Where among these levels the power lies varies from country to country. Consequently, the strategies most likely to bring about an appropriate balance or a temporary imbalance of power, or to augment one level and nullify another, and thus to effect evolution or revolution in the curriculum likewise vary from country to country. This is why the seminal innovation of one country is the abortion of another.

To summarize briefly what may appear to have been an airy and irrelevant digression, a conceptual model of the kind I have been discussing aids perspective on two counts. First, it provides substantive criteria for appraising current and recent curriculum planning efforts and for projecting ideological innovations for tomorrow. Second, it focuses attention on the curricular structure prior to posing innovations designed to remedy its shortcomings. Now, let me use it in continuing my Janus look.

Through a glass narrowly

By using this perhaps imprecise perspective and looking at the two recent eras through smaller panes of glass, some interesting differences come into view. First, in direct contrast to the '30s and '40s, the decades of the '50s and '60s have witnessed precious little dialogue about the commonplaces of curriculum among those forging the new curricula. There has been some discourse at the periphery by a handful of curriculum specialists but little of it has had vitality. Contrast this, however, with the spirited exchanges among George S. Counts, Harold Rugg, Boyd Bode, William Heard Kilpatrick, John Childs, and H. Gordon Hullfish. Paralleling the work of this group and particularly seminal in the '20s were the less flamboyant contributions of Henry C. Morrison, Franklin Bobbitt, and Charles H. Judd.

The differences between these groups are somewhat akin to the differences between the younger and the older Dewey who provided a bridge between the two. Admittedly, it was a bridge which from time to time suffered the fate of the Bridge on the River Kwai. The latter group had certain natural roots in Dewey (*circa* 1900) and Edward L. Thorndike. There are some present-day extensions in the work of those behavioural scientists who concern themselves with education (many of them now together in the National Academy of Education). The links to a curriculum past and present are weak but the pulse still beats and will beat stronger. The beat would be weaker if it were not for the personal bridge provided by Ralph W. Tyler whose roots in curriculum and in the behavioural sciences go back to Charters and Judd, in particular.

The former group—The Teachers College, Columbia, group in contrast to the Chicago group—began with Dewey and in many ways ended with Dewey, whose death in 1952 roughly coincided with the ending of one era and the beinning of another. One looks in vain today for powerful carriers of this great past. The group was philosophical rather than psychological in orientation but, by now, philosophy was turning in upon itself and away from its traditional preoccupation with the nature of man and the good life. Its thrusts have had no impelling resurgence but, thankfully, they are preserved and interpreted in the historical inquiry of Lawrence A. Cremin.

Whatever the differences between the Chicago and the Columbia groups—and they were at times monumental—they possessed in common one important characteristic: their deliberations took in a wide range of educational and, therefore, also of curricular commonplaces. What is education for? How are its ends to be achieved? What are the relevancies of society, learners, and subject-matter as data-sources for curriculum decisions? How are learning opportunities to be put together for most effective learning? The questions are still being asked but rhetorically and not in the right places.

This observation brings me to a recommendation for tomorrow. It is more of a plea than a recommendation because I have no specific target audience for it and little to suggest as means for bringing it about. *The curriculum planning process, at all levels of decision-making, must be enriched by lively, continuing dialogue, addressing itself systematically to defining the commonplaces of curriculum and alternatives stances toward them.* The problems of education and of mankind broadly are now so raw and bare that our energies are almost wholly devoted to treating them. The universities are becoming activist. Perhaps the kind of inquiry needed will emerge in them. But they probably need as catalyst some kind of centres for curriculum inquiry that concern themselves with the immediate and with training only for conceptual orientation. Be there a philanthropic foundation so bold as to found perhaps one such?

A second significant difference between the present and recent era and its predecessor is in political orientation. The Teachers College group (with Counts as leader in this instance) saw need for the schools to reform society itself.[15] Rugg, for example, viewed the schools as physical forums in the debate and educators as its leaders.[16] The change strategy was loose, perhaps even naive. But it was true unto the movement. It depended on ideas, in keeping with Dewey's doctrine that the most unsettling thing is a new idea. The movement sought to change the thinking of people—teachers, principals, superintendents, and the lay public—in the idealistic expectation that they in turn would change the schools. And improving the schools, for many progressives, was *the* means to improving education and society as a whole.

The discipline-centred curriculum reform movement has had no such broad and idealistic goals. It has been as pragmatic as its times. And it has been politically savvy. Its leaders got immediately to a source of enormous funds (enormous, at least, in contrast to those available in previous decades), the National Science Foundation. It influenced that source directly. Then, it bypassed the societal and institutional levels of curriclum decision-making and got directly to the instructional. Curriculum reformers did not seek to influence school boards or administrators. Teachers, not superintendents, were invited to summer institutes. And new textbooks—the most potent influencers of what boys and girls learn—were put into the hands of these teachers.[17]

A third difference between the two eras is a corollary of the second. In the progressive era, the components of curriculum were put together predominantly at an ideological level. The influence on real schools and classrooms was indirect and pervasive and often diluted until the original colours had been washed away. Furthermore, the concepts were complex, frequently obtuse, interrelated, and enormously difficult to implement. Theoretically-oriented interpreters and innovators were required; these always are in desperately short supply. The names of Carleton Washburne, Helen Parkhurst, and Corinne Seeds immediately come to mind. They depended, necessarily, on charisma; scientific tools of leadership were not available. Only a few of the mechanics of what they did are transferable. Meanwhile, most of the ideas remained in the minds of the devoted and entranced—probably fuzzily conceived there—and did not provide in the classroom the kind of expression that facilitated experimental comparisons or even filial identification.

In the discipline-centred era, by contrast, the components of curriculum have been put together at the instructional level, and here in the form of materials. Some of the instructional packages are designed to be so complete as to be 'teacher free.' But teachers intervene between students and materials, nonetheless. The limited conceptual and theoretical baggage is diverted; there is slippage from conception to implementation. To the extent that teachers do not understand or cannot implement the concepts of structure and inquiry to be acquired by the students, the goals of the curriculum projects are thwarted. Teachers brought upon deductive methods of teaching and learning do not take readily to the inductive requirements of the new materials.

A fourth difference between the two eras pertains to their significant omissions. Progressive education virtually eschewed textbooks. Its comprehensive view of the educational enterprise simply defied packaging. But teachers depend and have depended heavily on textbooks. They depended heavily on them during the progressive era, often being required by education authorities to use specific textbooks. Teachers were faced with an almost irreconcilable dilemma. They sat at the feet of William H. Kilpatrick and lesser exponents of progressivism, participating in discussions of some rather loosely defined concepts of project and activity methods for which there were few explicit models. Then they returned to the realities of their classrooms where the specifics of curriculum guides and textbooks won out. Progressive education remained virginal. One is tempted to say 'almost virginal,' since there was, indeed, an occasional breakthrough.

Whereas progressive education sought to shape the whole length and breadth of the school programme, the discipline-centred movement has sought to shape only subject matter for learning and teaching. It has neglected the institutional level of planning. We have not seen what model schools would look like, even if the best individual sequences of subjects were put together so as to use a week's or a year's time to best advantage. We lose sight of the fact that organizing a subject for learning and teaching and organizing the child's curriculum, to say nothing of his total education, are two different things.

Finally, both the progressive and the discipline-centred eras were deficient in the learning opportunities actually prepared for or with students. Progressive education, in seeking topics which were meaningful in the life of the child or to his larger world, stretched across many disciplines, often paying little attention to their structure or method. Mathematics, or art, or science, more often than not, was applied. In the graphic arts part of his social studies lesson, the child learned something about the shape of a pyramid but little about the shape of art. Progressive education needed the rigour of the subject-centred era that replaced it. But the time was not yet; progressive education was circumvented and passed by.

The discipline-centred movement, by contrast, in seeking topics to develop the structure and methods of the various fields, too often has overlooked the burgeoning interests of the child, many of which might have been picked up and used spontaneously. The child has been discovering the basic order of knowledge; but probably before he could appreciate its formalism. We have used as a criterion in determining what the child *should* learn what he *can* learn. Such a criterion is necessary but insufficient. The current curriculum era has needed the leavening of the era it so rudely thrust aside.

I said at the outset of this paper that curriculum is now ready for the tenets of progressive education. Let me now add that curriculum, *circa* 1950, was equally ready for the tenets of the discipline-centred era. Surely we are now ready for the tenets of both.

In conclusion

I conclude with a series of observations and proposals which emerge (logically and rationally, I trust!) from what has gone before. With these I conclude my Janus look.

First, the curriculum planning process, at all levels of decision-making, must be enlightened by a lively, continuing dialogue, addressing itself systematically to the commonplaces of curriculum and to alternative stances toward them. The problems of education and of mankind are now so raw and so bare that almost our full energies go into treating them, rather than into long-term inquiry. There should be curriculum study centres so set up that they cannot, indeed must not, succumb to activist pressure. A first order of business should be sustained, rigorous work that will make of curriculum a field of study. The practical benefits will follow but we must regard them as secondary for the present.

Second, the work that is to go on in such curriculum study centres must be carried at least one stage beyond verbal abstraction to a level of model building and simulation. It is possible, I think, to define and to agree upon a set of conceptual commonplaces in the field of curriculum. There are certain alternative sets but the overlap is likely to be substantial. However, the alternative stances with respect to each commonplace and each combination of commonplaces are many. Curriculum inquirers should play conceptual games with these alternatives, holding sets of alternatives constant long enough to see their shape and potential worth. Simulation techniques, aided by the computer, now make this possible.

Third, there must be experimental schools specifically charged with testing those simulated patterns or models believed to be most promising. The function of such schools would be experimentation; educating children would be an extremely important human by-product but not their prime function. Schools now existing, however good, do not meet this criterion. In effect, the schools I have in mind would collapse within themselves societal, institutional, and instructional levels of decision-making. They would reach out beyond themselves not for political sanctioning but for conceptual confirmation in the form of promising models already simulated but not refined and tested. Their commitment would be to remain true to concepts and from concepts their authority would be derived. Proceeding systematically, they would provide the substantiating or negating feedback so necessary to the systematic refinement of conceptual models.

I recognize that we should have, also, some free-wheeling experimental schools which would create their own concepts as well as develop models. The process described above would be reversed, with systematic model and theory building following rather than preceding the schools' innovative thrusts.

Experimental schools of both kinds probably are better tied into the structure they seek to agitate by linkages to co-operating demonstration schools than by direct linkages to public school systems. Thus, their responsibility for functions of explanation and dissemination would be markedly narrowed. But the fashioning of networks for broad-scale curricular change, networks which necessarily include public school systems, is still another story, one with which I shall not proceed here.

Fourth, one specific aspect of curriculum planning requires immediate attention if a new era of curriculum planning is to profit from the two eras that have been my targets. This is the business of assembling or integrating the learning opportunities with which students are to have their curricular romances. Progressive education suffered from an excess of learners' problems during one phase and society's problems during another.[18] The discipline-centred movement has suffered throughout from subject-matter myopia and surgical slicing of learning episodes. We now need experimentation with alternative modes of assembling the relevant and possible components of curricular structure. Not the structure of society, not the structure of human beings, not the structure of subject-matter, gives us *the* structure of a curriculum. It is some of all of these, with the mixtures varying according to time and place.

Fifth, and perhaps most important, reform of school and classroom curricula, whether according to progressive or discipline-centered concepts or a combination of the two, is not enough. There are other curricula: of television, of work experience, of leisure time activities central to the individual. Education is more than schools. And curriculum planning is much more than manipulating selected components until they become elegant curriculum designs. Curricula are individual and group tools that serve and, in fact, fashion human functions.

Our best hope is that all of our curricula together will make it possible to maintain a state of dynamic tension between our best dreams of what each of us as individuals and mankind in general might become and where we now stand on our various paths toward the realization of these dreams. The gap between expectations and present realities must never close; good education must see to that.

The future, like the past, must have its excesses. Excesses are the creative thrusts of individuals and of society, the counter-cyclical reactions to yesterday's excesses. But let us temper them with our lessons from the past so as to forestall crippling neuroses. Our excesses make of this sober educational pursuit our sport, our recreation. It is a tragedy that they are so often followed by painful retribution. But to have learned that life is tragedy is to begin to learn to live.

Notes

1. This paper was given as the opening paper at the Third International Curriculum Conference (1967) and is published by courtesy of the Schools Council.

2. However, exploratory work pertaining to 'the "new" mathematics for the schools' dates back to the 1940s, notably at the University of Chicago where a group of mathematicians and mathematics educators engaged in exploratory work in the early and mid-'40s. And, of course, the mathematics they proposed were not really 'new.'

3. See JAMES D. KOERNER, 'EDC: General Motors of Curriculum Reform,' *Saturday Review* (August 19, 1967), 56–58, 70–71.

4. See LAWRENCE A. CREMIN (1961), *The Transformation of the School*. New York: Alfred A. Knopf, Inc. I am indebted to Cremin but do not hold him responsible for these interpretative paragraphs.

5. See JOHN I. GOODLAD (1964), *School Curriculum Reform in the United States*. New York: Fund for the Advancement of Education; and JOHN I. GOODLAD (with Renata von Stoephasius and M. Frances Klein) (1966), *The Changing School Curriculum*. New York: Fund for the Advancement of Education.

6. BOYD H. BODE (1938), *Progressive Education at the Crossroads*. New York: Newson & Co., p. 44.

7. JEROME S. BRUNER (1960), *The Process of Education*. Cambridge: Harvard University Press.

8. UNITED STATES OFFICE OF EDUCATION (1951), *Vitalizing Secondary Education: Report of the First Commission on Life Adjustment Education for Youth*, Washington, p. 1.

9. LAWRENCE S. KUBIE (1958), *Neurotic Distortion of the Creative Process*. Lawrence, Kansas: The University of Kansas Press.

10. RALPH W. TYLER (1950), *Basic Principles of Curriculum and Instruction*. Chicago: University of Chicago Press.

11. The group consisted of Margaret P. Ammons, Alicja Iwanska, James A. Jordan, Maurice N, Richter, and John I. Goodlad. The work is reported in JOHN I. GOODLAD (with MAURICE N. RICHTER) (1966), *The Development of a Conceptual System for Dealing with Problems of Curriculum and Instruction*. Contract No. SAE-8024, Project No. 454, Co-operative Research Programme, United States Office of Education.

12. JAMES B. CONANT (1959), *The American High School Today*. New York: McGraw-Hill Book Co.; and, more recently, *The Comprehensive High School*. New York: McGraw-Hill Book Co., 1967.

13. JEROME S. BRUNER, *The Process of Education*, *op. cit.*

14. My first formulation of these levels was in 1960, when I sought to develop a framework around which to organize research in curriculum for the period, 1957–60. [See 'Curriculum: The State of the Field,' *Review of Educational Research*, XXX (June, 1960), 185–198.] I used them later in writing a volume for the NEA Project on Instruction (See *Planning and Organizing for Teaching*. Washington: National Education Association, 1963.) In preparing this paper, I encountered use of societal, institutional, and instructional levels by Derek Morrell, Joint Secretary, The Schools Council, London. (See 'The New Dynamic in Curriculum Development,' *New Dynamics in Curriculum Development*, pp. 25–40. Toronto: Ontario Curriculum Institute, 1965.) Perhaps a dialogue is begun!

15. GEORGE S. COUNTS (1932), *Dare the Schools Build a New Social Order?* New York: John Day Co.

16. HAROLD RUGG (1936), *American Life and the School Curriculum.* Boston: Glenn and Co.
17. See *The Principals Look at the Schools*, pp. 23–24. Washington: National Education Association, 1962.
18. RALPH W. TYLER (1957), 'Curriculum, Then and Now,' *Elementary School Journal*, 57 (April), 364–74.

The Impact of a Curriculum Project*

M. D. Shipman *Department of Education, University of Keele*

Introduction

This paper has been extracted from a follow-through study of 38 secondary schools involved in the trial of a Schools Council curriculum project. It is not concerned with the evaluation of curriculum materials or new teaching methods. It is focused only on the relation between the organization of the schools and the persistence of curriculum innovation.

The evaluation of current curriculum projects will provide evidence in this crucial but rather neglected area. In the case of the Schools Council Humanities Project, for example, this includes both intensive and extensive studies of the experiences of schools during innovation.[1] Already MacDonald and Rudduck have shown some of the difficulties in communication between schools and project team, even when this has been singled out for attention.[2] This confirms the findings of Gross and his co-workers, that, even where research and development support for an innovation has been intensive, the teachers concerned may still be confused about their new role.[3] The present author has argued that this arises out of the contrasting and changing definitions of the curriculum situation, not only among curriculum developers and teachers, but also among heads and local authority advisers.[4]

The object of the research into the Schools Council Integrated Studies Project based at Keele was to find how different aspects of school organization influence the success or failure of the trial of curriculum materials and new teaching methods. It was hypothesized that investment by teachers in innovation would be the crucial factor in

* This article is reproduced from the *Journal of Curriculum Studies* (5, 1, 1973) by permission of the author and Wm. Collins Sons and Company Ltd.

deciding the impact of a curriculum project. No precise measures of input or output could be made. Often the important factors were not detected in advance, not adequately defined, or too elusive for the techniques used in measuring. In retrospect, trying to detect the factors in schools that determine the success of curriculum innovation is like trying to repair a watch while wearing mittens.

Definitions of inputs, outputs and organizational factors
1. *Output*
a. *Contractual success* was defined as the fulfilment by the school of the 'contract' to try out integrated studies. Of 38 schools, 22 were, in this contractual sense, successes, seven were failures and five only entered in the second year of the trial. Another four schools did not complete the trial period but left to continue with their version of integrated studies independent of the project. These were contractual failures, although they were continuing with the innovation.

b. *Curriculum impact* was defined as the extent to which curriculum change had resulted from the trial experience. Each school was rated on one of four three-point scales. These measured the amount of trial materials in use after the end of the trial period, developments arising from the trial in integrated studies, developments in the related fields of the humanities and the persistence of forms of team teaching.

2. *Input*
a. *Time and energy* invested by teachers was measured on three three-point scales. These covered attendance at meetings, accumulation of supplementary materials and the provision of feedback to the project.

b. *Investment by the school* was measured on another three three-point scale covering the provision of a special team leader, adjustments to the timetable and the provision of special planning time for the integrated studies team.

c. *High level manpower* was measured by the extent to which head, deputy head or heads and heads of departments were involved in teaching integrated studies.

d. *Material resources* were measured by the provision and suitability of rooms and the availability of money and special facilities for the trial within the schools.

3. *The context of investment*
a. *The support of non-involved staff* was measured through their attitudes towards the trial in their schools.

b. *The basis for integrated studies* was assessed by the existence in the school curriculum of ongoing work before the trial in this or similar areas of the humanities.

c. *The climate of innovation* was a subjective assessment by the central project team of the esprit of the schools, on a scale derived from the *Organizational Climate Description Questionnaire,* Form IV, part III, developed by Halpin.[5]

The collection of data started in 1969 and was completed in the Spring of 1972 after the trial period had finished in August 1971. Information on the organization of the schools was collected by direct observation, through the routine returns of the project team and the feedback from the schools. Further information was provided by an interview programme. This was based on a schedule prepared on the basis of taped interviews with groups of teachers. The final interview programme involved 35 teachers, 14 head teachers and seven local authority advisers. Another 23 teachers returned the schedule by post. No attempt was made to select at random. The object was to contact those who had played an important part in the project. Data was compressed into two by two tables and hypotheses tested by *chi* squared. The reliability of these methods was probably low, particularly as variables contaminated each other as the author and project team collected new data in the light of old data collected across a period of over two years. Wherever possible different methods were triangulated and independent evidence, such as that collected by an observers' panel of advisers and College of Education lecturers as part of the evaluation, used as a check. Nevertheless, the results need to be interpreted with caution.

Results

The table shows the results of testing for association by *chi* squared.[6] Null hypotheses were confirmed (x) or rejected (beyond the five percent level) as follows.

Outputs	Inputs						
	2a	2b	2c	2d	3a	3b	3c
Contractual success	$\cdot01 > \cdot001$	$\cdot01 > \cdot001$	x	x	x	x	$\cdot01 > \cdot001$
Curriculum impact	$\cdot05 > \cdot02$	$\cdot01 > \cdot001$	x	x	x	x	x

The most predictive indices for the persistence of curriculum change within 2a and 2b were the feedback of information to the project, the accumulation of supplementary material by teachers and the provision of planning time by the school. The overall message of these statistics is that the net impact of this curriculum project seemed to depend on the commitment of the teachers involved. This confirms the now common finding that any innovation, means of organization or teaching method depends for success on the attitudes of the teachers, regardless of the intrinsic merits of the scheme.

Behind these superficially impressive significance levels lie measures of interest and effort that reflect the strains on teachers involved in innovations. At one extreme there were schools where the commitment to trial involved little disturbance to routine. At the other extreme were schools where teachers planned their team work in the vacations or in the evenings, integrated across a variety of subject boundaries, attended meetings at Keele and in teachers' centres, fed back new ideas, materials and evaluations and built up supplementary resources. In the latter the persistence of innovation seems to be ensured through the effort that had been put in.

There were also indications of a threshold beyond which schools seemed to break through into self-sustained innovation. They had not only invested enough to ensure sufficient momentum for further development, but had begun to experience the limelight of the innovator. Instead of feeling that it was a bore, nor worth the effort, teachers in these schools were appreciating the public recognition that innovation can bring. Observers, visitors, researchers, inspectors, advisers, students and journalists, often seen as inconvenient or hostile witnesses, were now welcomed. Nine of the 38 schools seemed to be in this category. All were building on the trial experience in the year after the project had finished in the schools.

The significance of 3c, the measure of organizational climate, is probably only another reflection of the commitment of teachers as the crucial factor. It consisted of measures of enthusiasm and drive. Indeed, it is misleading to suggest that indices can be separated into teacher and school investments. Thus the provision of timetabled time for team meetings had to be accompanied by effort by the teachers to be effective. Similarly timetables could be blocked to facilitate team teaching and inquiry methods, but teachers could still use blocked time in traditional ways. It is therefore probably safer to concentrate on what teachers actually do than to rely on the concept of school organization as if this can operate apart from the teachers who put it into practice.

The failure of the remaining investment indices to show significant correlations may have been due either to the blunt measuring instruments or their irrelevance to the organization of innovation. In one case, the effect of involvement of high level manpower on curriculum, there were conflicting influences. Probability level was $\cdot30 > \cdot20$, but in a negative direction. Breaking down this manpower showed that involvement of heads of departments increased the chance of successful curriculum innovation, but involvement of head teachers reduced the chance of success. Involvement of deputy heads seemed to make little difference.

The retrospective analysis based on information gathered after the trial project had ended uncovered three important influences not taken into account in designing this investigation.

1. *Turnover among staff*

Two of the seven schools that dropped out before completing the contracted trial and five of the 22 schools which completed it lost over half their integrated studies staff during the trial period. But this was not all loss. Seven teachers moved to other schools to take over or start integrated studies. But staff turnover, while not significantly related to failure to complete the trial, was significant (probability between $\cdot05$ and $\cdot02$) in determining the extent and persistence of curriculum change. Loss of staff on any scale stopped innovation. Three of the six schools with high investment by teachers and low curriculum impact and three of the five with high investment by school and low curriculum impact had lost over 50 per cent of their original integrated studies team.

2. *School re-organization*

Both actual and planned, or even anticipated, re-organization turned out to be important in determining whether the experiment with integrated studies survived beyond the trial period. Thus three of the five schools in one local authority area that had completed two years of trial gave up integrated studies in junior forms because re-organization meant that they received a 12-year-old entry instead of 11. In another area one school had successfully finished the trial, but re-organization finished off the innovation. However, the staff involved were moving to two other local schools to start up integrated studies for the first time.

3. *Press ganging*

It had been anticipated that the level of commitment would vary widely between schools. This was no doubt reflected in the investment indices. Some staff, interviewed after the end of the trial, firmly maintained that they had really not been part of the trial. They were 'helping out' or 'just interested'. But the interviews in the schools and with the local advisers revealed another anomaly. In three of the six schools that failed to complete the trial there was an enthusiastic head and un-enthusiastic staff. These teachers claimed to have been pressed into service. Local advisers confirmed this, Curiously however in the remaining three schools where teachers seemed to have been press ganged there was one with high teacher/high school investment and high curriculum impact, one with high teacher/high school investment and low curriculum impact, and another with low teacher/school investment and high curriculum impact.

Discussion

Gross *et al.* have detailed four barriers to change encountered by teachers.[7] One of these, the lack of the necessary materials, did not seem important in implementing the Keele Project. The remaining three barriers, lack of clarity in the new teaching role, lack of skills and knowledge to implement the innovation, and the existence of school organization incompatible with change may have been present. To Gross it seemed that these barriers resulted in a failure to implement the innovation. Hoyle has described this as tissue rejection.[8] The evidence collected here suggests both an elaboration of this problem and a possible way through the barriers.

The secondary changes in schools seem as likely to be beneficial as malignant, and change in one school can be beneficially infectious for others. In Britain at least, innovation has involved grass-roots efforts by teachers. Thus Brown has shown how innovation in primary schools often comes through the head teacher adopting ideas that have been found to work by other teachers.[9] Where there has been planned innovation this local enterprise can lead to unpredictable results. It may be that these unintentional side effects are as important as the planned change itself. The interview programme after the end of the Keele project revealed some aspects of this ripple effect of innovation. The teachers and head teachers saw innovation from their own viewpoint, as part of their school's future. The trial was of limited duration. Had all schools given up integrated studies it would have been no reflection on the success of the project which was concerned with the whole school system. But the experience of team teaching, of organizing inquiry based methods and of working in an integrated way, added another set of ideas and experiences to the planning of new curriculum, particularly to ensure a smoother transition from junior school and to design courses for school leavers. In only ten of the 38 schools entering the trial (four of the 22 who completed two years), was there a negligible impact. In all other schools there had been innovation, both at the curriculum level and in the attitudes of staff through the experience of involvement in planned curriculum change.

The impact of the project was not however confined to trial schools. The turnover of teachers in the project teams was a major disturbance, but it was not only those who moved to take up posts elsewhere who were spreading the ideas. There was also lateral movement of ideas between neighbouring trial schools, voluntarily sharing ideas. The teachers involved saw this exchange of information as the most important form of communication. Informal contacts and teacher centre meetings were appreciated more than meetings at Keele. But alongside the organized and informal groupings of trial schools was a spread of ideas to neighbouring schools not involved. Again this had occurred partly through informal contacts and local curriculum groups organized for RoSLA preparation.

The extent of this persisting influence on the teachers involved and on their schools was primarily determined by their own input. The final impact reflected early efforts. Where the project was accepted as a marginal activity and worked with minimum disturbance to established organization, or where staff had been reluctant to join, the failure rate was high and net impact low. It did not seem to matter whether schools accepted the philosophy of integration or not. The critical but involved teachers were often those who produced a lasting effect on their schools. The direction may not have always been identical with that recommended by the project team, but the resulting tension did not weaken the impact of the investment made. The failures were those schools where innovation was welcomed or just accepted but not as an opportunity to work at creating change.

The practical implication for overcoming resistance to change is that innovation must not be presented on a plate to schools. The successful organization of planned curriculum change may depend more on mobilizing teachers into planning and implementation than on getting schools to accept packaged materials. Given the way teachers plan their courses this will not be easy.[10] This was a dilemma for the project organizers at Keele. The schools had volunteered to enter the trial. The object was to test new materials and methods, not primarily to initiate changes in just these 38 schools. The project could have been a success if nothing had changed in these trial schools. As it was 28 out of the 38 involved had been affected. Curriculum projects may be important as initiators, stimulating and accelerating change, but not necessarily in the anticipated direction. The alien tissue may be transmuted not rejected.

So far the strategy has usually been to try out materials in trial schools and then hope that the published materials will be diffused under the stimulus of in-service courses and conferences. It might be better to concentrate on mobilizing teachers into the continuous development of these materials from the start. For curriculum projects this means local organization. Centralized projects may not be able to influence or even detect the actual extent of innovation. The strength of the Keele project was its local nature and the appointment of local co-ordinators to link project and schools. Without this close support the level of investment would have been lower, the trial could not have been monitored by the project and this research would have been impossible. But even more important, with one co-ordinator to some eight schools, the teachers felt that they were involved in the innovation. They felt that they were contributing. Significantly they wanted even more visits and were unanimous in their praise for the efforts of the co-ordinators.

It would be rash to generalize about the nature of the innovatory school from the evidence on the 38 investigated here. The salient points are that the school which is likely to introduce and implement successfully a planned innovation would:

—have teachers who would feed back information to the project
—have teachers who would accumulate supplementary material
—have teachers who had volunteered knowing that they would be involved in a lot of work
—re-organize its timetable to provide planning time for teachers involved in innovation
—have a head teacher who supported the innovation but did not insist on being personally involved
—have a low staff turnover among key personnel
—be free of any immediate need to reorganize as part of a changing local school structure.

It could be argued however that if you could find such a school there would be no point in trying to get it to change.

Notes

1. B. MacDonald (1971), 'The Evaluation of the Humanities Curriculum Project: A Holistic Approach', *Theory into Practice*, X, 3, June, pp. 163–167.
2. B. MacDonald and J. Ruddick (1971), 'Curriculum Research and Development Projects: Barriers to Success', *Brit. Jrn. Ed. Psych.*, 41, 2, June, pp. 148–154.
3. N. Gross, J. B. Giacquinta and M. Bernstein (1971), *Implementing Organizational Innovations*. Harper and Row.
4. M. D. Shipman (1972), 'Views of a Curriculum Project', *Journal Curr. Studs.*, 4, 2.
5. A. Halpin (1966), *Theory and Research in Administration*. Macmillan, pp. 131–249.
6. For some reservations on the technique employed, see H. Selvin, 'A critique of tests and significance in survey research', *Am. Soc. Rev.*, 1957, pp. 519–527. See also D. Gold, 'Statistical tests and substantive significance', *Am. Sociologist*, 1969, pp. 42–46.
7. Gross *et al.*, *op. cit.* pp. 196–198.
8. E. Hoyle (1970), 'Planned Organizational Change in Education', *Research in Ed.*, May, pp. 1–22.
9. M. R. Brown (1971), 'Some strategies used in primary schools for initiating and implementing change', unpub. MEd thesis, Univ. of Manchester.
10. P. H. Taylor (1970), *How teachers plan their courses.* Slough: NFER.

Summary Appraisal

The articles in this chapter deal with some of the problems faced by curriculum workers interested in changing schools. Goodlad suggests a set of procedures which take into account the relationships between schools and society and which, if followed, can lead to rational change and innovation. Shipman warns that curriculum change cannot be brought about without concern for the organizational variables inherent in schools. These articles map the terrain for the curriculum worker who is interested in the thoughtful reform of the schools. Even so, many questions are left unanswered. What societal factors inhibit or promote change? Which curriculum and instructional alternatives have a basis in theory and are desirable to change to? What are the organizational variables or social system variables in the school which must be considered if curriculum change is to be brought about? What change strategies exist that can be employed? The suggested readings which follow address themselves to questions such as these.

Suggested Readings

BENTZEN, MARY M. and Associates (1974). *Changing Schools: The Magic Feather Principle.* New York: McGraw-Hill, Inc.
The author describes a five-year study of change conducted in 18 elementary schools organized into a League of Co-operating Schools. The study was based upon the assumption that the single school is the key unit of educational change. Various organizational characteristics were measured as the school staffs attempted to improve their instructional programmes. Notable among these was the problem-solving process referred to as dialogue, decision making, action and evaluation (DDAE). (This is one of several books to be published from 1973 through 1975 in the *I/D/E/A series on Educational Change.**

TYE, KENNETH A. (1973). 'Effecting Change in Elementary Schools.' In: *The Elementary School in the United States,* The Seventy-second Yearbook of the National Society for the Study of Education, Part II, University of Chicago Press, Illinois.
This article reviews the current state of elementary education in the United States including the reasons why schools have a difficult time changing. Existing and emerging change strategies are discussed and the League of Co-operating Schools project is described in some detail.

CHASE, FRANCIS S. (1966). 'School Change in Perspective.' In: *The Changing American School,* The Sixty-fifth Yearbook of the National Society for the Study of Education, Part II, University of Chicago Press, Illinois.
In this chapter, Chase analyses the reasons for new societal demands upon education in the United States. He then proceeds to describe how the schools have or have not responded to these demands. Finally, he sets forth some possibilities for bringing societal needs and educational developments closer together.

EISNER, ELLIOT, W. (ed.) (1971) *Confronting Curriculum Reform.* Boston, Massachusetts: Little, Brown and Company (Inc.)
The articles in this book were originally prepared for presentation at the Cubberly Curriculum Conference held at Stanford University in 1969. They are written by leading curriculum workers in the United States. The book

---

* I/D/E/A/ (The Institute for Development of Educational Activities) is a non-profit organization focused upon improved schooling. It is funded by the C. F. Kettering Foundation. Other titles in the series are: *The Power to Change* (CULVER and HOBAN, eds.), *Effective Organizational Renewal in Schools* (WILLIAMS, WALL, MARTIN and BERCHIN), *Teachers on Individualization* (SHIPMAN, CULVER, LIEBERMAN, eds.), *The School in Transition* (TYE and NOVOTNEY), *The Dynamics of Educational Change* (GOODLAD), and *The Conduct of Research in School* (BENTZEN, et al.).

represents an effort to find out from those who have struggled with the tasks of curriculum making and curriculum implementation how they have gone about their work. It looks at problems indigenous to curriculum making to identify their common and unique characteristics and to suggest alternative approaches to curriculum development. Chapters by such authors as Benjamin Bloom, Lee Cronbach, Robert Karplus, Edward Begle, Michael Scriven and James Macdonald appear in the book.

GOODLAD, JOHN I., M. FRANCES KLEIN and Associates (1970). *Behind the Classroom Door*. Worthington, Ohio: Charles A. Jones Publishing Company.
This research report is based upon in-depth observations and interviews and interviews in 158 classrooms in 67 elementary schools in the United States. It begins by summarizing some of the organizational, curricular and instructional thrusts which have been widely recommended for schools. After describing the procedures for data collection, the authors then analyse their data. Finally, conclusions and generalizations about schools and classrooms are set forth. The book is appended with a valuable outline form for use in observing and interviewing in schools and classrooms.

JOYCE, BRUCE and MARSHA WEILL (1972). *Models of Teaching*. London: Prentice-Hall International.
The authors set forth 15 models of teaching based upon social interaction, information processing, personal and behaviour modification data sources. Examples of each model in use are given and methods for determining their appropriateness for teachers and learners in elementary and secondary schools are described. The book is so rich in ideas for curriculum development and is so well based in theory and practice that it should be required reading for all students of curriculum.

SARASON, SEYMOUR (1971). *The Culture of the School and the Problem of Change*. Boston, Massachusetts: Allyn and Bacon, Inc.
Sarason writes this book about change in schools from a social-psychological perspective. That is, he attempts to describe and to understand the aspects of the culture of the school, the roles played by actors in the school drama, and the consequences of interactions caused by the interaction of those actors and that culture. The focus of the book reflects a value judgment that among all the aspects of the school culture that are or may be the object of change, none is as important as the quality of life in the classroom and that the role of the teacher and principal are obviously crucial. This is not to say that curriculum workers should not attempt to bring about change. However, it does say that such attempts *must* be rooted in a deep understanding of the culture of the school. The book has a good bibliography.

Chapter 7

The Operational Curriculum

Introduction

The saying: 'Man proposes, God disposes' has its analogue when one comes to consider how the curriculum is dealt with in schools and classrooms, how what is prescribed as the content of teaching is handled by teachers, given reality in the classroom and understood by pupils and students. Curriculum proposals, whether in teachers' guides or plans for courses of study, suggest what should be taught, they do not determine what is taught let alone what is learned. What should be taught has to make an accommodation with many factors. With the varying competence of teachers, the interests of pupils, the physical and psychological conditions under which learning has to take place not to mention the ideology subsumed within the curricular proposals and implicit in the methods of teaching and learning adopted. It is with the nature of the accommodation of the intended curriculum to its context and with what results that we are concerned in this Chapter.

What results is termed the 'operational curriculum', the study of which is illustrated in the papers which follow.

The first paper by Barnes is a theoretical paper which by focusing on the uses of language in the classroom aims to illuminate a neglected factor in shaping what pupils and students learn in the classroom. This neglected factor is the teacher's talk and students' response to it, the language he uses and the part it plays as a major vehicle of student learning and a significant ingredient of the operational curriculum. By references to case studies Barnes suggests how language is used in the process of operationalizing the curriculum and shaping student learning.

Barnes argument is based on a model of teaching which accounts for the interrelationships of the major variables in classroom interaction—pupils' expectation, the context of the situation and the uses of language—and his major argument runs as follows: By his use of language in the classroom the teacher talks his students into those ways of thinking and understanding which the teacher considers correct. Just how this happens—what mechanism or process is involved—is still a matter for conjecture, but that it does is demonstrable, so Barnes claims. He goes on to argue that we can neither understand the nature of teaching nor how students give meaning to their curricular experience, until we appreciate the language of the classroom.

Walker's paper is also concerned with language as the medium for shaping the operational curriculum. Not the spoken language of the teacher and student but the written work set by teachers for students to do. What kind and approach to learning does the written work set in schools (and for that matter, in homework and other assignments) imply? Walker explores an answer to this question by examining different types of written work: student's explanatory accounts, the way they handle technical terms and jargon, and the use of secondary sources in their writing. Again, a case study approach is used and the material ranging from written work in Chemistry and History to English and Biology is used to illustrate the points made. Walker's thesis is that written work rather than being used as a means for deepening thought and feeling is used in a very limited way by teachers for evaluation and feedback, thus an important part of the operational curriculum is seen by students as a test and by teachers:

'as a measurement of "progress", not as a means of learning or coming to terms with new ideas, attitudes and values.'

Because of this one aspect of the curricular experience of students is narrowed, and in their written work they are forced to concentrate on what will pass the test and not on what will enable them to increase mastery over the subject matter and enhance their general cognitive capabilities.

Readings

---

*Language and Learning in the Classroom**

Douglas Barnes *University of Leeds Institute of Education*

Morton D. Waimon of Illinois State University pointed out in a recent article in this journal[1] that 40 years' research in the United States into 'teacher effectiveness' had been generally fruitless. Such research failed because it looked for the permanent characteristics of an ideal teacher, as all pupils responded best to the same teaching. The researchers were therefore unable to say anything to teachers which would help them improve their teaching.

Having thus dismissed earlier research into classroom behaviour, Dr Waimon turned to three more recent lines of research, those associated respectively with B. Othanel Smith, Arno Bellack, and Ned Flanders.[2] He pointed out that these studies have abandoned general statements about teachers in favour of the study of 'linguistic behaviour during teacher-pupil interaction'. Such studies of language in the classroom are based upon written transcriptions of tape-recordings made during lessons. By moving closer to the verbal give-and-take of lessons the researcher is more likely to be able to make statements which will be useful to teachers. 'Knowing what to observe about one's own teaching is the first step towards improving effectiveness.' So far one cannot but applaud.

It is when Dr Waimon goes on to demonstrate a method of analysis which he approves of—using methods very different from those of Bellack or Flanders—that one must dissent from his judgment. He quotes a short passage, but does not indicate whether it is constructed or comes from a real lesson. The teacher's statements have been analysed

---

* This article has been reproduced from the *Journal of Curriculum Studies* (3, 1, 1971) by permission of the author and Wm. Collins Sons and Company Ltd.

into large functional categories, such as gaining pupils' attention, disciplining pupils, making a statement about goals. The teacher's statements are also put into one of three categories derived from Thorndike: getting or maintaining readiness, helping pupils to emit an appropriate response, and rating pupil responses.

It is hard to see how either of these crude forms of categorizing teachers' language will be of any more help to teachers than the earlier researches which were so justly dismissed. In effect, the researcher, in his eagerness to find categories which will allow him to quantify, moves away too soon from the language itself into generalities, before he has found what it is that the teacher can most usefully perceive about his language. (This could be argued against Flanders's methods too.) Language functions not only on the large scale of whole utterances and their overt and deliberate meanings, but simultaneously at various lower levels which sometimes carry quite other messages through the details of formal organization and intonation. It seems likely that pupils interpret not only the teacher's overt statements about what he wants, and how he values what they say and do, but also interprets signals carried at other levels. Thus it is not enough to analyse the teacher's language only at the so-called 'functional' level. Some writers have used the phrase 'the hidden curriculum'[3] (by analogy perhaps with Thelen's 'the hidden agenda'[4]) to refer to any classroom learning which goes on in spite of the teacher's conscious aims, perhaps determined by the personalities of teachers or pupils, by the teacher's unacknowledged assumptions about classroom control, and so on. For example, many teachers who include amongst their curricular aims that of teaching pupils to 'think critically' can be shown to be encouraging pupils in passive habits of learning which are far from critical.[5]

The kinds of information likely to escape from Dr Waimon's analysis can be illustrated by an extract from a transcript of an actual lesson. A teacher of Religious Education was asking 11-year-old pupils to recapitulate information about life in New Testament Palestine.

T. How did they get the water from the well? . . . do you remember? . . . Yes?

P.1 They . . . ran the bucket down . . . er . . . and it was fastened on to this bit of string and it (*Here the words become inaudible for a phrase or two*) . . . other end to the water.

T. You might do it that way . . . Where did they put the water . . . John?

P.2 In a big . . . er . . . pitcher.
T.   Good . . . in a pitcher . . . which they carried on their . . .?
P.2 Heads.
T.   Good.

In Dr Waimon's system this might be categorized as:

Recall question
Neutral rating (or Negative Rating)
More effort
Positive rating

And these would go to swell the number of items in each of these categories. But this would totally miss what is of interest to the teacher in this episode.

An intuitive description of this episode might run like this: the teacher wants a one-word answer 'pitcher', but his first pupil interprets his question as an invitation to describe a mechanical device, thus translating a request for simple recall of information into a request to generate a sequence of reasoning. The teacher, his attention mainly on his own intentions, receives the pupil's reasoning with a neutral form of words but an intonation which is firmly rejective, and this rejection is intensified by the warm tone of approval with which he greets the answer which gives him the words he wants. If such a rejection were to happen several times during a lesson it would be likely to signal to children that this teacher valued the recall of names more highly than the use of language to go through a sequence of reasoning. What is interesting here is not that it is a rejection, but that it is a rejection of one activity in favour of another.

Now there is nothing in this account which could be proved, nor will this precise situation ever occur again. But this is not to say that this kind of examination of classroom language is of no use. It is much more likely to be useful to teachers—that is, to help them to inspect their own teaching—than that represented by Dr Waimon's example. Moreover, the future development of objective research may necessitate the detailed examination of recordings and transcriptions to elicit from them those dimensions of situation which affect children's performance.

What has so far been argued against Dr Waimon's approach is that it is over-rationalistic. The example just given was intended to illustrate how easily the essential nature of an exchange can be lost in such an analysis. Another inadequacy of this approach is that in focusing upon the teacher's intentions it totally ignores the pupils' contributions, and what lies behind them, that is, their interpretations of what the teacher says and does. (It is only fair to point out that this is not true of the work of Bellack and his associates.) The teacher's behaviour does not exist in a void, but answers on the one hand to his curricular objectives and on the other to his perceptions of what his pupils are saying and doing. Part of good teaching lies in perceiving how the language used by pupils is contributing to or inhibiting their learning.

To call Dr Waimon's approach over-rationalistic is not to abdicate responsibility for what goes on in one's classroom. Indeed, to recognize the 'hidden curriculum', to perceive that pupils are learning to cope with the teacher's demands and with one another's as well as (or instead of) with the demands of the subject matter, is a step towards taking responsibility for one's part in this. Although the personal interactions of the classroom will probably never fall completely under the deliberate control of even the best teachers, we all wish to take as much responsibility as possible for what is learnt in our lessons. To do this teachers must become more aware of their classroom behaviour: at the same time as they are helped to be clear about curricular objectives, they should be helped to be more sharply perceptive of their own and their pupils' behaviour, and the relationship of this to their aims.

It is not enough to see the language of the classroom merely as the medium of classroom communication. Two other aspects of language are of importance to the teacher, and awareness of these must inform studies of classroom language. Language is so deeply embedded in many subjects of the secondary curriculum that it is sometimes difficult to separate learning the concepts and processes of a subject from learning to use language to represent and use these concepts and processes. The second aspect of language is potentially even more important: to put it succinctly, language is a means of learning. The very act of verbalizing new knowledge often requires a re-organizing of the old and the new together.[6] For these reasons language in the classroom must be discussed in a wider context than that implied by Dr Waimon's interest in classroom interaction.

This paper is based upon the assumption that language is a major means of learning, and that the pupils' uses of language for learning are strongly influenced by the teacher's language, which prescribes to them their rôles as learners. (The degree to which they accept this prescription depends upon the socio-linguistic expectations which they have built up during their past experience.) The mother tongue has an ambiguous status in the curriculum, because 'English' at once indicates a subject area, and a medium of learning and teaching. For this reason, it is not easy in secondary schools to apportion responsibility for the mother tongue. A slogan such as 'Every lesson is an English lesson' does nothing to specify to teachers, primary or secondary, what kind of responsibility for language is theirs. It tells them nothing about how their uses of language expand or limit the kinds of participation in learning open to their pupils. Thus, a study of the language of classroom interaction can be seen as a contribution to curricular theory in a second respect, in that it can help teachers other than English specialists to define their responsibilities for their pupils' uses of language.

Any study of the uses of language for teaching and learning in classrooms is of more than theoretical interest. Teachers are only partly aware of their own uses of language, and still less aware of how and to what extent classroom language determines the kinds of involvement in learning which are open to their pupils. Nor are most teachers able to give a systematic account of which language activities best contribute to different kinds of learning, and this suggests that they may not be clearly perceptive of their pupils' uses of language. For example, most science teachers from time to time set their pupils practical work in small groups, but it is not easy to find any account of what kind of discussion will best help pupils to make explicit to themselves the principles exemplified in the practical work, nor of how the teacher can see to it that such discussion takes place. Similarly, some secondary schools are increasingly using 'packets' of materials accompanied by instructions addressed to pupils for work in the area of Humanities; there is need for theory about the effect of different verbal formulations of such instructions, about the contexts in which they are carried out, and about the teacher's rôle in such work.

There is an urgent need in educational discussion not only for a general theory of the part played by language in cognitive learning, but for special theories of language and learning in the classroom. This is not the place to discuss the debate about whether language enables or merely facilitates the growth of concepts; the importance of language in the classroom at secondary level cannot be denied.

Language as a means of learning has in the past been obscured by the stress laid on language as a means of teaching, and theoretical insights into language for learning have not yet made any strong impact upon classroom practice. Bruner[7] hints at the importance for learning of the difference between listener's choices and speaker's choices. By this he probably implies that a speaker, in order to express a logically connected sequence of ideas, has to select, organize, and relate them, at each point of choice selecting only one of a number of options. To do this he must operate more or less complex criteria, which he will not normally make explicit, or even be aware of. A listener, on the other hand, may be able to follow a speaker through a logically-connected sequence without being in the least aware of the many options not taken up, or of the criteria which informed the speaker's choices. He will only learn to operate these criteria when he himself becomes a speaker. Elsewhere Bruner emphasizes reciprocity in learning. By 'reciprocal learning' he refers to the way we learn in a dialogue: even while we are still talking we receive from our interlocutor information which enables us to reshape what we say while we are saying it. In reciprocal learning the learner in the very act of finding a verbal form for what he is learning receives promptings and modifications from the interlocutor's reactions and replies. Bruner argues that since the feedback occurs at the moment of choice such dialogue provides ideal circumstances for internalizing the interlocutor's criteria. Bruner is arguing for a greater emphasis upon spoken language in learning, and in doing so aligns himself with Vygotsky.[8] It is not clear, however, whether it is the demand to verbalize which is of primary importance, or whether a reciprocal dialogue with an adult is essential.

To emphasize that language is a major means of learning is not of course to deny that there are other means. Piaget and his followers hold that children learn to conceptualize first and that language comes in as a means of completing and representing such processes as classification and seriation.[9] Furth[10] suggests that deaf children develop non-linguistic means of conceptualizing. Nevertheless Piaget has never denied that language is essential to formal operations, when the adolescent's ability to set up hypothetical systems and to make his own thought-processes the object of attention requires a symbolic system which is 'creative',[11] in the sense that language is. Bruner has argued interestingly[12] that a child, having first organized experience through motor activities and visually, begins to learn a language and thereafter spends many years re-elaborating this experience of reality in ways made possible by the characteristics of the linguistic system. Whichever point of view one takes it is clear that learning to use language to think with is an essential part of most of the learning which goes on in both primary and and secondary schools.

It has been suggested that the very act of verbalizing demands, a reorganization of ideas which merits the name of learning. A moment's reflection, however, reminds us of occasions when we have used language not to accept but to avoid new perceptions. Thus we should ask under what conditions the act of putting something into words brings us into more full possession of it. All talking and writing is not equally fresh-minted: we vary in the extent to which we challenge ourselves to think (and feel) afresh. Indeed, Lawton[13] has shown that adolescents differ greatly one from another in this respect: one pupil may challenge himself to use language to think abstractly, while another may do so only in answer to a teacher's questions. Therefore it is not enough to tell teachers that their pupils' language is important; it is necessary to help them to understand how they can arrange discussion and writing in their classrooms so that their pupils benefit from them in the ways which they wish. Such advice—it is here argued—must be based upon a theory of learning which takes account of the socio-linguistic characteristics of classrooms.

A theory of language and classroom learning would have to take account of four aspects of classroom interaction, each partly depending on the previous one.

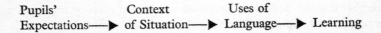

Pupils'   Context   Uses of
Expectations——▶ of Situation——▶ Language——▶ Learning

1. *Pupils' Expectations*

The classroom behaviour of pupils is heavily influenced by the expectations which they bring to the lesson. These have been set up both by the pupil's experience of language outside the classroom, and by his particular experience of language in lessons. These two require separate treatment. It is well established that pupils' uses of language vary with social class; these differences seem related to those expectations about the possible functions of language established in the social milieu to which the child belongs. Thus children from working class homes are likely to perceive differently from middle class children the demands for linguistic performance made upon them in school, and any theory must take this into account.[14] There are of course many other variations in children's uses of language besides those which correlate with social class. These expectations are not immutable, and one value of a close study of language in the classroom would be to help teachers to plan more systematically to influence their pupils' habitual uses of language, not for communication only but for thinking and feeling. Pupils' expectations are partly determined by what has happened in similar lessons, and this is controlled by the teachers.

These expectations are determined by such matters as the usual reception given to pupils' speech and writing, including the amount of explicit correction they receive, by the teacher's relative emphasis upon what has been said or how it has been said, by the interest he shows in the pupil's contributions. If a teacher asks only questions which require pupils to give back what they have been taught this is likely to affect their learning behaviour in all his lessons. If a teacher corrects spelling errors in writing but never comments on its content, this is likely to affect the kind of writing he receives. That is, the pupil's perception of the demands made on him, and the kinds of behaviour open to him, is partly determined by expectations set in previous lessons.

2. *Context of Situation*

The 'situation' in a lesson is not made of things but of meanings. These meanings arise as the pupils interpret the teacher's behaviour, one another's behaviour, and certain more objective matters (such as the size of the group) in the light of their expectations. Pupils' behaviour, including their language, is likely to be influenced by the way in which they perceive the subject matter and their rôle as learners of that subject, by the audience to which they are expected to address speech and writing, by the immediate task which they have been given (including how sharply it has been defined for them), by the presence or absence of non-verbal representations of the subject matter, by the relation of speech to any accompanying non-verbal activities, by the terms in which they are asked to speak or write, and so on. These aspects of the present situation are interpreted by the pupils in the light of their expectations about how much participation in the lesson is expected of them, and of what kinds, about the relevance of their own existing knowledge drawn from outside, in the light, that is, of their expectations about their rôles as learners in these lessons. Some secondary teachers abjure responsibility for the classroom contexts which they set up for their pupils' uses of language, and hold the English specialist responsible for all the linguistic behaviour of his pupils, even in contexts beyond his control.

3. *Uses of Language*

The uses to which language is put by the pupils in any lesson depend not merely on language tasks explicitly required by the teacher, but upon each pupil's perception of the whole situation which provides a context for language use. (Many teachers seem to be unaware of this, and treat language as if it were a skill which can be learnt and then be available for use whatever the context of situation.) Psychological studies of the development of older children's language have in the past assumed that either spoken or written language behaviour can be usefully represented as a single ability without reference to context of situation. Context has either been held constant, or a variety of contexts have been treated as if homogeneous. There is an urgent need for studies of children's language which indicate those dimensions of situation which correlate with formal and other characteristics of the language used. Not enough is at present known about how various uses of language function as means of learning, nor about the extent to which these are determined by the pupil's perception of the context for that language.

4. *Learning*

A theoretical account of language and classroom learning could not stop short at classroom language, but would relate different uses of language to different learning outcomes. (Britton,[15] for example, discusses particular group conversations with and without the presence of a teacher and makes surmises about the kinds of learning which such conversations make possible.) To see the learning outcomes in terms of the results of pencil and paper tests, however, would not necessarily be appropriate: such tests carry their own rigorous context of situation, and this limits their use as a means of defining the outcomes of a range of different contexts. For example, there is reason to believe that children differ one from another in the extent to which their performance is determined by context. When pupils' performances on tests have served as dependent variables in correlation studies of classroom interaction this has seldom produced convincing results: here is a considerable methodological problem.

Such a theory lies at the intersection of a number of academic disciplines. It is socio-linguistic in that it is concerned with the constraints upon pupils' language behaviour which arise from expectations brought from other social situations and from the characteristics of the classroom as a social setting. It lies within social psychology in that it is concerned with the manner in which certain social processes become transmuted into patterns of individual behaviour. It is necessarily evaluative rather than descriptive, since it must concern itself with making statements which might help teachers suit their means to their ends. In this context, however, it is most appropriate to note that this theory falls also into the field of curriculum theory. By beginning with the socio-linguistic constraints of the classroom, and moving from these to pupils' language and consequent learning, such a theory would invert the sequence which has become habitual in curriculum theory. A theory of language and classroom learning would begin with an analysis of some factors limiting pupils' performance in the classroom seen as a socio-linguistic context and then relate performance to kinds of learning. This sequence seems appropriate because classroom language, stemming from the language habits and assumptions of teacher and pupils, has a life of its own which is not entirely responsive to the immediate conscious intentions of the teacher.

Our understanding of how language acts as a means of classroom learning is so limited that naturalistic studies of classroom language at present provide insights quite out of proportion to their size. General descriptions of the language of lessons, uninformed by hypotheses about what dimensions of the language interaction are related to learning, are likely to be more time-consuming than fruitful. (This is to some degree true of the work of Bellack and his associates.) One value of naturalistic studies based upon the largely intuitive interpretation of language recorded in lessons is that they can provide the hypotheses for more systematic investigation. The present writer's study of 12 lessons taught during pupils' first term in secondary schools can be used to illustrate[16] the kinds of question raised by naturalistic studies of classroom language.

1. *The Pupils*

Eleven-year-old pupils' contributions to 12 lessons in various secondary subjects showed these characteristics:

(a) On only eleven occasions did a pupil, by asking a question, or by offering a statement that was not a reply to the teacher, initiate a sequence of interaction.

(b) There were few occasions when pupils could be said to be 'thinking aloud', that is, reorganizing learning or solving a problem by verbalizing it. Most contributions from pupils were of one word or a little longer.

(c) On only two occasions were there exploration of the meaning of a word, though definitions of technical terms were asked for and given.

(d) Only in one lesson (physics) did pupils frequently mention out-of-school experience in order to relate it to new ideas being learnt.

In sum, the pupils were on the whole passive recipients of instruction, their rôle being mainly confined to indicating in short answers that they could rehearse what had previously been taught. Could these and other characteristics of their rôle behaviour as learners be shown to relate to characteristics of the teacher's rôle behaviour?

2. *Teachers' Demands on Pupils*
Study of teachers' questions proved informative:

(a) In many of the lessons (particularly in arts subjects) a majority of the teacher's questions asked for factual replies.

(b) Teachers hardly ever asked questions in order to get information which they did not possess: they used questions mainly to test recollection of what had been taught previously.

(c) In some lessons pupils were asked to reason aloud: this often implied that they were to go over a sequence of thought given by the teacher. Teachers hardly ever followed a brief reply by requesting the pupil to expand it or make it more explicit. Teachers not infrequently interrupted pupils who did try to answer at length.

(d) Questions which asked pupils to refer to first-hand experience outside school were almost absent.

3. *Teachers' Use and Awareness of Language*

(a) With one exception these teachers did not make much use in these lessons of the technical terminology of their subject specialism: when they did they usually seemed to be aware of doing so.

(b) The teachers tended to use technical terms as labels rather than as instruments of thought.

(c) All but one of the teachers used a great deal of what might be called 'text-book language', which, though not specific to the subject, referred to important concepts and processes. (For example: 'the position of . . . in relation to . . .') They seemed unaware that they used this language, or that it might provide difficulties of comprehension, or otherwise affect pupils' participation in the lesson.

(*d*) The language of one teacher was much more colloquial and less like written prose than that of the others. (The fact that this was accompanied by an unusually high level of pupil-participation suggests a topic for investigation.)

(*e*) Teachers varied in the explicitness with which they gave instructions to classes. (A similar variation in mothers' teaching styles to their small children has been usefully investigated.[17])

(*f*) Some teachers worked from non-verbal representations of subject-matter: diagrams, working models, pictures. It seems possible that in these cases language was used more by pupils and less by teachers, because the non-verbal media made the subject-matter open to public discussion. Success in explanation could be checked against public criteria provided by the model or diagram.

These notes will suggest that it would not be difficult to hypothesize relationships between dimensions of teachers' classroom behaviour and dimensions of pupils' learning behaviour, and that these hypotheses could form the basis for more objective studies. Some less obvious lines of inquiry include:

(*a*) The rate of questioning[18] which might be related to
   (*i*) a taxonomical analysis of questions
   (*ii*) the syntactical complexity of questions[19] and
   (*iii*) the length and complexity of pupils' replies

(*b*) The extent to which pupils focus attention upon the given task or upon unintended signals from the teacher; this might be related to various dimensions of pupils' past experience and of the immediate context of situation. (Holt's unrigorous but perceptive books are suggestive here.[20])

(*c*) Teachers' linguistic styles,[21] which may relate to the level of pupil-participation, and especially to pupils' uses of language (i) for exploration as against providing expected answer, and (ii) for relating new knowledge to existing schemata.

(*d*) Syntactic and other characteristics of pupils' uses of language for learning, varying the context of situation, especially the presence and behaviour of the teacher.

This is not intended to suggest that the time for naturalistic studies is past. For example, it seems unlikely that (*d*) will be very valuable until informal studies of children's language have suggested significant dimensions of context of situation and ways of making them operational.

These suggestions, however, relate to only one aspect of Language in the Classroom, that is, to the effect of teachers' speech behaviour upon pupils' participation in learning. Other topics which would repay study include pupils' language in small group work, and variations in children's writing according to topic and context. But these possibilities cannot be developed here.

It would be absurd to suggest that an increased attention to classroom language will do miracles. Not only is there increasing evidence that teachers' non-verbal behaviour has an important influence on pupils' participation in lessons, but it is clearly possible that there are deeper levels of a child's personality which, by the time he first attends school, have already taken on an overall 'set' towards new experience. Notwithstanding Bernstein's work, it is not yet clear how far such personality patterns are available to change by new language experiences. In any case, pupils' lives outside school may be pushing them in quite other directions. It must also be admitted that some pupils do manage to learn passively from heavily directive teaching, perhaps entering into a silent dialogue with the lecturing teacher. Which pupils these are, and what previous experiences have lent them this ability, are also matters of interest.

Yet even when all these concessions have been made, the relationship between language and learning in the classroom remains a matter of great practical importance. If all teachers could learn to be as sensitive to language in the classroom as some already are, this might significantly raise the level of learning in all our schools.

Notes

1. M. D. WAIMON (1969), 'Judging the Effectiveness of Teaching,' *Journal of Curriculum Studies*, 1, 3 (November).
2. See A. A. BELLACK *et al.* (1966), *The Language of the Classroom*. New York: Teachers' College, Columbia. Papers by Smith and by Flanders can be seen in B. J. BIDDLE and W. J. ELLENA (eds.) (1964), *Contemporary Research on Teacher Effectiveness*. Holt, Rinehart and Winston.
3. See the valuable discussion of this in PHILIP W. JACKSON (1968), *Life in Classrooms*. Holt, Rinehart and Winston.
4. H. A. THELEN (1954), *Dynamics of Groups at Work*. University of Chicago Press.

5. As in D. R. GALLO (1968), 'Toward a more effective assessment of poetry teaching methods', *Research in the Teaching of English*, 2, 2.
6. See JAMES BRITTON and BERNARD NEWSOME (1968), 'What is learnt in English Lessons?', *Journal of Curriculum Studies*, 1, 1 (November).
7. J. S. BRUNER (1962), *On Knowing*. Cambridge, Mass.: Harvard University Press.
8. L. VYGOTSKY (1962), *Thought and Language*. (MIT).
9. e.g. B. INHELDER and J. PIAGET (1964), *The Early Growth of Logic in the Child*. London: Routledge.
10. H. FURTH (1966), *Thinking without Language*. Free Press.
11. NOAM CHOMSKY (1965), *Aspects of the Theory of Syntax*. MIT.
12. JEROME S. BRUNER et al. (1966), *Studies in Cognitive Growth*. New York: Wiley.
13. D. LAWTON (1968), *Social Class, Language and Education*. London: Routledge.
14. See LAWTON (1968), *op. cit.*
15. JAMES BRITTON (1969), 'Talking to Learn.' In: D. BARNES, J. N. BRITTON and H. ROSEN *Language, the Learner and the School*. Harmondsworth: Penguin.
16. D. BARNES (1969), 'Language in the Secondary Classroom'. In: BARNES, BRITTON and ROSEN (1969), *op. cit.*
17. R. D. HESS and V. C. SHIPMAN (1965), 'Early Experience and the Socialization of Cognitive Modes in Children', *Child Development*, 36, 4.
18. J. HOETKER (1968), 'Teacher questioning behaviour in nine Junior High School English classes', *Research in the Teaching of English*, 2, 2.
19. D. SCARBROUGH (1968), 'The Language of the Primary Teacher', *English for Immigrants*, 2, 1.
20. J. HOLT (1964), *How Children Fail*. Pitman.
21. A study by M. A. Fitzpatrick of the effect of different language styles in lecturing is described in G. KEMELFIELD, 'Progress Report of the Schools Television Research Project—111', *Educational Television International*, 3, 2, July, 1969.

Written Work and its Objectives: Attitudes to Written English in School*

Ralph G. Walker *City and Carnegie College of Education, Leeds*

Introduction to the study

This study of children's writing in school was undertaken with the purpose of distinguishing significant factors affecting pupils' writing activities.

---

* This article has been reproduced from the *Journal of Curriculum Studies* (4, 2, 1972) by permission of the author and Wm. Collins Sons and Company Ltd.

The material for the study was drawn from the work of six third-year pupils from a large comprehensive school, whose IQs ranged from 100–124. Three pupils were selected from a form in the 'A' band (Paul, Howard and Louise) and three from a form in the 'B' band (Paula, Stuart and Karen) to represent high, middle and low ability within each form. The 'A' band represented the top 120 children in the year arranged in four mixed ability classes; the 'B' band represented the middle 120 children in a year arranged in four mixed ability classes. Their writing in four subjects—English, History, Biology and Chemistry—was examined. All the writing carried out in the first term of the school year in each subject was read through and a record made of the amount and the kinds of writing involved. Photocopies were taken of at least three recent pieces of continuous writing in each of the four subjects for all six pupils. This was to constitute the sample for close analysis.

The eight members of staff who taught the relevant subjects to the pupils concerned were interviewed individually, and the pupils were interviewed in two groups of three. The resultant material provided an impression of the contexts in which writing took place and of attitudes towards it, so that a frame of reference for the analysis of the samples was available.

Teachers' views on writing

Generally the teachers interviewed seemed to expect competence in matters of spelling, punctuation, and paragraphing, though in most cases they did not penalize work for weaknesses in any of these three categories. What this means, I think, is that they expect children to be able to write fairly well by virtue of the fact that they are native speakers of the language, but that when poor spelling, punctuation and para-graphing occur—as they often do—they feel they must disregard most of these errors to concentrate on the content. Thus they are failing to pay much attention to technical language matters and generally ignoring the linguistic difficulties the children are encountering in dealing with the content.

None of the teachers said that they made any formal requirements about the kind of language the pupils were to use in their writing tasks. In most cases they wanted the pupils to feel free to express themselves in their own way. However, the teachers were not really aware of how the writing situations and their own habitual expectations and language use in class were in fact limiting the children's freedom in using language. Nor were they aware that children need positive help and guidance in adjusting to different types of writing tasks. To assume that children are free to express themselves when no formal language requirements are made upon them is to miss the essential issues involved.

The appearance of written work seems to be an important consideration for most teachers. But my impression is that their attention is more likely to be focused on superficial matters such as: correct headings underlined, work ruled off, neat and clear handwriting, and other general matters concerned with the look of the page, than on the selection and organizing of material and the expression of it. That is, I think they are looking for the required content presented in a neat and tidy fashion rather than looking for the individual organizing and expression of material.

The fact that teachers usually award a mark to each piece of written work tends to foster in pupils an unfortunate attitude towards the act of writing. Writing comes to be seen as a test, as a measurement of 'progress', not as a means of learning, or coming to terms with new ideas, attitudes and values.

Pupils' use of language in writing

From the analysis of the sample of pupils' writing, a number of categories emerged which seemed to form useful foci for raising relevant specific issues.

1. *Explanatory accounts*

For pupils one of the problems with an explanatory account lies in the question of to whom the explanation is addressed. Is is to be objective, directed at a diffuse general reader? Is it to be an expression of the pupil's attempt to understand the topic? Is it to be a means for the pupil to demonstrate to himself whether he can explain a particular process? Or is it to be a reproduction 'in the pupil's own words' of the teacher's form of explanation? It is obvious that the style of explanation adopted will change according to where the emphasis is placed.

The following extract from Howard's account in Biology suggests he is certainly in no position to explain: the material would appear to be too difficult for him to understand, and it is obvious that the teacher has not considered the problem of 'audience' and how this would affect the pupil's writing.

> Energy brakes off from the glucose and changes the ADP into ATP
> and the last phosphate ATP contains a lot of energy, which is
> liberated in the cells and the ATP changes back to ADP after the
> extra phosphates has been used as energy.

The breathless, syntactic rush of this sentence with its accumulation
of 'ands' reveals the minimum attempt (or ability) to relate together the
separate items of information. Furthermore, does it not seem confusing
to treat 'energy' as a chemical label like 'carbon', 'hydrogen', 'oxygen'
and 'phosphate'?

In general, the writing of scientific explanations is not easy for
children, and yet, not infrequently, pupils are expected to carry out such
tasks without the problems involved in this type of writing being
sufficiently considered by the teachers. For instance, an account of
respiration in the frog seemed to consist simply of filling in the spaces
between specialist terms like 'buccal cavity', 'muscular exertion',
'respire', 'respiratory surface', etc. The stiff, artificial style engendered
by this kind of impersonal writing shuts off contact with immediate
concrete experience. And the children cannot be said to be learning
much as it is not their 'own' language they are using. Knowing the
appropriate words does not mean that pupils understand the concepts
and processes.

Again in science children are too often expected to write in an
impersonal mode, i.e. a style appropriate to a vague general audience,
before they have progressed very far in the subject, and this mode is
often regarded by teachers as *the* scientific mode. However, there are
numerous ways of writing in science. The manner adopted usually for
scientific writing in schools is in many respects an outcome of the history
of the subject in schools and of the influence of textbooks, which act as
carriers of the traditional myth of what the appropriate form of writing
is for a particular subject.

In history pupils easily confuse the distinction—which admittedly
is not always easy to make—between explanatory accounts and narrative
or descriptive accounts. However, this is a distinction of which they
ought to be made aware, otherwise they accept ready-made explanations
as if they were unshakeable facts. The following example illustrates
how Howard is pasting together scraps of information, which are all
but meaningless to him, and in consequence writing an incoherent
explanation. What knowledge, if any, is gained will result from the
uncritical adoption of assertions presented to him.

Before 1914 Britain was in a fix. The TA of 1913 included Railway, Minery and Transport Union. The aim of the TA was to persuade the govt. and parl. This is political not industrial action. The GNCTU also wanted to do this.

One is forced to the conclusion that the role and purpose of explanatory accounts by pupils in schools needs more precise definition. The subject matter of an explanation needs to be within the intellectual grasp of the pupil; the means by which he gains the information necessary for the explanation needs careful consideration; and the form which an explanation is to take and the audience to whom it is addressed are crucial educational matters affecting the degree of learning the pupil acquires.

2. *Technical terms and subject jargon*

Another feature of language use which has a direct bearing upon the child's understanding of what he writes is subject jargon—the specialist technical terms and associated phraseology. For instance, in the pupils' accounts of a chemistry experiment—'The Preparation of Salt by Titration'—there is very little indication that the pupils understand what is entailed in the term 'titration'. In only one account did a pupil attempt to be explicit about the key idea of 'neutralization'.

There is a problem too in the pupils' use of general concept terms: such as, 'constant weight', 'energy', 'generates', 'liberated', 'can maintain health' in science; 'political levy', 'ballot', 'contracting out', 'revolution', 'political action not industrial action', 'government and parliament' in history. Pupils, intentionally or not, are prone to use such terms so glibly as to avoid the thought which greater explicitness would entail. This does not mean that pupils should be barred from using technical terms, but it does mean that teachers need to ensure that pupils are familiar with the significance of such terms through the means of class discussion and by providing opportunities for them to come to an understanding of the terms in free writing situations where they have a chance to work out the concepts in their own more personal language. Such strategies on the teachers' part might avoid the following: 'The enzymes act as catalysts, i.e. they speed up the *chemistry of digestion.*'

History textbooks often use 'concept' words to save pages of careful description of motive and action. Such abstractness conveys little to children of the concrete reality of the events and of the times, and often leads to consequent meaninglessness for them. This situation undoubtedly has a direct bearing on the kind of writing pupils employ themselves in history lessons, since in very many cases it is substantially dependent upon a limited number of textbooks.

An interesting instance of specialist language in an English context occurs in comprehension exercises. For instance, in a comprehension exercise on T. S. Eliot's poem *Macavity*, we find such examples of language use as the following: 'The adjective which best describes . . .', 'The main purposes . . .', 'The noun which could be used to describe . . .', 'parody'. A most striking feature of the language of the pupils' answer is the linguistic constraint arising from taking over the wording of the question. This linguistic constraint obviously mirrors cognitive constraint too. For instance, all the answers to the question: 'Which one word most appropriately sums up Macavity's behaviour?' take the form of a clumsy re-phrasing of the question with the word 'elusive' inserted into the right syntactical slot with little effort or thought. Since all the pupils use very much the same format and the key word 'elusive' it is unlikely that they have arrived individually, by the processes of thought, at the conclusion that 'elusive' was in fact the most appropriate word to sum up Macavity's behaviour. Most likely the word had come up in discussion or had circulated by means of a class whisper, so that the word was simply being used as a counter to fill the blank in the sentence formed from the original question.

Again, the following three answers to a comprehension question on the poem *Cynddylan* by R. S. Thomas illustrate how the pupils rephrase the question and prepare a total linguistic format into which they slot lexical information arrived at without much purposeful thought.

Question: Why is Cynddylan described as a 'knight at arms'?
Answers: (i) He is a knight because the clutches curse and the gears obey.
  (ii) Cynddylan is described as a knight at arms because he is always ready for the next days work.
  (iii) He is described as a knight at arms for he has all his farming equipment.

Indeed it would seem generally from the answers the children write that few of these pupils are exploring into the meaning of the words and phrases in terms of the poem.

3. *Loose compilations from secondary sources*

Much of the pupils' writing in history and in biology seemed to be little more than a mere tacking together of discrete items of information gleaned either from teacher or textbook. The following extracts reveal a clumsy manipulation of set phrases from a secondary source:

Karen

The insects have *breathing pores along the side of it*. These pores *lead into an extensive branching system of tubes called tracheae*. These *lead air right into the body* which alternately compress and release the main tracheae so that the tidal air flows in and out of them.

Paula

Along the sides of an insects are a number of *breathing pores* which *lead into an extensive branching system of tubes called tracheae*. These tubes *lead air right into the body*. The air is then renewed by pumping movements of the body, *which alternately compress and release the main tracheae so that air flows in and out* of them, this air is *tidal air*. (My italics draw attention to phrasing similarities.)

The second version, being more explicit, illustrates how the first pupil is confusing the sense by attempting to compress the information with little understanding of the meaning of the process she is describing. For instance, she confuses the pumping movements of the body and the contractions of the main tracheae, and she also unwarrantedly anticipates 'tidal' in 'the tidal air flows in and out of them'.

Even though the second account is fairly explicit and certainly comprehensible, the fact that so many phrases are little more than echoes from a secondary source suggests that the language this girl is using is not to any large extent being employed to make this meaningful to her; it is much more a matter of presenting the expected content in a form judged appropriate for the teacher.

An example from a historical account demonstrates a patchwork of discrete items of information, from which one gathers that Paul has little real idea of what was going on.

The Dockers were unskilled and uneducated workers. The people think that they would be difficult to organize into a union. So the dockers were doing casual work and getting payed about 4d. to 5d. a hour. The dockers want 6d. a hour and 4 hour day. The London

Dockers Strike was organized by Ben Tillett, John Burns and Tom
Mann. The strike was peaceful, well organized meeting processions
which won public sympathy. The contributions flowed in, £30,000
came from Australia. The strike last several weeks. This paved way
for New Unions of Unskilled Workers.

Paul is not making this material meaningful to himself in any significant
sense. There is no attempt to organize the material coherently; the
content simply follows a simple chronological narrative line. The
relationships between none of the separate items are made explicit in any
way. A further revealing feature is the fluctuations of tense between
present and past in the first half of the account; not a sign of strong
cognitive control. Even the choice of verbs—if indeed much choice
existed—is flat and conventional.

4. *Precision and degree of explicitness*

The acknowledgement by teachers of content without a complementary acknowledgement of the language with which it is expressed
does tend to lead to indecision on the question of the degree of accuracy
and explicitness required in children's writing.

The problem is essentially two-fold: pupils need to be encouraged
to be self-critical of their thoughts and the expression of them, but
they are not in a position to be self-critical unless they have a reasonable
understanding of what it is they are writing about. If teachers of science,
for instance, always require a 'finished' report of an experiment, and
allow little or no 'explanatory' investigation into the nature of the
experiment through discussion and individual 'personal' writing such
wholly inadequate accounts as the following by Paula are likely to
continue to occur.

'To find out what happens when we mix acids and alkalines'
    Method We put some hydrochloric acid into a burette and fixed the
            burette to a clamp stand.
            From a pipette we filled a beaker which contained 26 c.c.
            of sodium hydroxide, we placed the beaker underneath the
            burette to this we added 2.11 drops of acid (hydrochloric)
            into the beaker, we then added a few drops of Universal
            Indicator. The colour of the liquid slowly started to change
            to a neutral colour with the help of universal indicator.

Result   Acid is a lot more concentrated than alkalines, also it is a lot weaker. After this we evaporated it (the mixture we have now got) this result was a white powdery solid we then tested it and got a very good result; this result was SALT.

We could point out first that in sentence one the natural order of actions is reversed; the fixing ought to occur before the pouring. In sentence two 'From a pipette' is unnecessarily ambiguous; 'by means of' is clearer and more appropriate. In the same sentence 'which contained' is an anticipation of the completed action. The pupil is not relating the filling and containing correctly. And, furthermore, there is the confusion between 'filling', which suggests to the brim, and pouring in a set quantity of liquid, which might or might not fill the beaker. Following on from this, we again find the sequence of actions reversed; the Universal Indicator should be added to the alkaline solution before the acid is allowed to drop into it. Perhaps the most significant point is where the pupil seems to be confusing the concept of neutralization with the neutral colour of the solution: 'the liquid slowly started to change to a neutral colour'. Her thought seems to be focused on the change in colour rather than on the significance arising from the visible change. And, furthermore, what does she mean by a 'neutral colour'? She mentioned no specific colours in her account.

The following extract from Paul's biology account of 'The Essentials of a Healthy Diet' reveals a number of unsatisfactory features with regard to precision of thought and expression and acceptable explicitness.

These (referring to a list of six items) must be present in the food before a mammal can maintain health. Water is not really food since it is removed by sweat, urine and expired air. Water like oxygen is essential to mammals but it is not swallowed so as it is excluded from the term 'food'.

Another pupil, Howard, obviously assumes that the reader knows what he means and therefore takes little care over thought and language. One of his sentences in a chemistry account reads, 'the acid was run down to 20.9 c.c. and we then put the conical flask underneath with the tap on until it read 41.3.' 'Run down' is not appropriate in context, and the figure has no significance unless one knows how much acid one started with. Why doesn't he mention the precise amount of acid let out of the burette into the alkaline solution? 'With the tap on', of course, does not connect up syntactically with its correct antecedent, and this happens because the antecedent is not stated. The final clause is unacceptably ambiguous.

Consideration of these few examples would appear to indicate, among other possibilities, that the pupils have a grasp of the materials but are just not bothered to make a careful presentation of their work, or that the pupils simply have not sufficient grasp of the material to be self-critical of the expression of their thought. In the first instance the pupils are not interested in being precise and explicit; in the second they are in no position to apply any kind of criteria to what they write. It would seem that the two possible causes of weaknesses in pupils' writing to which I have just referred could be overcome, to some extent, by the teacher providing a better opportunity for pupils to pursue a more thorough 'personal' exploration of the material with which they are dealing. Through class and group discussion pupils might be led to develop criteria by reference to which they could produce written accounts which met the teachers' expectations satisfactorily and at the same time constituted valuable 'learning' experiences.

Conditions affecting the use of language by pupils

In many of the pieces of writing examined there seemed to be too much vagueness about their purpose. This was not entirely surprising since the teachers, when interviewed, had encountered difficulties on being asked to be explicit and precise on the purposes of the written work they set.

Science teachers placed an emphasis on the writing up of experiments as an aid to the training of observation. But what do they mean by observation? Is the pupil to write down everything he sees happening in an experiment? Or is he to write down only significant items he notices? If the latter, then where do the criteria come from to enable him to select significant features? If the criteria are provided solely by the teacher then the observation becomes merely observing what the teacher wants you to observe.

The scripts reveal on the whole that these pupils have only rudimentary criteria for inclusion and organization of material. Indeed few pupils seem to indicate much awareness of the meaning of what they are doing in a particular experiment. Does this arise because so many experiments are a matter of teacher's problem and teacher's method, with the pupil being excluded from the heart of the matter and simply going through the procedures mechanically?

Certainly it is interesting to note that rarely does a child formulate the nature of the problem he is investigating as a prelude in the written accounts of experiments. On those occasions when a pupil has attempted something of this nature, the ensuing account has appeared to gain in clarity.

One major purpose English teachers see for written work by pupils is a means for them to demonstrate their comprehension of what they have read. However, teachers do not think through sufficiently what is involved in comprehension, and pupils' written work of this kind shows too often a woeful lack of relevance to the significant aspects of understanding a piece of prose or a poem. There is a need for teachers to think more carefully what part writing could play in the process of helping children to respond to and understand the reading matter with which they are presented.

History teachers feel it important that their pupils should be trained in note-taking. This is an admirable aim, but how it is approached does have a significant bearing on the end product, and this is not generally recognized. For instance, the teachers in the school studied regard the presentation of a series of questions with page references as the most efficient method for guiding children to see the significance of selecting relevant material from books and arranging it clearly. However, such an unvaried procedure may well fail to produce the results they hope for. Are these notes for the teacher or are they for the pupil? And what purposes are they to serve? It seems that the question and reference technique is essentially only a means of checking whether or not the pupil has carried out the work set and the pupils are likely to regard questions as demanding right answers. This is hardly likely to educe notes which have personal significance for the pupil.

These few illustrations indicate that the varied purposes to which writing can be put are not sufficiently realized by many teachers, and the end result is a lack in efficiency in the use of the medium itself as an instrument of learning.

Conclusions

It would appear from this limited study that pupils' writing in secondary schools is viewed predominantly by teachers as a means of gaining feedback of what they have taught and only rarely is it seen as a means whereby a child can be given the opportunity to organize thoughts and feelings for himself. Moreover, since language written down has a degree of permanence which spoken language lacks (disregarding for the moment electronic recording) teachers have a tendency to view written work always in terms of a 'finished product'. Such views affect the teachers' attitudes to the writing tasks they set and their evaluation of them, and in turn affect the pupils' expectations of what they are to write and how they are to present their work.

There would appear to be a need for a less rigid attitude and practice with regard to the pupils' employment of written language. Pupils need opportunities for organizing new material in their own terms according to their own linguistic resources, and opportunities for helpful response to their tentative intellectual gropings both from teachers and other pupils. Until children are able to give the 'knowledge' they meet in schools 'personal significance' they will never be able to handle a subject adequately in objective and impersonal terms.

Writing in schools should be seen as more than the simple acquisition of a skill. It is, together with speech, one of the most powerful means to enable us to extend and deepen our powers of thought and feeling.

Summary Appraisal

In the preceding papers the teacher, his behaviour, especially his uses of language and the classroom as the context for learning have been the focus of attention. Each paper has suggested how the operational curriculum may be shaped, and pointed up implications for learning and teaching of changes in either teachers' behaviour—greater awareness of the uses of language both spoken and written in the classroom—or changes in the context of learning—more and better learning materials, and a different pattern for classroom teaching. Both papers have raised a wide range of issues: What in fact shapes the curricular experience of pupils? How is what it is intended to teach given an operational form? What research is needed to answer such questions? and do we yet understand the process by which classroom experience may determine how students think and feel? It is to the amplification of these issues that the Suggested Readings address themselves.

Suggested Readings

WALLER, W. (1932). *The Sociology of Teaching*. London and New York: John Wiley.
This is a classic study which sets out to appraise the conditions of teaching and the constraints imposed on teaching and learning by the social structure of schools and classrooms. It is a book to be sampled rather than read from start to finish. Of particular relevance to a study of the operational curriculum are Chapters 8 and 9, especially the latter: Attitudes and Roles in Classroom Situations.

JACKSON, P. (1968). *Life in Classrooms*. New York: Holt, Rinehart and Winston.
Not far short of classic in a minor key is Jackson's perceptive study of elementary school classrooms and the conditions which they impose on student learning. It is equally of interest for its methodological approach which is to characterize and quantify large aspects of the context of teaching and learning.

ADAMS, R. S. and BIDDLE, B. (1970). *The Realities of Teaching*. New York: Holt, Rinehart and Winston.
In recent years studying classroom interactions has become a research preoccupation and this book recounts the salient finding based on video recordings in classrooms. It also raises issues about the 'givens' of teaching and of translating the curriculum into operation, about those aspects of the process which tend to be taken for granted.

BARNES, D., BRITTON, J. and ROSEN, H. (1971). *Language, the Learner and the School*. Harmondsworth: Penguin Books.
This is a useful introduction to thinking about teaching as a form of language processing and to the issues which arise when the focus of attention is on how teachers use language to shape the content of the operational curriculum.

DREEBEN, R. (1968). *On What is Learned in Schools*. New York: Addison Wesley.
Schools and classrooms do not only traffic in knowledge, they also traffic in many kinds of values. In this book the author looks at how, by the ways in which relationships are transacted, pupils learn about 'fairness', 'tolerance', 'consideration', and 'trustfulness', and also about 'submerging their personal identity'. In many ways the argument of the book is a salutary one. The operational curriculum far from being a realization of good itentions could result in what was never intended.

Chapter 8

Curriculum Research

Introduction

Whenever substantial numbers of people recognize themselves as being engaged in a similar research enterprise, some will take upon themselves the role of clarifying the nature of the field to which they owe allegiance, and of charting possible courses for future endeavours, while others will carry on cultivating their chosen patches without much regard for the theorisers. Others still (possibly the largest group) will divide their attention between their research activity and attempts to reflect upon it, the better to understand what they are doing and to plan improvements to it. The ease with which such a dual interest can be fruitfully sustained is possibly an index of the health of the research enterprise. The papers in this chapter concentrate on theoretical aspects of the field, leaving specific research studies to be followed up from the references and the suggested readings.

Walker, in his paper *What Curriculum Research?* first assumes the role of clarifier of some fundamental issues, such as, what bases exist for defining curriculum research and why are some to be preferred to others? But next, and perhaps more importantly from the point of view of those who need to orient themselves in the poorly sign-posted area of curriculum research, he makes an objective attack on the central problem of the relationship between the kinds of research that get done and the kinds of research that seem most urgent in terms of a defensible set of propositions about the nature of the field. The nub of his argument is that curriculum research has suffered from '. . . misconceptions . . . of the nature and aims of empirical inquiry in a field concerned with practice', and that this has resulted in a dearth of relevant work. As Walker points out, the twin seductions of marching under a banner of 'scientific' research (probably in the tradition of experimental psychology), and engaging in programmes which are relatively inexpensive and readily funded are potent discouragements to anyone comtemplating a serious commitment to curriculum research as he defines it.

Adams presents a theoretical position having some rather different emphases and, in doing so, exemplifies the kinds of divergences of view which tend to be exhibited in curriculum research. Where Walker takes up a humanistic stance, Adams inclines to a more rigidly 'scientific' approach: Walker maintains that curriculum research can flourish only when the exclusive study of observable phenomena has been renounced, but for Adams this is the major data source. Far from being concerned to mark off curriculum from instruction or teaching, it is in the teacher-learner interaction that he discerns the locus of the central problems of curriculum research. Finally, while Walker would contend that there is a need to make the study of curriculum processes a priority, Adams considers that, if there is to be a research base for ongoing curriculum development, assumptions must be made and a model adopted as a first step towards data collection. Yet, in spite of some fundamental differences, both authors are agreed in some of their conclusions. Both, for example, stress the importance of studying the 'conceptual state of subject matter', in order to find bases for the optimal sequencing of learning experiences. Both recognize the role that value judgements must play in curriculum decision-making (though it is not clear that Adams would see these as presenting a suitable topic for research: one suspects not.)

Readings

What Curriculum Research?[1]* **

Decker F. Walker *University of Stanford*

My thesis in this paper is: we in the field of curriculum have failed to
conduct the empirical research needed to clarify the nature of the
phenomena and problems we address. This failure is due in part to
misconceptions we have uncritically accepted of the nature and aims of
empirical inquiry in a field concerned with practice. As one consequence
of these misconceptions, we lack faith in empirical inquiry as a means of
dealing with our concerns.

Let me clear the way for my main points with some definitions.
When I refer to the field of curriculum I mean the field of professional
study and practice in education which emerged from the generalized
matrix of pedagogy in the US around the turn of this century. Its
founders and early builders would undoubtedly include Franklin
Bobbitt, W. W. Charters, and Harold Rugg. Many others, such as
John Dewey, Hollis Caswell, and the McMurrys, are also frequently
mentioned as important formative influences. (The early years of the
field of curriculum have been chronicled by several authors, including
Caswell (1966), Kliebard (1968) and Seguel (1966).)

The school curriculum as a subject of study and an object of professional practice is more difficult to define. In the fraction of a century
since attempts to distinguish curriculum from other elements or aspects
of educational practice first began to be made, no consensus on the
proper basis for this distinction has been reached. But all agree that

---

* An earlier draft of this paper was presented to the American Educational
    Research Association in Chicago in April, 1972.
** This article is reproduced from the *Journal of Curriculum Studies* (5, 1, 1973)
    by permission of the author and Wm. Collins and Company Ltd.

curriculum is to be distinguished from instruction and teaching on the rough basis that it deals with questions of what items of content or skill or experience to include in the educational programme, whereas the latter fields deal more with questions of how best to present these items. It is not necessary to go beyond this rough distinction so far as this paper is concerned because the remarks I will make here about curriculum and curriculum research I would also make about instructional research and research on teaching.

In order to define the field in a positive way, rather than by its differences with other fields, it is necessary, I think, to consider the phenomena and problems of the field. Like medicine which studies the human body and how to make and keep it healthy, or architecture, which studies shelter and how to build and use it, or horticulture, which studies plants and how to make them grow and contribute to man's welfare, education, and curriculum as a part of education, is defined by what it studies and to what end rather than by the ideas, methods, theories, or techniques it uses or the identity, training, and organizational affiliations of its practitioners.

The phenomena of curriculum include all those activities and enterprises in which curricula are planned, created, adopted, presented, experienced, criticized, attacked, defended, and evaluated, as well as the objects which may be part of a curriculum, such as textbooks, apparatus and equipment, schedules, teachers guides, and so on.

In addition to these actual objects, events, and processes the phenomena of curriculum can be, and in my judgment should be, interpreted to include the plans, intentions, hopes, fears, dreams and the like of agents such as teachers, students, and curriculum developers or policy-makers.

The central problem of curriculum I take to be *'What should be taught, studied, and learned?'* This question takes many forms as it is asked in different situations. What should be taught to disadvantaged students? Considering the needs of the students in this community, what should be taught in their schools? Considering the characteristics of this particular topic within a school subject, to whom should it be taught? Given that a community wants this and this and this for its children, what should the school programme be like in that community? Answering these basic questions may require us to address other questions, such as, 'What has been or is being taught, studied or learned?' or 'What are the likely outcomes of teaching, studying, or learning this?'

Variants of this central problem and related questions of importance to the field include:

At what ages are various subjects or topics or skills most efficiently or effectively taught?

What patterns of personal characteristics—abilities, interests, etc.—predispose students to what sorts of reactions to studying, learning or being taught certain subjects, topics or skills?

What do children want to study, learn or be taught, and why do they want this?

What do parents, teachers, school board members and various other publics want children to study, learn and be taught?

Why do they want this?

In spite of differences about the proper definition of the field, people who identify themselves with the curriculum field would probably agree that these questions are centrally important.

By empirical research I mean systematic, disciplined study of observable phenomena. I distinguish this from watching or participating in the phenomenon without system and discipline, although such informal activities may lead to understanding and may even be vitally necessary to all inquiry. My definition of empirical research in curriculum also excludes the activities of creating curriculum materials, curriculum planning and policy-making, the implementation of curriculum plans and policies, and the criticism of existing, past, or proposed curricula. That is, these activities in themselves are not what I regard as empirical curriculum research. Research may be done in connection with them, or they may be the objects of research, but in themselves they are not curriculum research. (While I exclude these activities from my definition of empirical research, I accord them high places in the field.) When I speak of empirical research in curriculum, then, I mean systematic, disciplined study of curricular phenomena undertaken in an attempt to clarify our ideas about those phenomena or to help solve some curricular problem.

The dearth of curriculum research

It is my impression that relatively little empirical research is done in the curriculum field. This impression is based on my own experience in reading in the field and in talking with others who identify themselves with the field, though I certainly am not alone in this impression. When the *Review of Educational Research* followed the practice of devoting one issue every three years to a given topic, one of which was curriculum research, the editors of each curriculum issue could be depended upon to bemoan the lack of empirical research in the field during the three year period covered in their review. Goodlad (1969) was 'struck in preceding chapters with the paucity of ordered "findings" from curriculum research—findings in the sense either of scientific conclusions from cumulative inquiry or of tested guidelines for curriculum decisions.' (p. 368). Abramson (1966) referred to 'the continuing paucity of studies which can serve as models for curriculum research.' (p. 388). He also claimed that 'until recently there was considerable doubt as to whether curriculum research existed as a field at all, as distinguished from educational research in general or from the production of content and materials.' (p. 389). Macdonald and Raths (1963) said simply, 'reports of specific studies designed to attack this problem area (curriculum) are sparse indeed.' (p. 322).

Since the *Review* changed its policy two years ago and began to accept reviews individually, regardless of their subject, exactly one article reviewing research in curriculum has appeared. The card catalogue in Cubberley Library at Stanford University shows exactly one collection of research reports with the word 'curriculum' appearing in the title. I was unable to find a single book devoted entirely to methods or problems of research in curriculum, though I ran across several such books on instructional research. Three journals published in English regularly feature research reports in curriculum; *Journal of Curriculum Studies, Curriculum Theory Network*, and *Educational Leadership*. At least ten journals are devoted to research on media and methods of instruction. If further evidence of the dearth of empirical research is necessary, it would be asy enough to point to the length of the entries under 'curriculum' and 'teaching methods' and the number of research studies cited in each in the *Encyclopedia of Educational Research*, or the number of papers presented annually in each field at the meetings of American Educational Research Association, or any of a dozen other indices. All show the same result; not nearly as many studies reported in curriculum as in instruction or teaching.

In the final analysis, though, it is not the number of studies that should concern us, but the extent to which the studies, few or many, that are actually conducted illuminate the phenomena of concern to the field's practitioners, and deal in a satisfactory way with its major problems. Let us, then, examine some of the major phenomena and problems of the curriculum field, looking for the bodies of research that grow up around such foci of attention in fields with a vigorous tradition of empirical research.

I suspect many of us would agree with Hollis Caswell's statement that 'The fundamental problem facing curriculum specialists is to establish a consistent relationship between general goals, on the one hand, and specific objectives that guide teaching, on the other.' (Caswell, 1966, p. 5). Surely this relationship is not a purely logical one. Specific objectives do not follow logically and automatically from larger goals. It is not a matter purely of logic that making a living requires learning to read, or that learning to budget one's income requires learning economics or even mathematics. If it were, we could simply deduce the specific objectives from the general goals. So this relationship must be, at least in part, an empirical one to be discovered in actual observations of the outcomes of school programmes. But where in our journals are observations reported bearing on the relationship of general goals to specific objectives?

One of the first systematic studies in education in the United States, Joseph Mayer Rice's (1897) study of spelling, showed that the ability of students to spell a standard list of words did not increase with the amount of time they spent in school on spelling drills, thus showing that the specific objectives guiding daily teaching were not contributing to the attainment of the general goal of learning to spell. In the second and third decades of this century Thorndike, Judd, Rugg, and others launched a devasting attack on the doctrine of mental discipline in a series of studies that showed convincingly that the sort of general improvements in ability to memorize and to learn new facts claimed to result from tedious drill in such subjects as mathematics, spelling, and Latin were not produced by those activities.

These are genuine contributions to our understanding of the relationship between general goals and specific objectives. But they are half a century old. We continue to justify our practices by claims of general outcomes; better citizenship, more careful and rigorous habits of thought, greater ability to learn new things, new and more desirable attitudes toward any number of things. Yet we have almost no research which shows any connection between the particular things we do and these general outcomes, certainly nothing comparable in scope and quality to the earlier research on mental discipline.[1]

Let us proceed to another central problem of the field: to assess 'the educational potentialities of all fields of study at each level of instruction', to 'look impartially at the competing claims of various groups of specialists and to balance these interests in terms of the best service to students and society.' (Caswell, 1966, p. 9). Surely this task is in large measure empirical for how, short of looking for them in the actual conduct and consequences of schooling, are these potentialities to be determined? Yet where are the empirical studies which report on the relative benefits of teaching, studying and learning various subjects, topics, or skills? I have been unable to find even a recent systematic presentation of the arguments for and against the teaching of various subjects, though a model for such a work exists in Gilbert's *What Children Study and Why* (1913). Broudy, in a paper presented to the American Educational Research Association in 1970 and subsequently published in *Curriculum Theory Network*, pointed to a similar lack of research on what he called 'the life consequences of school learnings'. How can a field comprised of persons professionally concerned with the question 'What should be studied, taught, and learned?' not undertake the study of the consequences for life of studying various subjects?

Or consider the problem of sequence in learning: In what order should various subjects, topics, and skills be studied, taught, and learned? Travers (1968) judges that 'We are probably no nearer today than were the schoolmen of the Middle Ages to finding appropriate subject matter sequences within the disciplines.' He adds that 'those who talk most about the importance of sequencing subject matter have done little to solve the enormous difficulties that the practical application of this concept involves.' (p. 99). I fear this last remark is a direct hit on the curriculum field.

Perhaps these problems are too difficult. Researchers normally attack the most tractable problems first. The important curriculum problem which presents probably the least conceptual and methodological difficulty is the determination of what has been and is being taught (not learned necessarily) in schools. How many students of what kind are being asked to study economics or ecology or film-making, or, if the course unit is too large for your taste, the law of supply and demand in a free market or conservation of energy or *Moby Dick* or any of thousands of other topics. Without this basic information we cannot even argue cogently about the balance, comprehensiveness, up-to-dateness, or rate and direction of change in our educational programmes. Here, too, the field provides us with a series of models and precedents in older works—Payne (1905), Stout (1921), Bagley and Kyte (1926), Counts (1926), Mann (1928), Bruner (1941), Latimer (1958)—that form a veritable research tradition in the field; unfortunately, a neglected one. Economies construct a statistical market basket to represent what people buy so that changes in prices and patterns of consumption can be monitored. Surely the technical and practical problems of constructing a statistical curriculum which represents what we ask our children to study are no greater. Why have we not pursued this traditionally important and accessible area of study?

Finally, consider any of hundreds of important curricular problems that actually arise in practice where they fairly beg to be studied. What are the various responses to being asked to study something that teachers and students judge to be unnecessary, dull, too difficult or too easy? In short, what are the pathologies of content which we all as students and teachers felt so keenly; what are the responses it is possible to make to these pathologies; and what are the consequences of these responses? Or, to take a different problem in a different realm, how is it that a system which prides itself on diversity and local autonomy seems to have a single curriculum from coast to coast and from year to year? Why is it that the school curricula across the country are swept periodically by great waves of reform and innovation as pervasive and seemingly as permanent as changes in fashions or automobile design? Where are the empirical studies which would help us understand these problems?

I have overlooked important studies surely, though inadvertently, in this brief review. But a field of study should be able to exhibit bodies of empirical and theoretical work on the problems which preoccupy its members. And I doubt that I have overlooked several bodies of research.

Doubtless the dearth of empirical research in curriculum has many causes. The problems of curriculum are frequently normative and thought for that reason to be unsuited for empirical investigation. Many of the problems of curriculum also arise in particular situations where research seems uneconomic, because ungeneralizable. And, of course, we are all keenly aware of the complexity and multi-faceted nature of curricular phenomena and problems. But whatever the difficulties that lie in the way of research in curriculum, I cannot believe they are so much greater than the difficulties that confront other fields as to be so unyielding to determined assault by two generations of dedicated researchers. I conclude, therefore, that many of us in curriculum have at best a comparatively weak commitment to empirical research as a means of dealing with our professional problems.

Why have we in curriculum had such a weak commitment to empirical research? One important reason, I believe, is because we have misunderstood the nature and aims of empirical inquiry in education, a contention that I shall elaborate in the remainder of this paper.

Educational research is almost always classified as a branch of the social and behavioural sciences, and our conceptions of appropriate forms of research have come almost entirely from that tradition. Educators generally and we in curriculum in particular have accepted research in the behavioural and social sciences as the proper model of research in education. More accurately, we have adopted as our implicit ideal of empirical research a common but quite unsatisfactory reconstruction of social science research. Having accepted this reconstruction of what behavioural and social scientists do as our idea of what empirical research in curriculum must be, our distaste for and disavowal of empirical research is understandable.

Consider some common misconceptions.

1. *We have believed that we must study only overt behaviour*

And some of us have interpreted this to exlude even the study of the physical and social conditions under which the overt behaviour occurs. So when we think of studying textbooks, say, and how they influence their users, we eschew introspective accounts. And when we study classrooms, we look for 'behaviours', since we have been convinced that nothing but behaviour is observable. (Ironically, we do this in a time when methodologically rigorous psychologists study dreams, daydreams, fantasy, perception, and other phenomena relying wholly or primarily on introspective accounts (Klinger, 1971; Singer, 1966).)

Our problem here comes from our too ready acceptance of a philosophy of science which regards some data as objective and incorrigible. In physical science these are pointer readings. The pointer readings of behavioural science have been thought to be bodily motions, physical changes in the body. These are observable, objective and incorrigible. We build our science on them. We have known for some time in the physical sciences that this theory would not do, and we are now well on our way to understanding this in the social and behavioural sciences. Experiments on perception show that strict separation of observation and inference is impossible, that observations are theory-dependent from the very beginning. And studies in the history of science have shown that data are ignored, explained away, or reinterpreted to fit conceptions of the world that are powerful and otherwise coherent. So no matter what we do, our observations will be theory dependent. Our motto in this matter might well be: observation is selection in conformity with expectation.

In fact, what we observe are, even accepting philosophical behaviourism, patterns in behaviour: structured sequences of bodily motions interconnected with one another and adapted to other physical and behavioural circumstances frequently distant in space and time from the events we are watching. These structured patterns of behaviour are more often than not creations or inventions adapted to human purposes and to environmental circumstances. They are, in Herbert Simon's (1969) phrase, 'artificial', not natural. Some terms commonly used to mark out such artificial behavioural structures are 'performances', 'practices', 'policies', 'courses of action', and, misleadingly, 'behaviours'. Reading, writing, and doing arithmetic are performances, not 'behaviours'. They are rule-bound patterns of behaviour which are what they are because certain people made them that way and others have continued to follow their lead. These structured patterns of action, their influences on students, teachers and others, and the environmental conditions which sustain and affect them are the legitimate objects of our inquiries, not the bodily motions of students and teachers.

This may seem to be a trivial distinction, but it is really of the greatest importance. Even though the matters we are concerned with in education are all manifest in bodily motions (behaviour), the particular patterns of interest to us are not necessarily illuminated or clarified by being treated in behavioural terms. This is a difficult point to grasp, so an analogy may help. All material objects are made of atoms. So, in one sense, all we can observe about the material world are atoms. But an architect, city planner, builder, or interior designer would be ill-advised to think of his or her work as 'changing atoms', as would a barber, gardener, painter, dentist, or grocer, though the work of all these jobs can be so described correctly. Nor would the injunction to 'state their goals in atomic terms' be generally helpful. An architect deals entirely with atomic material, that is true, but the matters he or she really deals with are better expressed as entrances, exits, steps, doors, windows, roofs, walls, and, in general, the myriad terms developed over the centuries to describe the particular sorts of functional patterns of atomic organization of concern to architects. There is no necessary contradiction in maintaining that bodily motions are all we can observe about another person and at the same time using concepts like know-ledge, content, topic, life consequences of school learnings, integration or articulation of educational programmes, sequence, curriculum design, steering criterion group or any of the other myriad terms developed to describe the particular sorts of 'behaviour' of interest to people studying the curriculum. Nor are there any genuine problems in the field that are ruled out for study simply because of our incapacity to describe them in terms of bodily motions.

2. *We have believed that research must be entirely a matter of verification and proof*

'We may argue back and forth for years,' we say, 'but in the end research will show who's right. Research winnows the true from the false.' But this view looks at the final stages in a process and lays full credit for the result at the feet of the last step. As William Blake put it 200 years ago, 'What is now proved was once only imagined.' If research tests something, it must have something to test. How is this something to be obtained?

If the field of curriculum had a conceptual scheme for dealing with its central phenomena, a conceptual scheme which enabled inquirers to formulate and pursue fruitfully the important questions of the field in a verificational mode, then research-as-verification would be a limiting, but not crippling conception. But in the present state of the field this view strangles inquiry because we do not have the substructure of ideas and concepts needed to provide a rich store of plausible and interesting hypotheses to test. Instead of feverishly trying to think up hypotheses to be tested, would it not be better to do this thinking while observing and manipulating our phenomena and posing our questions rather than in the armchair beforehand?

I believe we must distinguish in our research between the context of discovery or invention and the context of verification or justification. Both are appropriate and necessary if empirical research is to progress. What we in curriculum sorely need are paradigms for conducting research in a context of discovery to match existing paradigms available from the research traditions of the behavioural and social sciences for the context of verification.

3. *We have believed that human judgments are unreliable, and therefore not fit objects for empirical research*

When we study curriculum development and planning we observe people making judgments about the value of certain topics or activities or objectives. Do we treat these judgments as data, as information about the phenomenon we are investigating? Or do we dismiss them as 'intuitive', 'guesswork' or 'personal prejudice'? We do not have to accept these judgments as valid indicators of the objective worth of the matters to which they are applied, but they are (or at least may be under some circumstances) expressions of the values people attach to those matters.

To think that we can study curriculum planning without reference to such judgments is like believing that it is possible to study piano playing without reference to any 'arbitrary' human standards of performance. What it means to play a piano well is in large part a matter of human preference. To think of these preferences as inadequate, judgmental indicators of some more objective criterion is a mistake. While people's judgments of the value of curriculum elements are not entirely pure expressions of subjective human preferences, neither are they entirely weak and fallible indicators of some objective values which can be uncovered by empirical study of facts as they are. In dealing with the question 'What should be studied, taught, and learned?' we have, I submit, already wandered into the realm of human judgment. We might as well recognize this fact and find ways to study these judgments and the factors that influence them.[2]

4. *We have believed that empirical research (at its best) means searching for isolated causes or cause-effect relations*

According to this view every event has an explanation in terms of a sequence of prior events each of which caused the next in the chain. And behavioural events are thought to be caused only by physical events, physiological events, or previous behavioural events. The task of empirical science in this view is to uncover the links in the causal chain leading up to the events to be explained. But of course one isolated event never causes another. It is always a complex 'initial' situation which leads to a complex 'final' situation. Our causal talk is just a convenient shorthand which singles out from the seamless web of events those that for one reason or another seem crucial to important other events. Too often we forget we have introduced this simplification and come to believe that 'the curriculum' *caused* this result, when in fact the curriculum is at best a crucial (and complex) factor in a complex situation which leads with some regularity to this result among others. The point here is not to urge abandonment of the search for courses of action which can give us control over educational results, but rather to urge acceptance of the view that such courses of action are elements in a larger situation and the 'result' produced is part of a pattern of consequence.

We must also remember that we single out parts of the seamless web of events as needing explanation and others as being well enough understood to serve as explanations for them. What serves as explicans from one point of view may be explicandum from another. Thus, some investigators regard the curriculum as a simple fact and seek to explain what social factors account for its being the way it is, while others seek to explain social phenomena by reference to the curriculum. Furthermore, entirely different modes of explanation can be applied to the same sequence of events. For example, a curricular 'effect' can be explained as the effect of 'studying physics' or of 'having been socialized into the norms of physics' or 'having mastered certain cognitive skills required in physics'. These explanations (actually brief sketches of explanations) are neither contradictory nor equivalent. They represent different selections from among the various possible self-consistent sets of terms in which an explanation may be couched. They are, in effect, different forms or levels of explanation. But we must live with all the actual consequences of our actions regardless of the particular descriptions given to both actions and consequences in some particular explanatory scheme. In curriculum the phenomena of interest to us are amenable to many forms of explanation—psychological, social, historical, moral, intellectual, physical. A causal shorthand which implies that these phenomena are simple effects of isolated causes is almost certain to have bad consequences serious enough to offset any benefits.

Many important questions in the curriculum field do not lend themselves to a causal formulation; some, for example, because they concern discovery of what people want to happen and why they want it. In those cases where a causal formulation of a problem is appropriate— notably, the study of curricular outcomes—we would do better, I believe, to speak of consequences, determinants, and influences rather than effects and results. The first set of terms should remind us that we must always think of complex situations leading to other complex situations rather than isolated causes leading to isolated results.

5. *We have believed that we must control our phenomena in order to study them scientifically*

So, when we puzzled over something like discovery learning, we took it into the laboratory where we could ensure that discovery would occur in only the experimental group. But in fact all that is necessary is control of the inferences we make from our observations. If it were necessary to control the phenomena, astronomy, the oldest of the sciences, would not be a science at all.

We must be able to make and substantiate arguments which show that some observation we have made is more consistent with one interpretation of the situation being studied than it is with another interpretation of this situation. This is the minimum condition for empirically testing such an interpretation. But we meet this condition as much by controlling what, where, when, and how we observe as we do by controlling the phenomenon being observed. And when our efforts to rule out alternative interpretations of a phenomenon interfere in unknown ways with the phenomenon, we are immediately presented with an unforeseen alternative interpretation: that our interference accounts for what we observe.

While controls are not absolutely necessary they may be extremely useful, so that we would be foolish to give them up altogether. But controls imply a 'theory of the phenomenon' which directs us in deciding what actions on the part of the inquirer rule out or make improbable what interpretations of the observed phenomena. Without such a theory no one can be sure that actions thought to control for some interpretations have not fundamentally altered the phenomenon being investigated.

Relatively uncontrolled approaches to a phenomenon are necessary in order to learn the terms on which the phenomenon will admit of being studied. And in my judgment we do not yet know these terms for curricular phenomena.

6. *We have believed that we must study one small thing at a time*

We cannot study everything at once, so the story goes. We must select bits of our phenomenon for intensive study, forgetting for the moment the other parts of it. So instead of studying a reasonable number of the important potential outcomes of a new curriculum we study only end-of-course performance on a standardized achievement test, hoping, perhaps that someone else will study other outcomes later.

Certainly it is necessary and helpful to place some aspects of what you are studying in the foreground of your attention and to relegate the rest to the background. But it is equally necessary to appreciate that one's actions implicate not merely the foreground aspects that one has studied, but the whole from which these aspects were abstracted. Educational policies and practices necessarily operate on the whole child, the whole staff, the whole school and the whole community, not just on those aspects which were singled out for study.

At some stage in an educational inquiry someone will have to use the knowledge obtained in intensive studies of particular aspects of an educational phenomenon to devise and determine wise policies. When this stage is reached it will be necessary to weigh in the same scale the results of various studies carried on from different points of view, with different techniques, and perhaps within the traditions of different disciplines. If each of these studies was conducted in a way that ignored the other, how will this ultimate coordination in use be possible?

This is a major recurring problem in curriculum, indeed, in all fields of practical endeavour. Perhaps medical research offers a useful model and an alternative to the one-variable-at-a-time research strategy. A medical researcher specializing in the gastro-intestinal tract is not a biochemist, or psychologist, or physiologist. But he uses the terms and techniques of these and other disciplines when they illuminate his phenomenon. And when he studies the secretions of the stomach, he is not acting as a biochemist or as anything but a medical researcher honouring his phenomenon and trying to understand it from any vantage point that offers a clear view. Empirical researchers in curriculum seem to me better advised to take the medical specialist as their model rather than his colleagues in the disciplines. (They might copy the medical specialist in another way, too, by working in inter-disciplinary teams.)

Significantly, the gastro-intestinal specialist and the biochemist have inherited independent traditions of careful data collection and analysis, medicine and the natural sciences, which have over years accommodated themselves to one another in a mutually complementary way. We need to develop a tradition of synthetic and integrative research which will complement the work of our colleagues in related disciplines.

Each of these misconceptions has a legitimate concern behind it. It is important to have objective evidence for empirical claims, and this evidence must ultimately come from observations of people's actions. It is important to conduct research that will verify empirical claims. Human judgments of matters of fact are frequently unreliable. Research should help identify factors that can be manipulated to achieve what we want educationally. Research must control for confounding variables. And we must always limit our attention in any study. Trouble comes when, through excess of zeal or lack of insight, we carry these legitimate concerns too far or insist unnecessarily on particular ways of handling them. The restrictions we place on our inquiry in this way can be so great that they make intelligent study of our phenomena and problems impossible.

Is it any wonder really that people who think of empirical research as the search for isolated causes of overt behaviour in controlled situations, one variable at a time, for the purpose of verifying hypotheses not concerned with human judgments or preferences find little use for empirical research in their study of the phenomena and problems of curriculum? But empirical research does not have to be this sort of enterprise. In accepting such a conception we give it power over us. If we reject this image of empirical research, and set about finding more appropriate ways of getting and using factual information to help us formulate and resolve our problems, we will find, I believe, that empirical research can be extremely useful. In fact, I believe it to be ultimately indispensible. As S. S. Tomkins (1963) put it, 'the word we perceive is a dream we learn to have from a script we have not written'. The trouble with so much of the literature of curriculum is that the author has written the script, so the dream is entirely a work of imagination undisciplined by reality. Empirical research give us access to a common source of scripts outside ourselves. We cannot afford to be scared away from that source by the nightmarish image of research that we are told we should honour.

If the field of curriculum is to develop and sustain a rich and vital tradition of disciplined inquiry, those of us who work in the field will have to reverse some trends of the past decades. We will need to develop a stronger commitment to empirical inquiry as a means of dealing with our professional affairs. We will need to discard some widespread misconceptions about the nature and purpose of empirical inquiry and to find or develop modes of inquiry that meet the legitimate concerns that lie behind these misconceptions in ways that are not unduly restricting. We would be wise, I think, to cultivate the research tradition handed down to us from our predecessors, and to honour it with criticism, imitation, or revision as circumstances require. Most importantly, we will need to keep our attention fixed on the phenomena and problems of the field at all costs. If we make no progress in elucidating these, if we turn instead to the phenomena and problems of instruction or administration or philosophy or sociology, because these seem more accessible, we will have abandoned the most powerful justification for our existence as a field: the importance of the phenomena and problems with which we deal.

Notes

1. The work based on Gagne's hierarchical task analysis technique is probably the most ambitious modern attempt to deal with the problem of relating specific goals to more general ones. The basic idea in this procedure is to identify simple, specific capabilities that are prerequisite to more complex and general ones. The more complex and general capabilities are then taught by proceeding carefully and sequentially through each of the prerequisite tasks, making sure that the student has mastered the prerequisites for each new task. This is a promising beginning, but it seems to be limited to the teaching of skills and knowledge—it is not clear that attitudes, elements of character, or creative enterprises requiring novel responses can be analysed in this way—and it needs to be empirically tested. Gagne's own work shows that this sort of analysis can be performed, but whether such an analysis yields curricula that are more effective or efficient than ones produced in some other way is not known.

2. Anyone interested in the systematic study of educational judgments should consult ROBERT STAKE's article, 'Objectives, Priorities, and Other Judgment Data', *Review of Educational Research*, 40: 181–212, April, 1970. The work reviewed there is a fine start towards the serious study of educational judgments.

Bibliography

ABRAMSON, DAVID A. (1966). 'Curriculum Research and Evaluation', *Review of Educational Research*, 36: June, pp. 388–395.

BAGLEY, WILLIAM C. and KYTE, GEORGE C. (1926). *The California Curriculum Study*. Berkeley: University of California.

BROUDY, HARRY (1970). 'Components and Constraints of Curriculum Research', *Curriculum Theory Network*, 5: Spring, pp. 16–31.

BRUNER, HERBERT *et al.* (1941). *What Our Schools Are Teaching*. New York: Teachers College Press.

CASWELL, HOLLIS (1966). 'Emergence of Curriculum as a Field of Professional Work and Study', *Precedents and Promises in the Curriculum Field*, (edited by HELEN F. ROBISON). New York: Teachers College Press, pp. 1–11.

COUNTS, GEORGE S. (1926). *The Senior High School Curriculum*. Chicago: The University of Chicago Press.

GILBERT, CHARLES B. (1913). *What Children Study and Why*. Boston: Silver, Burdett.

GOODLAD, JOHN (1969). 'Curriculum: The State of the Field', *Review of Educational Research*, 39: June, pp. 367–375.

KLIEBARD, HERBERT (1968). 'The Curriculum Field in Retrospect'. In: WITT, P. W. F. (edited by) (1968), *Technology and the Curriculum*. New York: Teachers College Press, pp. 69–84.

KLINGER, ERIC (1971). *Structure and Functions of Fantasy*. New York: Wiley.

LATIMER, JOHN (1958). *What's Happened to Our High Schools?* Washington, D.C.: Public Affairs Press.

MACDONALD, JAMES and RATHS, JAMES (1963). 'Curriculum Research: Problems, Techniques, and Prospects', *Review of Educational Research*, 33: June, pp. 322–329.

MANN, CARLETON (1928). *How Schools Use Their Time*. New York: Teachers College Press.

PAYNE, BRUCE R. (1905). *Public Elementary School Curricula*. Boston: Silver, Burdett.

RICE, JOSEPH MAYER (1897). 'The Futility of the Spelling Grind', *Forum*, 23, pp. 163–172, 409–419.

SCHWAB, JOSEPH (1969). 'The Practical: A Language for Curriculum', *School Review*, 78: November, p. 1023.

SEGUEL, MARY LOUISE (1966). *The Curriculum Field, Its Formative Years*. New York: Teachers College Press.

SIMON, HERBERT (1969). *The Sciences of the Artificial*. Cambridge, Massachusetts: MIT Press.

SINGER, JEROME (1966). *Daydreaming*. New York: Random House.

STOUT, JOHN E. (1921). *The Development of High School Curricula in the North Central States: 1860–1918*. Chicago: University of Chicago (Supplementary Monographs).

TOMKINS, SILVAN S. (1963). *Affect, Imagery, Consciousness*. New York: Academic Press.

TRAVERS, ROBERT M. W. (1968). 'Directions for the Development of an Educational Technology', *Technology and the Curriculum*, (edited by P. W. F. Witt), New York: Teachers College Press, pp. 83–103.

*Curriculum Development and Research—A Question of Fit**

Raymond S. Adams, *University of Missouri*

This paper explores a curriculum model in order to consider its implications for research. Preceding discussion of the model is an attempt to set the stage.

* This article has been reproduced from the *Journal of Curriculum Studies* (5, 1, 1973) by permission of the author and Wm. Collins Sons and Company Ltd.

Definition

As it used here, curriculum means *a set of experiences serving to restructure response predispositions*. Several comments need to be made about this definition.

The definition accepts first, that any experience is potentially a learning experience. It assumes second, that any learning experience results in a restructing of mental, emotional or physical response predispositions. It assumes third, that evidence that learning has occurred can only be gleaned from the observation of subsequent behaviour. It assumes fourth, that behaviour is a form of response triggered by predispositional factors representing the individual's interpretation of the reality of the situation at the time. It also assumes that from observations of behaviour can be inferred this 'response predisposition.'[1]

This rather roomy definition of curriculum can be confined by specifying the context in which the curriculum occurs. This paper is concerned with school curricula and, *ipso facto* with the classroom setting where the curricula are manifested.

Curriculum in context

In the classroom, the structuring of response predispositions occurs through stimuli which impinge on the members and which emanate from a variety of origins, some animate, some inanimate, some contrived, some accidental. The classroom, is of course, a multi-stimulus environment. The teacher is one source of stimuli, so are the other members of the setting, so are the various physical properties of the setting—its books, chairs, blackboards, etc.—and so, it must be admitted, are the concealed thoughts of the members themselves. The transactional process that occurs between members and the stimuli, involves stimuli and counter-stimuli in continuous apposition and opposition. The complexity of the classroom as a learning environment is obviously immense. Currently no learning theory has been able to accommodate to its multi-stimulus complexity. A full appreciation of this complexity thus is likely to elude us for some considerable time yet. Meanwhile, as victims of an unavoidable myopia, we are forced to perceive the situation in simplistic terms.

For the sake of this presentation, the transactional procedures of the classroom are seen to be under considerable control of the teacher. In real life this may not be the case. Teachers may at times be quite incidental to the process and may serve no response restructuring function at all. At other times, they may be rather accidental to it as their actions turn out to be at odds with their intentions. At other times again, their actions and intentions may be in nice harmony. On most occasions, however, they are likely to be all of these at once, as different pupils with uniquely different perceptual predispositions, perceive the teacher's actions uniquely.

The last assessment represents the learning-teacher problem writ large. However, its magnitude is the result of having to accommodate a number of learners simultaneously. The problem writ small, is essentially the problem of transaction between learner and teacher. It is this problem that must be confronted first.

The teaching-learning transaction

It was implied earlier that human beings carry with them response predisposition structures that enable them to interpret reality and to react to it. In the teaching-learning situation then, we have transactions between a 'teacher' and a 'pupil,' both of whom can be inferred as having their own structured response predispositions. However, for learning to have occurred, at least one of the structures must undergo change. Assume that only one structure does change—that only one person learns—then the change may occur in two directions, towards the other's structure (convergently) or away from it (divergently). If both learner and teacher change then four alternative combinations of direction are possible. When the prospect of 'no change at all,' is included, nine alternatives result. Figure 1 below, presents a factorial design in which all the alternatives are taken into account.

Fig. 1. Transactional Restructuring

		TEACHER		
		No Change	Convergent	Divergent
	No Change	1.1	1.2	1.3
PUPIL	Convergent	2.1	2.2	2.3
	Divergent	3.1	3.2	3.3

Presumably, in most learning situations the teacher's structure of response predisposition (concerning whatever is being transacted) undergoes no change while the pupil's is restructured convergently—type 2.1 in Figure 1. Occasionally, when both teacher and pupil are seeking an unknown solution to a mutual problem, 2.2 occurs, and occasionally again, when pupil and teacher are at odds with each other, 2.3 occurs. A situation completely devoid of restructuring (type 1.1) is typified by complete lack of effective communication, while type 3.3 is characterized by complete misunderstanding. When the pupil manifests no change but the teacher converges (1.2), then the pupil learns nothing but the teacher appreciates the pupil's position better. In the case of type 1.3, the pupil still learns nothing but the teacher succeeds in misunderstanding the pupil's position even more. On the other hand, when the teacher learns nothing and the pupil diverges (3.1) it is the pupil this time who misunderstands the teacher more than before. In the final case (3.2), the pupil still succeeds in misunderstanding the teacher more, but the teacher gains a clearer understanding of the pupil's position.

At this point it is possible to inject a value judgment into the discussion. It might seem that some of the transactional types would be 'better' than the others—they would be more efficient from an educational point of view. For instance, would not type 2.1 represent effective teaching? Not necessarily so. If the teacher is more misinformed than the pupil, then the pupil's convergence results in learned 'ignorance.' Under such circumstances, 3.1 (teacher, no change; pupil, divergent) *might* be better—it might be worse too. But *all* the pupil 'no change' categories (1.1, 1.2, 1.3) will be better for the pupil, and 1.2 (pupil, no change; teacher, convergent) might be better for the teacher.

Transitional criteria

This discussion implies that there is some yardstick external to the situation, by which the resulted learning (restructuring) has to be measured. Assuming that what-is-to-be-taught has been predetermined, the external yardstick is, whether what-is-to-be-taught is itself, 'right.' In other words, sitting on top of any teacher's structuring of the reality of what-is-to-be-taught, is the meta-structuring of that same what-is-to-be-taught reality that can be used to determine whether the teacher is right or wrong. To illustrate, for many years Darwin's theory of evolution could not be discussed in schools. Generations of pupils grew up ignorant of the theory but aware of the emotional controversy it occasioned. Today those pupils are teachers themselves, and evolutionary theory has become educationally legitimate. Understandably, then, teachers are often able to present only confused and erroneous versions to their pupils.

Fairly obviously, this idea of rightness can be employed at different levels of sophistication. For instance, it may be a matter of whether a specific fact (sic) is correct or not. It may also be a matter of whether a whole domain of knowledge is ordered 'correctly' or not. For example, currently we are being exposed to world-wide reform in the teaching of arithmetic. Newly ordered theoretical systems for understanding the domain of arithmetic are being used. 'Rightness' in these cases is often a matter of whether or not the teachers understand the system— whether the teachers' behaviours are consistent with the premises, procedures, and conclusions of the systems.

At this point it is appropriate to acknowledge another assumption that underlies this paper. It is assumed that the subject matters of education can be treated as coherent, ordered, and rational systems. These systems consist basically of: a conceptual posture, the concepts which result, procedures for relating the concepts and the propositions generated. Thus social studies for its conceptual posture focuses in a semi-sociological way on man-in-society. Its concepts include variations on the theme 'man' (brown-white, peaceful-agressive), and upon the concept society (agrarian-industrial, democratic-autocratic). Its procedures include comparing and contrasting different societies. In the process of refining categories and applying procedures, new sub-concepts (kinship, occupation, ritual, etc.) emerge, and conclusions are reached about their inter-relationships (e.g., the connection between economic development and educational provision).

At any point in time, it is possible for the present status of a given subject matter to be explicated with, at least, some degree of precision.

There are then three elements that have to be taken into account in any curriculum development model—the pupil's current structure of response predisposition, the teacher's structure, and what might be called the meta-conceptual structure of the subject-matter itself.

The problem of fit

In the best of all possible educational worlds, the teacher would succeed in restructuring the pupil's response predisposition so that it became identical with the conceptual structure of the subject matter. However, the teacher himself is an intervening variable whose success (presumably) depends on the closeness of fit between *his* structure and the conceptual structure of the subject. Thus the process of individual learning or restructuring can be seen as a succession of changes in structuring whose ultimate form is to a large degree dependent on

(i) the teacher's response predisposition structure and (ii) his ability to communicate it. This process has been illustrated in Figure 2.

The figure illustrates the effects of transactional process on the pupil over time. Two teacher structures are exhibited in the figure. Structure A is in harmony with the conceptual structure of the subject matter and has the potential for leading the pupil *towards* 'true' knowledge. Structure B is at odds with the conceptual structure of the subject

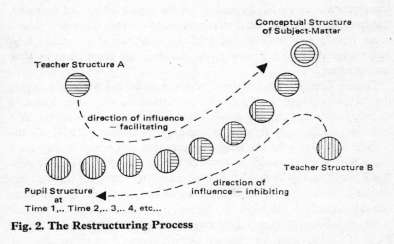

Fig. 2. The Restructuring Process

matter and has the potential for leading the pupil in the opposite direction. How far the pupil proceeds towards the goal of complete restructuring of understanding is a function of the teacher's behaviour as a facilitating or inhibiting agent.

Research on curriculum

Contriving closeness of fit between the pupil's response predisposition and the subject-matter's structure then seems to demand knowledge of four phenomena: (i) The present response predispositional state of the pupil, (ii) the present response predispositional state of the teacher, (iii) the transactional procedures which bring about change in the pupil's state, (iv) the conceptual state of the subject-matter.

Gaining knowledge on these phenomena represents the four main tasks of curriculum development research. Each is considered in turn.

Pupil Condition. Piaget (1924) (1926) and his followers (Inhelder, 1958) have provided us with insights into the nature of children's thinking. They have demonstrated with dramatic clarity that children at different stages perceive the world differently from the conventional adult interpretation of it. Research stimulated by their insights continues. Without doubt its range and scope will expand until we know much more not only about the conventions that children employ to 'comprehend' weight, and number, special relationships and language, but interpersonal, and social relationships too. From this research will come both a new understanding of the child world and ultimately, devices for determining how given children at a given point in time are operating.

Teacher Condition. Educational research so far has neglected to give the teacher's structure of response predisposition the same degree of attention. It is theoretically possible that teachers (and people) manifest different 'thinking styles.' The recognition by Guilford (1959) of convergent and divergent thinking, suggests that some people may have characteristic predispositions towards one or the other. The Siegels' (1967) work on the 'factual' and 'conceptual' objectives of teachers has similar implications. At the moment some work is being done on what might be called teaching styles by Ryans (1960) and Solomon and Miller (1961) but the effort to map the thought processes of adults lacks the fine focus of similar work on children. At the moment to all intents and purposes, 'a teacher is a teacher is a teacher.'

Transactional Processes. However, no matter how the various inhabitants of learning situations structure their response predispositions, there still remains the very critical problem of how the structures are communicated. The teacher's understanding of the subject matter may be ideal but without the techniques of effective communication, of what avail is it? The legend of the brilliant academic who is patently ineffectual as a teacher is not without substance. Currently, more and more educational research is being concerned with the teacher in action—with the transactional process of the classroom. Stimulated by the earlier work of Anderson and Brewer (1939) (1945) (1946 a.b.c.), researchers like Withall (1949) (1956), Medley and Mitzel (1958), and Flanders (1960) (1961) have begun a trend that has since been complemented by the more complicated research work of Bellack *et al.* (1966), Biddle and Adams (1967), and the like. These studies are serving to provide new insights into the process of real-life teaching and learning.

Their work has the potential for describing the means by which closeness of response predispositional fit may be achieved.

Subject Matter. Perhaps most challenging of the four research areas is the remaining one—the conceptual structure of subject matter. Fine examples of what can be done are to be found in Gattengo's Piaget-derived structuring arithmetic, in the 'new math,' in PSSC, etc. New reading methods, for example like 'ita,' represent a much more sophisticated approach to subject-matter delineation than we have had in the past. However it is predictable that such attempts only represent a beginning. Other subjects will be streamlined similarly. Eventually the boundaries of the existing subject matter-domains will become blurred and just as rhetoric and dialectic gave way to Greek and Latin, and Greek and Latin (grudgingly) gave way to chemistry and physics, chemistry and physics may well give way to other 'subjects.' This time, however, the 'subject' may be defined in terms of conceptual catorgories, or common conceptual postures, or common concept related procedures. In the meantime, it remains the special problem of educational research to make articulate the essential conceptual character of the existing subject-matters.

Comment

There are two last points that should be made. Throughout, substantive discussion has been concerned with the simple transaction—between one teacher and one pupil—and with *one restructuring problem* at a time. It is quite possible that at any given time, the transactors may be working simultaneously on two or more restructuring problems. However, it is likely that these problems will be in different dimensions from each other. For example, on one dimension the restructuring problem is concerned with an aspect of subject-matter, say characteristics of right-angled triangles. At the same time, both teacher and pupil can also be restructuring in an *affectional* domain as they reform their attitudes towards each other—or towards the subject matter. At the same time they might both also be refining their language skills, thus restructuring there as well. In addition, both teacher and pupil may be restructuring their respective perceptions of each other's personality. Basically, however, the problem is the same—a problem of fit between pupil structure and teacher structure. It must be admitted, that the meta-conceptual structures of affectional 'subject-matter' and personality 'subject-matter' are relatively poorly articulated.

If introducing more dimensions complicates the model (and the researcher's life), so does recognizing the true multi-person condition of the classroom. Fairly obviously, children are different from each other, and in the real educational world, the teacher seldom can afford the luxury of an exclusive one-at-a-time relationship with his pupils. Consequently, the task of adapting to the various response predispositions of his various charges, faces the teacher with a king-sized problem. No doubt, programmed learning devices and computers themselves will provide him with some measure of assistance in the future—both in diagnosing pupil structure and providing appropriate learning programmes. So will the new organizational skills that he will have to acquire. However, the day is far off when computers will be adaptable enough to provide for all individual learners packaged programmes that are able to take into account the multi-dimensional character of the teaching learning transaction.

It is perhaps worth noting in passing, that the reason for the teacher's survival in the machine age is also the major source for most of his frustration and concern. If teaching were not a complicated and socially demanding task, then the teacher would be redundant, the machines would take over, and 1984 would indeed be upon us.

Notes

1. Fairly obviously, the definition used goes to great pains to avoid the phrase, cognitive structure. There is good reason. Not all learning is cognitive, even though much is accomplished by cognitive means. But physical skills are learned, so are emotional responses. The somewhat clumsy term, response predisposition has been used to accommodate these and other kinds of learning as well.

Bibliography

ADAMS, R. S. and BIDDLE, B. J. (1968). *Diagnosis of Teaching*. New York: Holt, Rinehart & Winston.

ANDERSON, H. H. (1939). 'The measurement of domination and of socially integrative behaviour in teachers' contacts with children,' *Child Development*, X, 73–89.

ANDERSON, H. H. and BREWER, HELEN M. (1945). 'Studies of teachers' classroom personalities. I: Dominative and socially integrative behaviour of kindergarten teachers,' *Psychological Monographs*, 6.

ANDERSON, H. H. and BREWER, J. E. (1946). 'Studies of teachers' dominative and integrated contacts on children's classroom behaviour,' *Psychological Monographs*, 8.

ANDERSON, H. H., BREWER, J. E. and REED, MARY F. (1946). 'Studies of teachers' classroom personalities. III: Follow-up studies of the effects of dominative and integrative contacts on children's behaviour.' *Applied Psychological Monograph* II.

ANDERSON, H. H. and BREWER, J. E. (1946). *Studies of teachers' classroom personalities. III: Effects of teachers' dominative and integrative contacts on children's classroom behaviour.* Stanford, California: Stanford University Press.

BELLACK, A. A., KLIEBARD, H. M., HYMAN, R. T. and SMITH, F. L. Jr. (1966). *The Language of the Classroom*, 47. New York: Teachers College Press, Columbia University.

BIDDLE, B. J. and ADAMS, R. S. *An Analysis of Classroom Activities*. Final Report Contract No. 3–02–002. USOE, Columbia, Mo.: University of Missouri.

FLANDERS, N. A. (1960). *Interaction Analysis in the Classroom*. Minn.: University of Minnesota.

FLANDERS, N. A. (1961). 'Analysing teacher behaviour as part of the teacher-learning process,' *Educational Leadership*, December.

GUILDFORD, J. P. (1959). 'Three faces of intellect,' *American Psychologist*, XIV, 469–47.

INHELDER, B. and PIAGET, J. (1956). *The Growth of Logical Thinking from Childhood to Adolescence*. New York: Basic Books.

MEDLEY, D. M. and MITZEL, H. E. (1958). 'A technique for measuring classroom behaviour,' *Journal of Educational Psychology*, XLIX, 86–92.

PIAGET, J. (1923). *Le Language et la pensee chez l'enfant*. Neuchatel-Paris: Delachaux & Niestle.

PIAGET, J. (1926). *La representation du monde chez l'enfant*. Paris: F. Alcan.

SIEGEL, LAWRENCE and SIEGAL, LILA CORKLAND (1967). Chapter 9 in SIEGAL, LAWRENCE (Ed.) *Interaction: Some Contemporary Viewpoints*. San Francisco: Chandler.

SOLOMAN, D. and MILLER, N. L. (1961). *Exploration in teaching styles: report of preliminary investigations and development of categories*. Chicago: Center for the Study of Liberal Education for Adults.

WITHALL, J. (1949). 'The development of a technique for the measurement of social-emotional climate in classrooms,' *Journal of Experimental Education*, XVII, 347–361.

WITHALL, J. (1956). 'An objective measurement of a teacher's classroom interactions,' *Journal of Educational Psychology*, XLVII, 203–12.

Summary Appraisal

In the two papers the emphasis is on theoretical aspect of research. Taken together, they illustrate the dialectical quality of much discussion of curriculum research: should it seek for understanding ('pure' research), or try to answer to the immediate, practical needs of curriculum development ('applied' research)? Is it fundamentally a scientific or a humanistic enterprise? A matter of amassing facts, or arriving at insights or theoretical formulations? The suggested readings provide an introduction to pieces of research undertaken from a variety of backgrounds, and from widely diverging viewpoints.

Suggested Readings

GAGNE, R. M. (1970). *The Condition of Learning*. London and New York: Holt, Rinehart, Winston (2nd ed.).
This is not in itself a work of research, but it is a useful attempt to draw together a range of studies with implications for the optimal design of instructional programmes. Its orientation is psychological and experimental. Extensive references are provided.

HODGETTS, A. B. (1968). *What Culture? What Heritage? A Study of Civic Education in Canada*. Toronto: Ontario Institute for Studies in Education.
One of the few systematic attempts to answer the question 'What is *in fact* taught in schools?' The research techniques are simple, the writing lucid and straightforward. An atheoretical, but none the less insightful study of how a curriculum is experienced by students in classrooms.

HUSEN, T. and BOALT, G. (1968). *Educational Research and Change: The Case of Sweden*. Stockholm: Almqvist and Wiksell.
An important tradition of educational research has grown up in Sweden in recent years. This volume, which provides a well written introduction to it, contains a chapter on 'Curriculum Research', outlining a number of studies of how the curriculum is implemented (instructional procedures, allocation of time to various topics), what learning outcomes result, and what demands for specific skills are placed on students by employers, upper schools, and institutions of higher education. (For a recent, theoretically oriented Swedish contribution to curriculum research, see Lundgren U.P., (1972). *Frame Factors and the Teaching Process: A Contribution to Curriculum Theory and Theory on Teaching*. Stockholm: Almqvist and Wiksell (Contains a very full bibliography.).)

SMITH, L. M. and KEITH, P. M. (1971). *Anatomy of an Educational Innovation: An Organisational Analysis of an Elementary School*. New York: Wiley.
From the point of view of curriculum research this study presents a number of interesting features: it adopts a 'case study' approach in which a wide variety of sociological perspectives are brought to bear on curriculum issues; it investigates the curriculum in its institutional context, and it focuses on the question of innovation, which is a central concern of curriculum studies. Good bibliography, especially for works on organizational analysis and innovation.

Young, M. F. D. (ed.) (1971). *Knowledge and Control: New Directions for the Sociology of Education*. London: Collier-Macmillan.

Knowledge has traditionally been regarded as a commodity available for incorporation in curricula according to principles of a logical or psychological, rather than moral or sociological order. The quite different tone of this volume is set by Young's opening essay 'An approach to the Study of Curricula as Socially Organised Knowledge'. Other contributors suggest how such a perspective might be fruitfully applied in curriculum research. Many useful references.

General Bibliography for Part Two

Books

GOODLAD, JOHN I. (1975). *The Dynamics of Educational Change: Toward Responsive Schools.* New York: McGraw-Hill.

BENTZEN, MARY M. (1974). *Changing Schools: The Magic Feather Principle.* New York: McGraw-Hill.

OWEN, J. G. (1973). *The Management of Curriculum Development.* Cambridge: Cambridge University Press.

REID, W. A. (1972). *The Universities and the Sixth Form Curriculum.* London: Macmillan Educational.

REID, W. A. and WALKER, D. F. (eds.) (1975). *Case Studies in Curriculum Change.* London: Routledge and Kegan Paul.

SARASON, S. B. (1971). *The Culture of the School and the Problem of Change.* Boston: Allyn and Bacon.

SCHOOLS COUNCIL (1973). *Pattern and Variation in Curriculum Development Projects.* London: Macmillan Educational.

SHELDRAKE, P. and BERRY, S. (1975). *Looking at Innovation.* Slough: NFER.

SHIPMAN, M. (1974). *Inside a Curriculum Project.* London: Methuen.

SMITH, L. M. and KEITH, P. M. (1971). *Anatomy of Educational Innovation: An Organizational Analysis of an Elementary School.* New York: Wiley.

STENHOUSE, L. (1975). *An Introduction to Curriculum Research and Development.* London: Heinemann.

TAYLOR, P. H. (ed.) (1975). *Aims, Influence and Change in the Primary School Curriculum.* Slough: NFER.

TAYLOR, P. H., REID, W. A. and HOLLEY, B. J. (1974). *The English Sixth Form.* London: Routledge and Kegan Paul.

TYE, K. A. and NOVOTNEY, J. M. (1975). *Schools in Transition: The Practitioner as Change Agent.* New York: McGraw-Hill.

Articles

BROUDY, H. S. (1970). 'Components and constraints in curriculum research,' *Curr. Th. Network*, 5.

CONNELLY, F. M. (1972). 'The functions of curriculum development,' *Interchange*, 3, 161–177.

EISNER, E. (1975). 'Curriculum development in Stanford University's Kettering Project,' *J. Curr. St.*, 7, 1, 26–41.

FENSHAM, P. J. (1974). 'Science curricula and the organization of secondary schooling,' *J. Curric. St.*, **6**, 1, 61–72.

GOODLAD, J. I. (1972). 'Staff development, the League Model,' *Theory into Practice*, XI (October) 207–214.

JOHNSON, M. (1970). 'Appropriate research directions in curriculum and instruction,' *Curr. Th. Network*, 6, 24–37.

KELLY, P. J. (1970). 'The process of curriculum innovation,' *Paedagogica Europaea*, 6, 84–106.

KIRST, M. and WALKER, D. F. (1971). 'An analysis of curriculum policy-making,' *Rev. Ed. Res.*, **41**, 5, 201–237.

McDONALD, B. and RUDDUCK, J. (1971). 'Curriculum research and development projects: barriers to success,' *Brit. J. Ed. Psych.*, **41**, 2, 148-154.